Cricket in Wales

BERNARD HEDGES
The Player from 'Ponty'

Stephen Hedges

ST DAVID'S PRESS
Cardiff

Published in Wales by St. David's Press, an imprint of

Ashley Drake Publishing Ltd
PO Box 733
Cardiff
CF14 2YX

www.st-davids-press.wales

First Impression – 2019

ISBN
978-1-902719-56-6

British Library Cataloguing-in-Publication Data.
A CIP catalogue for this book is available from the British Library.

Typeset by Prepress Plus, India (www.prepressplus.in)
Cover designed by Siôn Ilar, Welsh Books Council, Aberystwyth.

CONTENTS

In memory of my father, Bernard Hedges,
and his roommate for 18 seasons, the late Don Shepherd.
Like hundreds of others, they typified
'the finest characteristics of professional cricketers.'

ACKNOWLEDGEMENTS

As this is the first published book I have ever written there is a strong desire to thank everyone that has ever helped me as a writer, from my teachers through to the many authors whose books have enthralled and inspired me. Please take as read my indebtedness to them all, from Mr Pollard, my English teacher at Blake Comprehensive School (1975-80), to Philip Pullman, author of the *Northern Lights* trilogy and to Duncan Hamilton, journalist and winner, more than once, of the William Hill Sports Book of the Year Award. There are many more cricket writers I have learnt from and borrowed from. I hope these borrowings have been clearly signposted.

In a book about your father, family must play a significant first part, and Dad's early years in Pontypridd came to life through a number of conversations I had with Peter Hedges, Margaret Baker, Jean Warne, Joan McGrath and Lynne Roberts. These are all Dad's surviving siblings. His two other brothers, John and Gerald, were remembered too during these chats. My mother, Jean Hedges, also helped with her reflections on being married to a county cricketer. I hope I have done our conversations justice and my thanks to her, also, for allowing me to use photos from her wedding and other albums. I also met and talked with two old school friends of Dad, Alan Oliver and Maurice Stallworthy. Both helped me understand the sporting culture that existed at Pontypridd County School for Boys and much else besides. Maurice gave me some insight into the great Glynn Davies who shared a classroom with him and Bernard, and who had who died too soon.

For Dad's days as a rugby player with Pontypridd RFC, I was lucky enough to spend a couple of hours with Wales and British Lions star Russell Robins. His insights and stories brought me closer to seeing this bit of Bernard's sporting life which has, inevitably, remained hidden behind his cricketing career. Thanks too must go to Alan Granfield, author of the club's official history *Black and White* and to ex-players Dai Love and Stan Thomas whom I met at Sardis Road before a Pontypridd RFC home match. Their warm reflections reinforced what I had already assumed about those days in the late 1940s and early 1950s.

Taking inspiration from Stephen Chalke's conversational books, *Caught in the Memory* and *Runs in the Memory*, this book includes large extracts from meetings I had with ex-cricketers of Dad's era. I met with Alan Jones, Roger Davis, Tony Lewis, Peter Walker, Ossie Wheatley, Lawrence Williams and the late Don Shepherd. They were all very kind in their assessment of my father as a man and honest in their assessment of him as a cricketer. I hope the pleasure I had in having those discussions comes through in the editing. Outside of Glamorgan, I spoke to M.J.K. Smith, Alan Oakman, Peter Richardson, Geoff Pullar, Ron Headley, Jimmy Gray as well as corresponding with Norman Hill. This was primarily about the 1961 season, but as with all cricket discussions, we ended up talking about a whole lot more. Sadly, Geoff, Jimmy, Alan and Peter have all passed away whilst the book has been awaiting publication. A whole generation of cricketers is leaving us. They take a great deal with them, most of which is the best of cricket. They will all be missed. There were other cricketers, both of Glamorgan and other counties, who I did not get an opportunity to talk to. My apologies to them. The lack of diligence that comes with being a novice hampered me many times. In this instance, it cost me the chance to speak to some great players.

You never quite realise how useful libraries and librarians are until you have to do a bit of research. Many thanks must go to Edwina Smart and the other staff of Pontypridd Library who guided me towards books and archives that proved extremely helpful. Thanks, too, to John Smart for showing me around the Pontypridd CC pavilion and a guided tour of Ynysangharad Park. Colwyn Bay Library helped give some flesh to the bones of the first Wales XI match that took place there in 1969. Glamorgan Archives gave me access to the Glamorgan CCC minutes for the years of Dad's career. These were, in some instances, a real eye-opener. I visited the National Library of Wales in Aberystwyth where I spent several days ploughing through old editions of the *Western Mail* which were in pristine condition. I visited RAF Halton, the site of Dad's posting whilst on National Sevice between 1946 and 1949. Wing Commander Mick Perry was most helpful in guiding me to areas of interest.

The Boundary of Wales Walk took place less than six months after Dad had passed away. It was an emotional experience for me but one that would not have felt half as fulfilling without the efforts of the following people. Peter Hybart, Chief Executive of Cricket Wales was an enthusiastic backer of the walk from the very first and his media colleague, Andrew Weltch of Weltch Media worked hard to get the walk a wider audience. Martyn Bicknell at Glamorgan CCC did a similar job and Hugh Morris, the Chief Executive, was happy for the club to offer support and assistance where it could. All of these people were involved in Welsh cricket so perhaps had a professional interest in the walk. Greater thanks are due to those who helped because they just remembered Dad and wanted to help. Paul and Bev Rogers, neighbours of my father in his later years, were unstinting and, sometimes, evangelical, in their promotion of the walk. They pushed at doors that I would have walked by. My brother David and his partner Julie, arranged the key experiences with local cricketers in Neyland, in Pembrokeshire, and Menai Bridge on Anglesey. They, too, were great at promoting the walk and its messages. The Donalds looked after me for a couple of nights and I got an inkling of what it's like being a current first-class cricketer. Jocelyn is my cousin and their son, Aneurin, played for Glamorgan before moving to Hampshire. I think that makes us second cousins. Whatever. All I know is that there is a hell of a lot of kit. My mum would have sunk under the weight of it all!

Publishing is more a mystery to me than writing. The garnering of testimonials appears to be a significant feature of pre-publication. I am deeply grateful to the four men who provided testimonials for this book. Alan Jones, Tom David, Neil Kinnock and Gareth Edwards suggest, in part at least, the wide appeal my father had as a player and the currency that cricket had in the 1950s. I know their kind words will be burning coal in the hearths of Dad's sisters and brother.

There are two names that I have held back to this point. Ashley Drake, owner of St. David's Press has made the process of publishing the book feel like a straightforward five-minute bus journey. He has asked little of me but is providing the greatest thing in return. His confidence in me and willingness to accept everything I laid before him is due to his relationship with the second name, Andrew Hignell. As the chief historian of Glamorgan cricket and the writer of numerous books on the game in Wales, Andrew's encouragement and support was vital in convincing Ashley that the book was worth publishing. His firm editing and gentle persuasion has kept me clear of the rocks of controversy, allowing me to express Dad's story in an accessible and interesting way. His commitment to Glamorgan, its present and its past, is truly remarkable. I hope I have sustained the honour of the Club, as well as my dad, in the writing of *The Player From 'Ponty'*. Every boy must dream of honouring their father in some way. Andrew has enabled me to do that. I will never be able to thank him enough.

Every writer has a family. I am no exception. Loving thanks go to Cheryl, my wife, and my two sons Ellis and Lewis, who have seen me through this three-year process. None of us would have believed it. We still might not with the first copy in our hands.

Whilst writing the book, I read Jamling Tenzing Norgay's account of his climb to the top of the highest mountain in the world. He had done it in memory of his father who had been the first man to summit with Sir Edmund Hillary in 1953. Writing after the climb, he said something that is at once astonishing and yet would make sense to many sons:

Stepping on the summit of Everest freed me from the confinement of my ambitions[1]

I never felt any pressure to follow in my father's footsteps although I would have loved to have been a first-class cricketer. I did feel that after his death I wanted to honour him, to recognise his passing and with my actions to convey the love that, perhaps, like many sons, I found difficult to express to him whilst he was alive. Writing a book is not climbing a mountain. Neither is walking around the whole of Wales comparable to conquering the highest mountain in the world. But they are of the same order; the same kind of acts. I never saw these acts as confining. My ambition to make my dad proud never constrained me. Rather, it was what felt like my obligations that freed me up to experience the greatest intellectual and spiritual experience of my adult life.

There are many mistakes that I made in the writing of the book but most I would hazard were errors of omission. Dad was well known throughout the valleys and 'Ponty' in particular. There were hundreds who would have had stories about him or the times that I did not get around to recording. I regret that. I was also unable to source a recording of *Down Your Way* which featured Dad in the episode from Pontypridd. Perhaps someone, somewhere, will make that available soon. It would be great to hear it. Any errors of fact and of reporting I have made along the way are mine alone. I hope you enjoy reading the book.

---

1. Jamling Tenzing Norgay with Broughton Cobourn, *Touching My Father's Soul*, Harper San Francisco, 2001, p.290.

FOREWORD
By Don Shepherd (Glamorgan 1950-1972)

It seems such a long time ago now, when Bernard and I first played together for Glamorgan. The world of cricket and, indeed, the world itself has changed beyond recognition since then. It was a totally different era for sport and sportsmen. We played because we loved the game, not because of any expectations of fame or fortune. There were no big money purses or win bonuses. Neither were there fielding coaches, sports nutritionists or batting and bowling analysts. The nearest I got to advice on what to eat and drink was when Wilf Wooller, offering me a pint of beer, told me that I would never bowl quick on orangeade. In those days, the umpires would sometimes give you a few tips, suggesting a change to your action or telling you that you were leaving the 'gate open' and so on. You would not have that now. Today, they spend more time training than playing. Our training was done during a match. With two three-day matches a week plus charity or other games on a Sunday we played a lot. The season could be a hard grind.

Bernard and I came together from different places, me from the Gower and the tranquil coast and him from Pontypridd in the heart of the industrial valleys. I remember playing with him in Glamorgan's 2nd XI when J.T. Morgan was the captain. We went to Bristol on a bitterly cold morning at the start of the season. We were a bit late arriving and

Don Shepherd, photographed in 1950, when both he and Bernard made their first-class debuts for Glamorgan. (© Glamorgan CCC)

Colonel Henson, the Gloucestershire secretary, informed us that they would not be able to serve us tea in the changing rooms. J.T. Morgan insisted, politely of course, on the team having that cup of tea before we went out to play and, in due course, the tea arrived. 'JT' was a proper gentleman who greeted every new player with the question, 'And what is it that you do, my man?' That was how the game was then. It was fiercely contested on the pitch, but off it, there was always room for the characters of the game plus a lot of fairness and respect.

Bernard, like fast bowler Ken Lewis and me was a new player and we tended to get shuffled about a lot. We were just glad to be there, playing but not saying anything. We were all just doing our best. I certainly would not have offered advice to anyone senior to me and we were all used to taking orders. As part of National Service, you had to accept some of the most ridiculous things, so being a junior professional was not so difficult. Bernard did not start his Glamorgan life as an opening batsman. It was the tradition to learn the trade in those days. We had Emrys Davies, Phil Clift and Gilbert Parkhouse who were all capable of opening the batting so you had to take a place lower down the batting order and when you got your chance you had to take it. Glamorgan were not the best batting side in the world so there were plenty of situations where a batsman could make his mark.

We had been County Champions in 1948, but the team had never beaten Middlesex or Yorkshire either at home or away. We managed to do both of those things in the early years of our first-class careers. It was very satisfying for Bernard and me to be in the teams which secured these famous victories and we all did something of note. We both played in the historic victory over the South African tourists at Swansea in 1951, although our contributions did not amount to much. Bernard was caught van Ryneveld, bowled Rowan in the first innings. Rowan was one of the best off-spinners in the world. Jim McConnon got most of the credit because of the hat-trick he took but Len Muncer got the most wickets in the match. The crowd was phenomenal.

As far as batting technique was concerned, Bernard concentrated on making his runs off the back foot, either pushing or guiding the ball away or cutting and pulling. He had all the shots but I do not think he took on the quicker bowlers with the hook like Gilbert Parkhouse. Survival, plus runs on the back foot. That was Bernard. Like a number of Glamorgan batsmen of that time, he adapted his game to cope with the numerous slow pitches that we played on. Having uncovered pitches meant we played on lots of slow, turning pitches. He was always very realistic about his ability; always very level headed. I never saw him sulking or worrying if things were not going too well.

Gilbert and Bernard were great together. Twice during the 1959 season they got the fastest 200 in the first innings. There was also a match against Northants in 1961 where Bernard got a hundred in the second innings before he and Gilbert set about scoring 214 in the second innings in two and a quarter hours. We got them with half an hour to spare. They were quite something to behold when they were chasing a target and both firing on all cylinders.

I was also there in 1963 when he won his man-of-the-match award in the Gillette Cup. I was not playing but I watched him score his hundred and take a couple of wickets. It was one of those proper professional innings played in really difficult circumstances because nobody knew what was a good score. It was the first time we had played limited-overs cricket. As for his bowling, a lot of batsmen could do that. Just bowl a length with a little bit of movement. Bernard was used to it. He spent his winters in the indoor school at Neath bowling ball after ball at club and up-and-coming cricketers. I always remember George Lavis writing to me to tell me I had found a way to become a 'match winner'. He could have said it about Bernard on that day. We were both very fond of George and he was our first coach when we started playing for Glamorgan.

George Lavis, who made 206 appearances for Glamorgan between the wars and just after, batting for the county against Surrey in 1936. He was coach to both Bernard and Don in their early days at Glamorgan. (© Glamorgan CCC)

Bernard was a true sportsman and played the game with an honesty and sense of fair play that stood out. I think that was one of the reasons that he lost faith in the game in the end. It has changed, there has been so much cheating and fiddling going on that he lost all respect for the game that he had played with such honesty. It was not the game that he knew and it was not the way he had played. He seemed to lose interest not only in the game but also his part in its history with Glamorgan. I believe he lost himself a lot of pleasure. A lot of the old players would turn up at the ex-players reunions. I can only think he had made his mind up and when he had done that he took a bit of shifting.

I remember the last time I saw him. He was bed-ridden but still as bright as a button. I asked him what he thought was his best innings. I thought he was going to say the hundred at Llanelli facing spinner Bruce Dooland on a big turner. But, instead, he said it was at Broadmoor Hospital. What were we doing there? Well, Bill Edwards, who was on the committee, knew the padre and he had arranged for us to travel there for a match against the patients. It was a high security facility for mental health patients who had committed some serious crimes. It was quite an experience to have every door unlocked for you and then locked behind you as you passed through the corridors. We played against a Broadmoor team and they had some pretty handy cricketers. Bernard said we were about 41 for 4 so he could not have gone in first. He got enough runs for us to win, maybe 80 or 90. There was a lovely big field where we played with plenty of protection around it. A wire fence circled the sports area. One of the patients had adopted me for the day to pass the time away while we were there. All the patients did the same, pairing off with one of the players. He had made a ship's reading lamp which he presented to me as I recall. Anyway, this chap said at the end of the match that they had had the Broadmoor Sports Day the previous week. 'They let us play every sport except one' he related, 'the pole vault!'

That was an incredible thing for Bernard to say that this was his best innings because he played many notable ones. But it was just like him. Playing the game was always the most important thing for him and it did not matter whether he was against Test players at The Oval or club players at Ebbw Vale. He was a good player but perhaps more than that he was a good bloke, easy company and willing to do anything for anyone. When you contribute as much to cricket in general and Glamorgan cricket in particular, as Bernard did, you are entitled to enjoy those memories. I know Bernard did do a little bit of that in his later years with his family and others. Perhaps this book can be seen as an extra little 'entitlement' for all those years of loyal service to the game he loved and to Glamorgan County Cricket Club.

Don Shepherd

INTRODUCTION

'Anything involving a ball. He was good at it. He had a gift.'

Inscribed on the doorway of a house in Newton near the Mumbles is the first line of Dylan Thomas' poem *Fern Hill*. The doorway and the inscription are unremarkable in themselves and would go unnoticed by the casual passer-by. They mark the place where Wales' most famous poet spent some time as a child.

It was a line well remembered by Bernard Hedges, who lived for so many years in the area where the famous writer and poet grew up and was often repeated to his family as they gathered at his home. 'Now as I was young and easy under the apple boughs...' It was a line that was always delivered

Bernard and Don in the early years of their careers, with a Glamorgan supporter.
(© Mrs M.J. Hedges)

with the cultured solemnity that was reminiscent of Thomas' own voice but the recital would begin and end with those words. Familiarity with the first line had not, as with so many other lovers of the lyricism of poetry, led to an intimate knowledge of the poem. If Bernard had been able to continue his recitation, he would have arrived at Thomas' resounding confession that reaches out in appeal to every reader, imploring them to find ways of celebrating their time on this earth:

> *'Oh as I was young and easy in the mercy of his means,*
> *Time held me green and dying*
> *Though I sang in my chains like the sea.'*

Bernard Hedges was one of those lucky few for whom the discovery of what to 'sing in my chains' came without any need for searching. He was a gifted all-round sportsman and, from an early age, showed a great affinity with a range of ball games.

'Anything involving a ball, hitting it and stroking it. Whatever. He was good at it. He had a gift.'

The photograph of Bernard during his playing days that was used at his funeral. (© Glamorgan CCC)

These are the words of his schoolboy friend, Maurice Stallworthy, but many who saw Bernard play would have said similar things. 'A great ball player' was how British Lion and Pontypridd back row forward Russell Robbins remembered him. 'A good cricketer' was how he was described, in understated terms, by Ossie Wheatley, the Glamorgan captain from 1961 to 1966.

Primarily, he is remembered as a cricketer and a batsman of some repute. During an 18-year career in first-class cricket with Glamorgan CCC, he amassed 17,733 runs in 422 appearances. All were in the days of uncovered wickets where bowlers often arrived at a ground with conditions stacked heavily in their favour. They were the days, as well, of three-day matches, with captains frequently negotiating run-chases on the final afternoon, and eschewing the opportunity for batsmen to 'fill their boots', as is often the case today in four-day matches, *en route* to bloated totals and maximum bonus points.

It is a measure of Bernard's talents with the bat that he remains seventh in Glamorgan's all-time list of run scorers and is still one of only six Glamorgan batsmen to ever score over 2,000 runs in a season, getting 2,026 in 1961. He wrote his name into the club's record books during his Benefit Year of 1963 by scoring the county's first century in a one-day game with an unbeaten 103. The one-day games back in 1963 had innings that spanned 65 overs, without any fielding restrictions or other regulations, which in the modern game greatly assist the batsmen. This was a proper hundred!

Before he became a professional cricketer, Bernard played rugby for Pontypridd and Swansea as well as captaining the Wales ATC XV against the England ATC XV at the Arms Park in 1945. He was also good enough to secure a final rugby trial for Wales during 1950, something that in these modern days of professional sport would be impossible with seasons overlapping and players specialising in just one game. For good measure, he also represented Great Britain ATC in an international football tournament in 1946, and it was therefore no surprise this man who shone in both summer and winter sports was inducted in 2004 into the Rhondda Cynon Taff Sporting Hall of Fame alongside other sporting legends of the valleys; Russell Robbins, Bleddyn Williams, Tom David and Neil Jenkins; men who reached the top of their game in just one sport.

Yet despite his outstanding career as a sporting all-rounder, in the sometimes cruel, clear light of the statisticians gaze, his cricketing career may not appear that exceptional. It was sandwiched between Glamorgan's two Championship winning seasons of 1948 and 1969. The nearest Glamorgan came to winning any silverware with Bernard in the team was 1963 when, under the leadership of Ossie Wheatley, they were runners-up in the County Championship.

He was missing from the line-up through illness when the Glamorgan team took on and beat the 1964 Australians at Swansea, and he had retired by the time the Welsh county repeated the trick four years later at St. Helen's. He was the first to admit that there were too many times when he got out too cheaply. In the second innings of Championship games, he freely gave his wicket away in the pursuit of quick runs ahead of a declaration. As a true 'team man', it was collective glory and the pursuit of a victory rather than more conservatively playing for his average that meant most to Bernard. Indeed, his closing career average of 25.22 reflects the fact that he put the team's needs ahead of his personal goals.

There were never stories of England call-ups, selection on MCC winter tours or newspaper editorials proclaiming 'Glamorgan player overlooked'. For much of his career, Glamorgan were an unfashionable county and Bernard remained, first and foremost, someone who rarely grabbed the headlines. But there is always more to the true story than meets the statistical eye. As colleagues and opponents have testified time and again, Bernard was a most reliable and brave opening batsman who forged vibrant opening partnerships, initially with Gilbert Parkhouse and subsequently with Alan Jones. Indeed, Bernard was someone who never shirked away from the challenges of facing the fury of pace bowlers such as Fred Trueman, Frank Tyson, Brian Statham or the country's other fast bowlers. They thrived on green, damp and spiteful wickets in the days when batsmen played without helmets and the other body armour used by modern players. This was a time when a good eye, swift reflexes and a calm head would prevent a batsman being knocked black and blue by a volley of short deliveries.

There was more to his game than dour defence and a safety-first approach. He could dominate the bowling with a range of powerful strokes, often outscoring more illustrious batting partners. The cut and the pull were the strongest weapons in his armoury but his straight drives and 'punched' off drives brought applause from many a crowd and opponents alike. He could also apply himself on the turning wickets that proliferated in the era of uncovered pitches, and Bernard's good technique allied to his level-headed temperament, helped him effectively counter the wiles of the greatest spin bowlers of the time.

He was therefore the kind of player that every county team needed; solid, loyal and dependable as a batsman whilst, in the field, he was a swift presence in the deep besides being a safe and assured pair of hands close to the wicket. Rarely a match winner or a game changer, he was a stalwart rather than a star, a man who might rarely have won selection for an all-time best-ever Glamorgan XI, but a team of Bernard Hedges' would have given any county team a very good run for their money and more often than not come out on top.

Bernard was also a very proud Welsh sportsman, that second adjective being just as important as the first. He was the first native of Pontypridd to gain sustained recognition with Glamorgan CCC. The acclaim, celebrity and distinction given to him in the town took him beyond normal sporting pre-eminence into the realm of folk hero status. He became part of the sporting patchwork of the town, forever woven into the fabric of the past. The Welsh national anthem, co-written by father and son Evan and James James, was composed in Pontypridd in 1856. A memorial to them, in the form of two figures representing poetry and music, was erected and stands still, in Ynysangharad Park, the sporting and, in many ways, spiritual heart of the town. It was here that a hundred years after the anthem was penned, that Bernard graced the same park with his cricketing prowess, playing first, for his school, and later for Glamorgan.

Such coincidences are a given in Wales. The country prides itself on being, in the translated words of *Hen Wlad Fy Nhadau*, a land of bards and singers, and famous men of renown. Pontypridd, and Wales as a whole, is small enough and, perhaps, talented enough for there always to be someone whose notoriety would allow you to point at them and say, 'He lived down my street' or 'I used to go to school with him'. That phrase, 'famous men of renown', an anachronism today, anticipated those countless men of Wales who would take to the sporting fields like 'warring defenders, so gallant and brave'. Throughout the 20th century they were, for the duration of their careers, the standard bearers of a nation. Bernard was one such man. In a small corner of Wales, for a brief period of time, and in a game more 'English' than any other, he acquired that quality of being widely honoured and acclaimed. He was a 'man of renown.'

His individual achievements during the 1950s and 1960s may have faded in the memory; his part in something larger, for many who lived through them, remains. That something larger, some may say, was a golden era of sport when the game was played by men overwhelmingly because they loved it and wanted to be good at it. That pursuit of sporting excellence took place without the distractions of high wages and a celebrity culture which all too often seem to dominate discussions of sport and sporting heroes today.

Sportsmen and women of Bernard's era were seen as proud representatives of the community they came from and sport was a noble pursuit that both

Bernard cuts for four playing against the touring Pakistanis in 1962. (© Glamorgan CCC)

reflected and shaped their character It was the era of Tom Finney, the one-club footballer who was never booked or sent off. In rugby, Jackie Kyle and Cliff Morgan did battle on the pitch, but behaved like friends as they did so. In cricket, Len Hutton, Denis Compton and Peter May all led successive England teams to victories over Australia in the Ashes. The players delighted in the battle of ball against bat with little, if any, of the animosity that had earlier accompanied these contests, most notably the Bodyline series of 1932-33. The simple philosophy was to play the game. No game plans, no clever ploys, no sledging. Just two teams wrestling for supremacy without recourse to dirty tricks. An Irish rugby captain's team talk summed up the approach: "I think a subtle mix of runnin', jinkin' and kickin' should just work out fine." Such a game plan would be viewed today, in the era of tactical awareness, as hopelessly inadequate, if not recklessly naïve.

If sport was so much simpler and more honest back in those days, then Bernard, too, was remembered for the simple and honest way in which he played his sport. His willingness to give himself out lbw and to start walking back to the pavilion before the umpire had upheld the bowlers appeal was, in Ossie Wheatley's eyes, unprecedented as well as being something of a source of eternal frustration for the Glamorgan captain. Dickie Bird, writing in the second instalment of his autobiography *White Cap and Bails* recollected the way in which this Welshman played the game of cricket:

> *'Bernie Hedges opened the innings with Gilbert Parkhouse for Glamorgan at the time I was playing and both did a fine job for the county. Bernie is one of the nicest men I have ever come across in county cricket. I have seen him walk off, without waiting for the umpire's decision, to be met by colleagues in the dressing room questioning whether or not he had got a nick. 'Didn't think you touched that one Bernie', they would say. 'Neither did I 'would come the startling reply, 'But somebody appealed so I must have done.' With the massive appealing that has crept into the game since then, I doubt that he would ever score a run these days.'*

This Corinthian approach was in marked contrast to his first Glamorgan captain, the combative and irascible Wilf Wooller. Standing at short-leg, and snarling a mix of encouragement and criticism to his players, plus a volley of abuse – modern day sledging – to opponents. Wilf was the absolute antithesis of the Corinthian sportsman that Bernard represented. Whilst their approaches to county cricket were polar opposites, for each the goal was identical. If their manner was worlds apart, for both Wilf and Bernard, the result was the same, with the pair sharing the same desire and passion – that Glamorgan should be successful.

Wilf's determination to win and his inclination to see the game in military terms sometimes led him to dispense with the unwritten 'spirit of cricket' in favour of that much more prosaic philosophy; 'whatever is expedient is right'. However, there is nothing to suggest that the two men ever came into conflict about any aspect of the game. Bernard was a player who was never outspoken and who never sought confrontation. There is no evidence to suggest that Bernard ever fell out with *any* of his captains, although he was not afraid to make his views known. He was a captain's dream – loyal, reliable and prepared to do anything for the Glamorgan cause. Despite his standing as a professional, he was a gentleman player and one whose approach was akin more to those amateurs rather than his colleagues in the paid ranks.

Whilst rarely grabbing the headlines himself, Bernard's sporting career placed him alongside some of the greats of Welsh sport. He mixed with a generation of men who were talented rugby players and soccer players as well as cricketers who went on to win higher honours for MCC and England. He rubbed shoulders with some of the giants of English and world cricket. His first-class career, though by no means outstanding, was good enough to secure him a permanent place in the annals at Glamorgan. Sport, and in particular, cricket had been the *leitmotif* of his life. Yet he seemed, strangely, ambivalent about it. Despite the offers and encouragement of others, especially Don Shepherd with whom he roomed for most of his county career, he remained aloof from the Glamorgan Former Players Association. They met annually to remember the cricketing days gone by, and to, once again, enjoy shared memories of proudly wearing the daffodil sweater. Bernard would profess a lack of interest in the modern game to anyone that would care to ask. That apparent ambivalence appears perplexing. Why would someone who seemed to have had so much enjoyment from life on the county circuit remain so singularly silent about it?

One explanation could be that the closing years of his career saw the most dramatic changes in the game with the end, in 1963, of the distinction between Gentlemen and Players. The distinction between amateurs and professional players had dominated the game since the time of W.G. Grace, though to many it was largely symbolic, as amateurs, like the good doctor himself, had received generous payment in some shape or form for many years. However, the emergence of the professional cricketer gave greater impetus to the forces that would

Wilf Wooller. A great leader, tenacious opponent and the inspiration for Glamorgan's County Championship success in 1948. He was club captain from 1947 to 1960. (© Glamorgan CCC)

ultimately threaten to tear the game apart during the following decades. Some cricketing historians draw a line from the Packer Circus of the late 1970s back to the MCC's decision in 1963 to abolish amateurism. As a working class boy barely making a living from professional cricket, much of this would have passed Bernard by, but as a traditionalist, he found it difficult to accept changes to the game. These difficulties led him to cutting himself off from those players with whom he had spent so much time and experienced so much.

If cricket was changing, then the world was changing at an even greater pace. Bernard was born into a valley town whose essential nature had not altered since the mid-1850s, with heavy industry and coal-mining dominating the local economy. Pontypridd and Wales would go through the most dramatic economic and social transformation during Bernard's lifetime. From industrial heartland to industrial wasteland, the communities of the valleys were slowly strangled by economic decline and government diktat.

The departure of economic prosperity was combined with the arrival of cultural and technological changes that undermined the old community ties. Television, advertising, pop music and the emergence of teenage culture all created tensions in Welsh communities. Bernard would have placed himself firmly in the 'pre-Elvis camp' where these changes were concerned. He would willingly have stayed in the world before rock 'n' roll and the 'white heat' of the technological revolution.

It is somewhat ironic, therefore, that his second career, after retiring as a professional cricketer, was with Barclaycard, the company at the forefront of the credit card revolution in the United Kingdom. Yet he remained a man from the pre-technological age. His television diet went little beyond live sport and an extensive range of comedy programmes. Whilst the fish and chip shops in Pontypridd which Bernard had frequented as a young boy were replaced by Chinese and Indian takeaways, and the shelves of the supermarkets accommodated a far wider range of international foods, his diet in later life did not stray beyond the boundaries of plain, Welsh cooking. He would still sing songs from the 1930s as he stood washing the dishes at the sink. He was a man who, for all intents and purposes, got stuck in the immediate post-war years that were his 'hey-day'. His unwillingness to embrace the modern world was, at turns, endearing and frustrating for those around him.

An admirer of Herbert Sutcliffe – the great Yorkshire and England batsman – once explained how cricketers are preserved in the mind of those that saw them play. 'I saw him immediately in my mind as I'd seen him at Headingley, Bradford and Sheffield. He was never old, never frail to me. Your heroes stay as you first saw them'.

Bernard died at home in the Mumbles aged 86. He had become frail and eventually succumbed to old age and disease. It is not how anyone who knew him, especially those that saw him play, would want to remember him. The picture of him that was placed in front of the congregation at his funeral was of a young, handsome man with lightly tanned skin. It was an outdoor face; the face of a cricketer who had just spent several days in the field. His eyes glinted and hinted at an untold depth of character, his jet black hair parted and swept backwards from his face, encouraging you to take in all of his features. The intensity of Bernard's expression would not have appeared out of place on a Hollywood film set or one of the film moguls' billboards.

The brochure from Bernard's Benefit Year in 1963. (© Glamorgan CCC)

This book is an attempt to preserve Bernard Hedges in that time and place when his life was in full flood. A Welshman and a true sportsman who excelled at a number of sports – a man with a Corinthian spirit who played games the way they should be played. He continued to see the world in that way throughout his life. He was a coach, a husband, a father and a friend but, primarily, he was a player. He carried no flags nor made any great boasts about either his talent or his back story.

Nevertheless, he was seen as a boy from the valleys, 'me old butty from Pontypridd' as Basil Easterbrook wrote of him. He was a player of the people - *The Player from 'Ponty'*.

Bernard pulls for four in the match against Kent at Dartford, June 1959. He and Gilbert hit 207 for the first wicket scoring at over four an over. (© Glamorgan CCC)

1

The Early Years

'The odds against him becoming a county cricketer were not merely astronomical, they were laughable.'

Bernard's sister Jean lived for many years in the village of Rhydyfelin, little more than a run around the boundary rope away from where the Hedges family lived in Chestnut Street in 1936. On her kitchen wall there was a drawing, in ink, of the town of Pontypridd. The closely drawn lines had a certain hypnotic quality and you found yourself, after a few seconds, staring 'goggle-eyed' at the picture. Its terraced houses, like so many broken ranks of toy soldiers, sketched as if they were hidden in the folds of a blanket; for all the world a battlefield to the eyes of a young child. The hill tops, inkless on the drawing, huddle round the town's limits at all points of the compass.

The writer Alun Richards, born in Pontypridd in 1929, described the town as he saw it in the years before the Second World War. To him it was,

'a higgledy-piggledy collection of awkward jutting buildings, some big, some small, some minute and whitewashed like pieces of confectionary, some Victorian in style, some Rhondda baronial with forests of drainpipes and guttering, some straight marzipan Cardiff Rialto, the whole a representation of architectural untidiness and looked as if the entire town had been carelessly dropped from the sky and had come together by accident around the leaden river which trailed like a black slug through the centre.'

Pontypridd is a 'confluence town', and a place at once blessed and cursed by its geography. It developed at the point where the River Rhondda, originating from its Rhondda Fawr and Rhondda Fach tributaries, joined the River Taff which flowed down from Merthyr to Cardiff. There had been a bridge over the River Taff since 1756 when William Edwards built an arched, stone footbridge which remains as a symbol of the town and its rugby club today. But it was the building of the Glamorganshire Canal during 1794 and the creation of the railway line in 1841 that gave great impetus to the forces that were transforming Pontypridd from a rural village into an industrial market town.

One of the first large firms to locate in Pontypridd was the Brown Lennox Chainworks, in 1815. The firm produced a stud-linked wrought iron chain that was suitable as a ship's anchor cable and Pontypridd was its second factory. The site provided easy access to the high quantities of pig iron and coal needed in production. Two canal basins were constructed, one for the receipt of raw materials, the other for the dispatching of finished goods. The 20 foot difference between these two basins also allowed the works to be powered entirely through water wheels and turbines.

From 1818, both Brown Lennox factories started manufacturing suspension bridge chains. Through the second half of the 19th century, they were the sole suppliers of chains to the Royal Navy. The Brown Lenox plant at Pontypridd was reputedly where the anchor chain for the RMS Titanic was manufactured and there is a monument near the site of the factory acknowledging this. Isambard Kingdom Brunel was famously photographed in front of chains made by Brown Lennox for his ship the SS Great Eastern. It is no surprise that the company was to play a significant role in the development of sport and recreation in the town.

If iron and steel were the first major industries of the town, coal mining was its most decisive and extensive employer. 'King coal' was the driving force behind the expansion of Pontypridd and its development came in two waves. The first, in the 1840s and 1850s saw the sinking of the Maritime Colliery in 1841, Newbridge Colliery in 1844, Tŷ Mawr Colliery in 1848, and the Great Western Colliery in 1851. The second wave mirrored the great expansion of the Rhondda during the 1870s and 1880s and was marked by the sinking of Dan's Muck Hole or the Pwllgwaun colliery and the Naval Colliery in Penygraig in 1875 and the Albion Colliery, Cilfynydd, in 1884.

The population of the Rhondda grew from 542 in 1801 to 113,735 in 1902. Pontypridd's share of that growth saw the town grow from 2,200 in 1847 to 38,000 in 1899 but this growth had no masterplan. Fields were transformed into villages that grew and expanded along the valleys as identical rows of cheaply constructed terraced houses, with few amenities, clung to the hillsides. Hopkinstown, Cilfynydd, Pwllgaun and Maesycoed all grew up around the local pits, extending like bony black fingers pointing to the top of the Rhondda. These fingernails were cracked and chipped. No varnish, no gloss; just bricks, mortar, men and their families.

With this huge influx of men drawn to the lucrative but dangerous work underground also came that frequent and dreaded caller to valley homes: serious injury and death. During the second half of the 19th century it was estimated that a miner died every six hours somewhere in Britain's coalmines. In 1893, 63 men and boys aged between 14 and 61 lost their lives at the Great Western pit and a year later, 290 were killed in an explosion at the Albion Colliery. Of the 125 horses that worked underground there, only two survived and one family in Howell Street, Cilfynydd, lost 11 members: the father, his four sons and six lodgers. Fatal and near-fatal accidents became a regular part of the town's life, the blinds being drawn by families in the streets where a victim of the struggle for 'black gold' lived. Tragedy remained close at hand in the life of the town and it was to touch Bernard's life in its own way.

Life was tough and uncompromising in Pontypridd and, similar to other mining communities, it bred hard drinking, God-fearing men. The non-conformist chapels thrived throughout the town, where women brought up large families in cramped conditions, with nothing in the way of support from the state. It was a community where the men drank like devils but sang like angels; the town giving birth not only to *Hen Wlad fy Nhadau* but also *Cwm Rhondda*, penned by John Hughes, a clerk at the Great Western Colliery. Pontypridd was a place that lived for, and in, the moment, enjoying its simple pleasures like a Sunday school trip to Barry Island, a bike ride or a boxing match. This was, in the vivid phraseology of Gwyn Alf Williams, 'the distinctive, sardonic, complex, warm, picaresque, soft-hearted and malicious, hard-headed and cock-eyed, ambitious and heroic and daft world of the miners.'

Sport was an integral part of this society. Gambling often went along with it, and with one sport in particular, boxing. The town produced many champion boxers, the most famous of which was Freddie Welsh, who held the World Lightweight title during the years of the First World War, and the Moody brothers, Frank and Glenn, who both won Welsh boxing titles. Promoter Ted E. Lewis, manager of the Moody brothers and co-founder of the Boxing Board of Control, stated in 1932, 'within a 20 mile radius of the fountain (in Taff Street, Pontypridd) each of the nine Welshmen who won British titles were born and bred ... if ever boxing should determine the point, Pontypridd would easily be entitled to the description of capital of Wales.'

Team sports were popular with the miners, so rugby and football provided a release from the drudgery of work at the pit.

The cricket pavilion, Ynysangharad Park, Pontypridd (© Rhondda Cynon Taff Libraries)

The memorial to Evan and James James, co-writers of The Welsh National Anthem Mae Hen Wlad Fy Nhadau, erected in Ynysangharad Park. (© Rhondda Cynon Taff Libraries)

A range of sports provided a means by which this emerging community could forge a measure of local identity and collective pride. A cricket club had been formed in 1870, but references to cricket in Pontypridd date back to 1858. Like many other clubs in these close-knit industrial communities, its origin was the result of the influx into the valleys of English-born and educated migrants. The early games of the newly formed club were staged in the grounds of Gelliwasted House, before a move in 1873 to a more spacious area of farmland owned by Gordon Lenox, the resident director of Brown Lenox. Gordon Lenox oversaw the laying of a decent wicket in one of the fields at Ynysangharad Farm alongside the River Taff. The company also acted as generous philanthropists by giving the cricket club money to buy equipment and kit, knowing that many of the club`s members were men of quite modest means and could not afford kit of their own. Given this help, the number of members increased and in 1897, Pontypridd were able to enter the newly-formed Glamorgan Cricket League, playing fixtures against clubs from Treherbert, Treorchy, Merthyr Tydfil, Ferndale and Mountain Ash.

The farmland home of Pontypridd CC was transformed into an attractive parkland after the Great War. When hostilities ended, plans were set in motion for the creation of a war memorial for Pontypridd and, in keeping with their role as generous patrons to the town, Brown Lenox offered their farmland at Ynysangharad. Public subscriptions and grants from the Miners Welfare Fund helped to finance the conversion of the farmland into a spacious park and public recreation ground. The war memorial was opened on August Bank Holiday Monday 1923 and, over the following years, a bowling green, rugby pitch, swimming pool, tennis courts and bandstand were added to the already existing cricket pitch and small pavilion.

Pontypridd RFC had been formed in 1876, and was sufficiently well established by March 1880 to be one of nine clubs that met at the Tenby Hotel, Swansea, to discuss the formation of a national union. In 1886-87 the headquarters of the club was the Maltsers Arms, near the stone footbridge that that has become a symbol of the town. It played its home matches at the Ynysangharad and Trallwn Fields. In 1890-91 the club moved to a field alongside the River Taff at Treforest, and began the development of the famous Taff Vale Park. The final Welsh trial was held there in December 1892 'to encourage the rising valley club.' The club then moved to the People's Park in Mill Street in 1901, where it stayed for three seasons. Then, on 1 October 1904, it played Caerphilly in the first game on a new pitch at Ynysangharad Fields. Although the club later returned to Taff Vale Park for a short time, it was back at Ynysangharad by 1908 and stayed there for 66 years.

The Hedges family were migrants of a sort. Bernard's great grandfather had been a publican, owning the Royal Exchange public house in Llandaff North, a popular suburb of Cardiff. His grandfather had worked at the Melingriffith Tin Works at Whitchurch before moving north to Pontypridd as an engine driver in the 1890s. Bernard's great uncle, John, born in 1855, succumbed to the pressures to survive and ended up in the Pontypridd workhouse, his presence there being recorded in the 1911 census. A contemporaneous account of the conditions in the workhouse leaves the reader in no doubt about the nature of the place:

'Hygiene was unheard of, stores were empty and inmates were sometimes barefooted. Many had no change of clothing; their underclothes were in rags and were overrun with vermin. The main diet of 'stew' contained oatmeal with obvious evidence of rats droppings ... the healthy stole what was eatable from the sick, the strong from the weak, all were degraded in the battle for survival.'

Bernard's father John (or Jack as he was known) was born in 1893, the same year as the pit disaster at the Great Western Colliery. He started work in the pits, first at the Maritime Colliery and later, at the Great Western, from an early age. After the First World War, Jack found himself

Jack Hedges, Bernard's father, photographed (front row centre) on a walk with friends in the years immediately after The Great War. (© Peter Hedges)

The Graigwen Working Men's Institute Committee photographed in 1921. Jack Hedges is standing far left. (© Peter Hedges)

Pontypridd RFC before their 1920 tour of the West Country. Jack Hedges is sitting on the grass, front right.

not only contributing to the work of the colliery but also the working men's institute. He was a keen rugby player and played at scrum-half for Pontypridd.

Bernard was Jack's first son, born in 1927 and named after his brother who had died fighting for the King's Shropshire Light Infantry in April 1916. The body of the 21-year-old soldier was never recovered so the name B. Hedges appears on the famous stone gate memorial at Ypres. The street into which Jack was bringing his young family was known locally as the chain works cottages and stood less than a cricket field away from the pitch at Ynysangharad. Three sisters for Bernard followed over the next few years, with Margaret, then Joan, and finally Jean. Three brothers: John, Gerald and Peter were added to the family during the 1930s and before the beginning of the Second World War.

Jack's eighth child, a daughter christened Lynne, did not arrive until 1948, when Bernard was 21 years old. Big families were not unusual in those days. Indeed, when the family moved to Rhydyfelin in 1934 they joked about all the big families in Pontypridd being moved to the same street. With the depression causing widespread hardship in the industrial valleys, Jack and his wife Gwen faced a real struggle to raise their ever-growing family. For several years, Gwen worked in the Greyhound public house and ended up practically running the place. It gave her a lifelong disgust of the evils of drink, a feeling she clearly passed on to her eldest son. Whilst Bernard was willing to have a drink well into old age, he was always reluctant to drink in excess and showed his dislike of the effects of too much alcohol.

Living conditions were basic. Peter remembered that there was no running water and an outside toilet in the old cottage in Ynysangharad Road where the family lived until 1934. All the same, the daily necessities of wholesome meals and clean clothes always seemed to be available. 'I don't know how my mum managed. The boys outside playing; the girls in here working with Gran. The boys in one bedroom; the girls in the other. We always ate well. Sunday morning breakfast was salt fish. We never missed a Sunday lunch. My mum was quite strong willed. It must have been terribly hard for here between the wars.'

The years before moving to Rhydyfelin was the period of the General Strike and the Hunger Marches, of grinding poverty and widespread disease and ill health. Alun Richards would write, looking back on this time in Pontypridd:

Jack and Gwen Hedges photographed on holiday in Porthcawl during the early 1950s. (© Peter Hedges)

'Even those born in comparatively affluent circumstances were aware of the long lines of the unemployed threading their way in shabby queues along the main street, while no one who attended a council school in the 1930s could be unaware of malnutrition, of leg irons masking rickets and the sight of undernourished ragged children shivering damply in inadequate playground shelters in the winter when it seemed to rain incessantly.'

Bernard did not escape his childhood without succumbing to these difficult conditions. Basil Easterbrook, writing nearly 30 years later in Bernard's Benefit brochure, noted that, 'When he was eight he was bed ridden for seven months. The future Glamorgan stalwart could not walk. Doctors and specialists looked at him and the discovery of a groin abscess led to the long search for a tubercular bone, which fortunately was not revealed and after special treatment at a Pontypridd Clinic Bernard Hedges became a normal lively boy.'

That could have been the clinic at Ynysangharad Park that also treated the scourges of scabies and rickets. Bernard remembered being operated on at the kitchen table. Local doctors at that time would charge for their visits as well as making their own remedies for their own dispensary. Gwen told one

The Hedges family photographed outside their house in Chestnut Street, Rhydyfelin. From left: Jean, Gwen, Peter (being held by Gwen), Bernard, John, Jack, Margaret, Gerald (being held by Margaret), Joan. Lynne was yet to be born which dates the photo to the years immediately after the Second World War. (© Hedges family)

doctor never to visit the house again after he was rude about one of the children. Name and reputation would not get in the way of Gwen's determination to look after her own.

It was no wonder that Basil Easterbrook could state in his profile of Bernard that, 'From his birth in 1927 the odds against him becoming a county cricketer were not merely astronomical, they were laughable.'

In the wake of the General Strike, one of Jack's brothers, Thomas, was so desperate to find work that he left the Rhondda on foot and did not stop walking until he had reached London, where a branch of the Hedges family made a new home in the English capital's East End. The strong family connection nevertheless remained and one of Tom's children, Gwyneth, had a son, Trahaearn, who visited Bernard while studying at Swansea University during the 1990s.

Trahaearn always fondly remembered the time he spent with Bernard. As a keen cricketer with aspirations to play first-class cricket, he had come hoping to get good advice from his mother's cousin. What he got was Bernard's gentle admonitions to try harder and his reflections that a career in cricket was hard and probably best not to be entered into. This was something of his childhood that stayed with him always. Life was hard and setbacks were to be expected. It was not so much a fatalistic and pessimistic outlook as a pragmatic accommodation to what he saw as the truth: life was like war, so why place yourself in the firing line.

Despite widespread unemployment, Jack retained his job at the pit, and was a strong and influential character not only in his own house but in the community as well. When King Edward VIII visited the valleys in 1936, Jack made sure that the street was bedecked with bunting. One house at the end of the terrace and occupied by a local communist sympathiser remained 'bunting free'. After a visit from Jack and some strong words, the bunting went up. Peter recalls his father:

'He was a straight man. He didn't take any messing from anybody. You'd be out playing and you'd break somebody's window. He'd be round with glass and fix it the next day and you would have to pay for it out of your own pocket money for the next few weeks.'

He was a strong disciplinarian but he loved his children and always tried to give them a childhood filled with memories other than those imposed on them by their circumstances. Margaret remembered him putting up a series of tents one summer for all the Hedges children and their friends. Peter remembered the period just after the war:

Bernard, aged 18, with younger brother Peter outside the front door at Chestnut Street. (© Hedges family)

'There was a lot more fun in those days. We didn't have Playstations or computers. We were the first on the estate to have a TV. There used to be about 20 kids in here. It was a rental. Every Friday there was a pewter mug. All the kids put their half a crown in. "No excuses", he would say. "Everybody pays or the TV goes back."'

Jack was involved in an accident at the pit in the early 1930s. Despite the seriousness of his injuries, he refused to be taken back to the house in an ambulance. He got out at the end of the street and walked the last few hundred yards home. Peter, again:

'When I remember him, he worked at the Treforest Industrial Estate in a factory making glass. He hated it. "It wasn't a job for a man," he said. He was trapped in a fall at the pit. There was no social security so he had to get better to go back to work. He always walked to work. We never had a car.'

The town of Pontypridd was a seething urban backdrop to all the developments of the Hedges family. Described by broadcaster Gwyn Thomas as the 'Damascus of the valleys' it was a social and commercial pole of attraction for the hundreds of pit villages that lay around it. In 1939, there were 259 regular tenants of the indoor market including 61 fruit and veg stalls, 49 selling second-hand clothes, 37 butchers, 12 selling cakes and biscuits, and four that

Bernard, aged 16, camping with best friend Bernard Cummings. 'I thought I had two brothers called Bernard' Peter Hedges recalled. (Courtesy the Hedges Family)

just sold bacon. A trip to 'Ponty' was an opportunity to revel in the excitement of this heaving hub of retail outlets. Besides all of that, there was always playing. 'It was all day and everyday out on the field. Football, 30-a-side. We couldn't play when they were marking the field.'

Even Bernard's sisters would join in these games, although Jack had some doubts about their effectiveness. A regular player was Bernard Cummings, a local boy and Bernard's best friend. Peter remembers thinking that he had a second brother called Bernard he was at the house so often! All were made welcome by Gwen, a kindness that would see her welcoming some of the best sportsman in Wales in the years ahead. Russell Robbins, Cliff Morgan and Don Shepherd would all receive a taste of her hospitality. Bernard had undergone a tough start to his life but he had survived. Passing the 11-plus exam, he must have thought that things were looking up for him. However, before he arrived at the local grammar school, his life chances were affected in a far more significant way with the start of the Second World War.

2

The War and The County School

'The road from the pit had three lanes, with one leading through books and the other two leading through the rugby pitch and the cricket pavilion.'

'I have nothing to offer but blood, toil, tears and sweat': the words of Winston Churchill speaking in the Houses of Parliament in May 1940, days after assuming the leadership of Britain from Neville Chamberlain. The 'phoney war' was over and the whole country was fearful of what lay ahead. Pontypridd was no different to elsewhere in the UK. The threat of invasion had been made abundantly clear throughout the second half of 1939 with campaign posters going up around the town and signposts being dismantled. There was already rationing on a wide scale – butter, bacon, chocolates, sweets, meat, sugar, clothes and petrol were all in short supply – and, by 1940, the town was receiving its first evacuees; it was soon to experience its first bombings.

For an 11-year-old boy about to move into his secondary schooling it must have been quite bewildering. Life during the 1930s had been tough enough for the Hedges family but now it was becoming even tougher. Gwen's sister moved into the house. Jack, now carrying his injuries from the pit, could only serve at home but was a gunner as part of the detachment of the Welsh Guards which defended Windsor Castle. He would return on leave with stories of conversations with King George and Queen Elizabeth the Queen Mother as they walked the ramparts each evening.

Pontypridd, despite being a home of radicalism and agitation around unemployment and the mines, threw its weight fully behind the war effort. The Home Guard made its impact known in the town and surrounding areas. An unemployed actor by the name of Arthur Lowe, who was to subsequently make his name gently lampooning the organisation he was part of, in the BBC series *Dad's Army*, was billeted in Treforest, just a stone's throw from the factory where Jack worked. Bevin Boys and later, American soldiers came to stay and were welcomed. One evacuee, remembering their time in the town, later said: 'My recollections of Wales are of great kindness. We were received into the homes of strangers with complete openness.'

Through force of circumstance, if not inclination, the people of Wales were drawn towards their neighbours in England. Martin Johnes, in his history, *Wales Since 1939*, believes that 'the Welsh people perhaps felt more British than at any other time during their history.' This sense that we were 'all in it together' was perhaps summed up best by a fictional character, the vicar in the 1942 film, *Mrs Miniver*. As the film reaches its conclusion, the vicar speaks to all those watching as well as his immediate audience at the graveside when he says,

> 'this is not only a war of soldiers in uniform. It is the war of the people, of all the people. And it must be fought not only on the battlefield but in the cities and in the villages, in the factories and on the farms, in the home and in the heart of every man, woman and child who loves freedom. Well, we have buried our dead, but we shall not forget them. Instead they will inspire us with an unbreakable determination to free ourselves, and those who come after us, from the tyranny and terror that threaten to strike us down. This is the People's War. It is our war. We are the fighters. Fight it then. Fight it with all that is in us.'

With everyone urged to 'Dig for Victory' the cricket pitch at Ynysangharad was given over to growing vegetables to supply the 'British Restaurant' which had opened in the Tabernacle Hall in the centre of the town. This was part of a network of 1,500 eating places opened to supply cheap nutritious food for workers who could not get home because of the Blitz. And, of course, the bombs came. On 29 August 1940, at the beginning of the Battle of Britain, a large number of incendiary bombs and 13 high explosive bombs were dropped on the town, with the Luftwaffe hoping to damage the town's centres of commerce and trade, its rows of terraced housing and, perhaps most important of all, its factories that were a vital cog in the munitions trade. Fortunately, there was no obliteration with few landmarks of note, as unlike other Welsh towns which suffered heavy bombing, in Pontypridd there was just row upon row of brick and mortar, and very little to assist the Nazi air crew and their navigational equipment for their grim deeds.

There was one large building to the north of the town which did not interest the Luftwaffe navigators. It was the County School for Boys. This would become the centre of interest for young Bernard for the next seven years. Built halfway up the hill, and overlooking Ynysangharad, it nestled under the mountain top like a climber seeking refuge from the elements. After passing his 11-plus, this was where Bernard started his secondary school life in September

1939. The school was one of a number of grammar schools in the valleys and surrounding areas. They took their ethos and their outlook from the English public schools. The school motto, *Ymdrech a Lwydda*, could not have been more apt for the times the school community now found itself in. 'Success through Effort' was, essentially, 'blood, toil, sweat and tears' for all the boys.

The headmaster, Mr E.R. Thomas, (or 'Piggy' as he was known to all the boys, though none would dare call him that to his face), was caught up in the drama of the bombings. The windows of his house on Tyfica Road were shattered. Reporting back to the school assembly, with Bernard looking on, he commented, 'Well I'm sure you are all pleased to see that I have survived.' A mixture of boos and cheers greeted the head's announcement, reflecting the conflicting attitudes the pupils had towards him.

Writer Alun Richards, who started at the school two years below Bernard, saw Mr Thomas in a rather Dickensian way; 'He was a concerned, engaged, and forthright man, never diffident or aloof, often wrong, but always moving forward, making a two fisted attack on life, unafraid of its abrasions to the end.'

Richards also talked more plainly about Mr Thomas. 'He beat you, harangued you and found you out,' but reverted to comparison to complete the picture of this overbearing school master. 'Like Stalin, or Mao Tse Tung, or Field Marshall Kitchener on the famous wartime recruiting poster, his eyes were always on you. He did not leave you alone, ever. And there was The Stick . . '. Others, such as Russell Robbins the British Lion and old boy of the school, remembered him purely in relation to that stick as 'the bugger who caned us'. Maurice Stallworthy recalled crossing the head when he went for a football trial instead of playing for the school rugby team. The conversation went something like this: 'I understand you cried off rugby on Saturday'. 'Yes Sir'. 'So you put this *Youth Club* before the school?' 'Yes Sir.' 'You will not play rugby for the school team for the rest of the season. Get out!'

Maurice was so upset that, after telling his father, he also came into the school the following day to try and smooth things out for his son, but even Mr Stallworthy senior was sent home with his tail between his legs. The message was clear and simple – school comes first. By all accounts, Bernard avoided too much confrontation with Mr Thomas and was a conscientious pupil. Used to a disciplined life at home, he applied himself with diligence to his life at school. Whilst he was not outstanding academically, he did gain a school certificate from the Central Welsh Education Board for being very good in chemistry in 1945. He would have been 17 years old.

For every boy at the County School (and possibly some of the staff as well!), it was the activities outside the classroom that proved the most rewarding and inspiring. The playing of sport ran through the school like the seams of coal that permeated the rock beneath it. But the sporting life back then was very simple; you played rugby in the winter and cricket in the summer, with inter-form competitions in both sports, plus an established fixture list with the other grammar schools in the locality.

As Maurice recalled, 'I can vividly remember at lunch time going up on to the asphalt plateau where there used to be tennis courts but nobody played tennis. We used to cut a hazel stick and play touch rugby. It was a brilliant foundation to the game. No kicking. It was run, run, run. As soon as we finished lunch, we were back up there playing.'

It was this collective enthusiasm which stood the school in good stead on the sporting fields, and more than made up for the fact that many young and able-bodied men were away on military service, leaving others – less mobile or gifted – to take charge of the next generation of Pontypridd sportsmen. There was a great tradition in these sports, and Bernard proudly witnessed the 1st XV of 1944-1945 enjoy a record-breaking season, unequalled in the history of rugby at the school. They won all 20 of their games, and, in so doing, amassed 666 points and only conceded 43, with Wynford Davies, the team's captain, also leading the Welsh Schools side against the English Public Schools. Bernard was a regular in the 2nd XV, watching on in awe at some of the players he would subsequently play alongside or against in Pontypridd colours. These included Wynford, who would play for Newport as well as the full Welsh side, and Glyn Davies, who would partner Wynford at fly half for Wales in the Victory Internationals of 1946.

As winter gave way to spring and summer, so rugby gave way to cricket, with Bernard being named vice-captain of the 1st XI. The summer of 1945 saw the side win eight of their games, only losing one, with three others being drawn. The number of victories might have been higher, but as he grew accustomed in future years with Glamorgan, the fickle nature of the summer weather in the Taff Valley saw five other games being cancelled due to rain. At the time, Bernard enjoyed more success with the ball than the bat, a not uncommon trait in the development of professional talent with the 17-year-old delivering 59.5 overs, the most by anyone in the 1st XI – and claiming 15 wickets at a mere eight runs apiece. In his seven innings, he amassed 107 runs with an average of a shade under 18.

When assessing the true merit of these figures, we should not forget that these were not the day-long games enjoyed by those at boarding schools elsewhere in England and Wales. All were played in the early evening after school and, in essence, were more akin to Twenty20 matches than other forms of limited-overs games. Just like every other aspect of life in the UK at the time, time at the crease was rationed, so scoring hundreds and playing lengthy innings was out of the question. Nevertheless, Bernard's potential for batting

The County School for Boys, Pontypridd, 1st XI in 1945. Glyn Davies is seated far left, Bernard is standing far right. The Master standing in the back row was Mr P.R. Jones (French). Seated (centre) is Mr J.L. Thomas who, during the war, would announce casualties in assembly and would also chart its progress, calling for three cheers on D-Day. (Courtesy Mrs MJ Hedges)

was clear to everyone, and the highlight of his summer for the grammar school was an unbeaten 53 against Porth County School. It was an innings that ensured that he, and his school teammate George Yeomans, were selected in the Glamorgan schoolboy's team which went on to decisively defeat their counterparts from Monmouthshire.

At the end of that Summer Term, Bernard attended the school Air Training Corps (ATC) Squadron Summer Camp at St. Athan. The huge RAF base was only 25 miles away but it must have felt like a different world to Bernard and his friends. The sprawling base, built within sight of the Bristol Channel coastline and surrounded by open countryside, stood in stark contrast to the confined spaces of Rhydyfelin and Pontypridd. The ATC had formed in the town in 1941 and three years later had set up its headquarters at the school with Mr Thomas acting as Flight Lieutenant. Not only were their activities a way of encouraging discipline and service into young boys, they were also a means of fostering greater sporting competition. 557 Squadron played several other south Wales Squadrons at rugby and the ATC was soon to give Bernard his most meritorious moments to date.

Meanwhile, in his aircraftsman's uniform, he had already been involved in a series of huge parades through the town which brought Pontypridd to a standstill. These were led by despatch riders, the Welsh regimental goat, Cymmer military band, Ynysybwl Silver Band, the WAAF band, American soldiers, Sea Cadets, Sea Rangers, Army Cadets, ATC Cadets, Women's Land Army, the Glamorgan Constabulary, the ARP wardens and so on. In May 1944, the 'Save for the Soldier Week' culminated with one such parade, the highlight of which was a parachute drop onto the cricket pitch at Ynysangharad Park. There were five paratroopers in total, though their drop met with mixed results: the first landed in the River Taff, the second in a potato patch and the third in some bushes, before the final two managed to land successfully on the outfield of the cricket ground. It was hoped, by all, that future military operations with slightly more at stake would have a higher rate of success!

On VE Day, 8 May 1945, Pontypridd joined in the celebrations throughout the country. Churchill's victory broadcast was amplified through loudspeakers at the Rediffusion shop in Market Street and the town was illuminated that night as family friends and school mates mingled together to celebrate the end of the war. As one account outlined, 'Strings of multi-coloured lights sparkled from the Tumble end of the town and along Taff Street to the Old Bridge. They culminated there in a huge crown scintillating with red, white, blue and green lamps supported on brightly lit arms which formed an arch over the adjacent Victorian bridge across the River Taff.'

On VJ Day in August, Bernard found himself in St. Athan. Large bonfires were built and the ATC band was called out. Everyone followed the band, 'Pied

The County School 1st XI. Here, Headmaster Mr E.R. Thomas is flanked by Bernard (left) and Glyn Davies (right). (© Mrs M.J. Hedges)

Piper fashion', through the station, finishing by the main gate, where they were greeted by the fire and smoke which engulfed the nearby fireman's hut.

A week later, Bernard was back in cricketing action, having been chosen in the Welsh Secondary Schools XI against Glamorgan Colts at Cardiff Arms Park. The game was a showcase of the emerging talent in the region. The county club, tragically struck by the death of their captain Maurice Turnbull shortly after the Normandy Landings, was striving to prepare for the future and life without their inspirational figurehead. Once again, George Yeomans was in the Welsh side, but Bernard's friend, as well as fellow opener Graham Crimp, departed early and it was left to Bernard, batting at number three, to provide the bulwark of the 28-over innings, striking an unbeaten 54.

His efforts were not enough to build a match-winning total as the county's colts won the game comfortably by nine wickets, with their only wicket to fall being that of Derek Williams, the future Wales rugby international, who despite having played in the county's 1st XI during some of their wartime friendlies was snared by Bernard's gentle medium pace. It was quite a feather in the cap of the Pontypridd schoolboy to claim Derek's wicket.

Out of school, Bernard spent a lot of his time playing football for St Dyfrig's Youth Club and any sport he cared to play on Acacia Green outside his house. Lots of local children in Rhydyfelin used to spend some of their evenings on the

Wartime football. St. Dyfrig's Youth Club football team photographed during the 1944/45 season. The 16-year-old Bernard is third from right on the back row. His best friend, Bernard Cummings, is holding the ball. (© Mrs M.J. Hedges)

railway embankment watching the greyhounds being raced on the local track, as Alan Oliver recalled:

> 'We used to sit there and watch all the races. We were thrilled when the lights went on. Most went down there to bet. We used to make tuppence of thruppence by looking after somebody's car or bike. When there was nobody there we would nip down over the fence and go onto the tracks. The traps were activated with thick rubber bands. We would cut them off to make slings.'

The older boys would get the job of looking after the dogs in the moments before they were put into the traps. They could see at close quarters, the rough tactics employed by the dog owners to try and affect the result. Some overfed their dogs so they would lose one race to get better odds in the next. Some squeezed their dog's testicles or gave their dog a nip of whiskey immediately before they were placed inside. This was meant to make them run faster but often the only thing it made them do was yelp more loudly!

The Wales ATC XV that played England ATC at Cardiff Arms Park in May 1946. Bernard captained the side and is seen holding the match ball. Wales won 18-5. (© Mrs M.J. Hedges)

In the 1946 edition of the school magazine, *The Pontypriddian*, Bernard is prominently mentioned in the section on the Air Training Corps: 'The Flight has distinguished itself in sport and has seen one of its members, B. Hedges, reach a most enviable position ... Bernard Hedges captained the Welsh Team which defeated the English side by 18 points to 5. In April, Hedges had a very memorable experience. With the other members of a representative British ATC side he was flown to Switzerland to take part in a series of six games against Swiss Youth Clubs.'

That Welsh ATC side was a truly representative rugby team. It included Ian McJennett, who later played for Cardiff RFC between 1946 and 1950 before transferring to Newport where he played prop, served on the committee and acted as coach. Known as 'Blondie', John Thorley played for Neath and Wales before turning professional and playing rugby league for Halifax and Great Britain. He played in the 1954 Challenge Cup final against Warrington in front of 100,000

Bernard in ATC uniform with a friend in Berne, Switzerland, for an international football tournament in April 1946. (© Hedges family)

plus fans at Odsal Stadium in Bradford. Peter Evans played as a flanker. He was from 556 Squadron Llanelli. He played twice for Wales in the 1950-51 season and was Llanelli club captain from 1953 to 1955.

The captain of the British Soccer ATC side was a 17-year-old called Jimmy Wardaugh, who was to make his debut for Hearts later that year. He became known as an integral part of the 'Terrible Trio', the Hearts forward line of the 1950s, alongside Willie Bauld and Alfie Conn. He was the club's record League goal-scorer for almost 40 years, until his tally of 206 was surpassed by John Robertson in 1997. Bernard played at inside right and, according to those who saw him, was 'very clever', with close control and good pace, both of which were to serve him well in his days playing rugby for Pontypridd.

Alan Oliver remembers hearing of Bernard's selection for the British ATC side:

'I remember Piggy, that's what we disrespectfully called him, at the school assembly. We were all there and he had all these announcements to make. How the rugby team were doing, this, that and the other and I'll never forget him saying "and Bernard Hedges, he's been picked to play association football". Now we didn't bloody know what association football was, it was soccer to us!'

Bernard was already well known as a sportsman in the school, so much so that his opinion and assistance was sought after by the other boys. Again, Alan recalls:

'I lived about 200 yards away from Bernard and he had to pass our house every day to go to school or go to 'Ponty'. There was an alleyway past the end of the house. We were all keen on cricket, we used to play on the grass with a tennis ball: me, my old man, my brothers and my brother in law. Bernard would stop to watch when he passed. "Olly, you're hopeless!" he'd shout. Once or twice we persuaded him to come in and he showed us how to square cut properly. He would show us how to bowl an off-break or a 'leggie'. We always called him in.'

After their record-breaking ventures the previous winter, the 1st XV of 1945-46 had quite something to live up to, but the rugby season, once again, saw a wholly dominant side from Pontypridd Boys Grammar School. They won 22 of the 24 games, with one draw and a defeat. Bernard played occasionally for the team, and again shared in their collective success, but any sadness which he had felt on missing out on a regular place was more than compensated for in April when he was appointed captain for the school's cricket 1st XI.

It was a decent summer for both Bernard and the school team, who were presented with a cricket bat by Glamorgan's George Lavis, one of several of the county's pre-war players who had answered the call to arms raised by veteran Johnnie Clay. Despite being nearer 50 than 40, Johnnie had agreed to lead the team in 1946 as the County Championship resumed, and to oversee the county's off-field operations. These included coaching and talent-spotting, with George being one of the players who agreed to help out by returning to south Wales after a short spell in Scotland. He duly became a significant influence on Bernard and it was on George's advice that Glamorgan offered Bernard his first professional contract in 1950.

Under Bernard's leadership, the school won seven of its matches, and emulated the rugby side by drawing one and losing one. Perhaps having been inspired by the donation of the bat from George, or some of his wise words, 1946 saw a marked improvement in Bernard's batting with 243 runs at an average of 43. But this wasn't to the detriment of his bowling, as he continued to shine with the ball, taking 16 wickets at seven runs apiece, besides producing career-best figures of 7-8 against Penarth County School who were dismissed for a paltry 19.

The highlight for everyone associated with the County School was the selection of Wynford and Glyn Davies to play for Wales against England at the Arms Park in February. Wales' youngest ever half back partnership was front

An Aerial View of Ynysangharad Park (taken in 1959) where Bernard played his early schools cricket. The ground had hosted county cricket since 1924. See the circular Bandstand area just below the cricket pavilion and field. The park is boundaried by the River Taff and beyond it you see the arc of the railway station platform with the hills beyond that. (© RCAHMW)

page news in Pontypridd and the 'grand little pair' as Mr E.R. Thomas called them in the *Pontypridd Observer*, would not be attending the game on their own. The school duly hired several buses to take its pupils, Bernard included, down to the match. Mysteriously, the school bell, used to signal the end of lessons and lunch time, had gone missing. With the game under way the Arms Park, as well as hearing the roar of the crowd, was treated to the unmistakeable sound of the Pontypridd County School for Boys Bell ringing out whenever Glyn or Wynford made a contribution to the game. Stealing the bell, under normal circumstances, would be more than enough reason for an audience with the headmaster and to feel the whip of his cane. On the Monday following the game, the bell found its way back to its rightful place and Mr Thomas never made mention of its disappearance!

Bernard certainly never allowed any of his sporting success to go to his head. At school, there were others who went on to win a string of Welsh schoolboy rugby caps, and they were the king-pins in the school's sporting hierarchy. At home, Bernard's feet were very firmly kept on the ground by his father, who strove to ensure that none of his boys ended up down the pit. He would have been pleased with the aphorism 'the road out of the pit led through a school book'. In Bernard's case, that road may have had three

The ATC football team at an international tournament in Switzerland, April 1946. Bernard is standing in the back row (far right). Jimmy Wardaugh is seated between two officers (third from left). (© Mrs M.J. Hedges)

lanes with, in addition to the one leading through his classroom, another two leading through the rugby pitch and the cricket pavilion.

Had he grown up in the modern era, Bernard's prowess on the cricket field, and his contact with county coaches would have seen him join the Glamorgan Academy. Life in south Wales in 1946 was very different. The Welsh county were still operating on a shoestring budget and had to make do, for many years after the war. With indoor nets along a corridor of the North Stand at the Arms Park. Thoughts about a career in sport were furthest from Bernard's mind as his school days drew to a close. For him, like the majority of the other leavers from the County School, his immediate future lay in National Service, and dutifully following the founding article of faith, which he had recited so many times with the ATC – 'I further promise to be a good citizen and do my duty to God and the Queen, my country and my flag.'

It was with this sense of service that he duly departed home for the first time for an extended period, to begin his RAF National Service. It was the first time he remembered ever having felt the touch of his father's hand. The handshake told him he was now a man and was expected to act as one, with strong principles and commitment. That commitment would involve, to his father's eternal pride, the playing of the games of rugby and cricket.

3

National Service

'I could have got those runs with this hose pipe.'

When Bernard started his National Service with the RAF during the autumn of 1946 he was joining organisations that were already steeped in traditions of competitive sport. During the Second World War there was not only a range of opportunities for servicemen to engage in sport, from boxing to football, but also for professional players to find themselves involved in representative games against other services and scratch teams from other countries. Football led the way with the British Army of the Rhine (BAOR) but cricket was not far behind with the RAF playing the Army and the Navy as well as the Royal Australian Air Force. Top players were withdrawn from areas of conflict to allow them to play in some of these games. Bleddyn Williams, who would grace the shirt of Wales and the British Lions and was a near neighbour of Bernard's in Taff's Well, was recalled from his slit trench in Germany to play rugby for Britain against the Dominions at Leicester. His CO, who had ordered him to attend the match, was Major Hugh Bartlett, an attacking left-handed batsman and captain of Sussex after the war.

After his initial training, Bernard was posted to St. Athan, a place he already knew through his involvement in the Air Cadets. The station had been ordained as a technical training school just before the war. It was where the young Don Shepherd would also be sent on a training course for his profession as a mechanic, a rather alien workplace for the man, raised in in the peaceful surroundings of the Gower, who went on to become Glamorgan's most successful bowler. After seeing out the extreme winter of 1947 Bernard settled into the routine of station life which, in St. Athan, was equivalent to that of a small town:

'Entertainments and welfare activities for the station's population of nearly 10,000 were centred in the Amenities Building on East Camp which contained under one roof a modern cinema with a seating capacity of 1,255, also used as a theatre for the presentation of plays and concerts, a heated swimming pool 100ft by 50ft with diving boards, a gymnasium 300ft by 120ft, an indoor drill hall and two churches. There was also a cinema on West Camp with a seating capacity of 580.'

In June 1947 the Administrative Apprentices Training School was opened and visited by Chief of the Air Staff, Marshal of the Royal Air Force, Lord Tedder G.C.B., D.C.L, LL.D. Shortly after this, Bernard was given an administrative posting to RAF Halton in Buckinghamshire. If St. Athan had been a different kind of place for Bernard, at least it was near to home. Halton must have felt like landing on Mars. Used to the narrow confines and sharp contours of his valleys home, Bernard arrived at a station at the eastern end of the Vale of Aylesbury, pancake flat with the only features towards the horizon being field boundaries. The Chiltern Hills, which marked the eastern end of the station, were diminutive when compared with the steep rising inclines of the Rhondda. Britain was a country still in the grips of wartime austerity and the services were not exempt from shortages. The catering bulletin, a publication

The RAF v Minor Counties, Jesmond, 28 July 1948. A happy Bernard before the match (middle row, third from right). He was still smiling after day two, when he had scored a confident 143, an innings that did not go unnoticed in Wales. (© Mrs M.J. Hedges)

An athletics event at RAF Halton. An all-round athlete, Bernard looks a cut above the other participants in the race. (© Mrs M.J. Hedges)

circulated widely on RAF stations, as well as containing top tips from chefs, carried the news, in February 1948, of the latest reductions in rations. Bacon, meat and cheese were all available in smaller quantities, with the meat ration for men reduced from 29 ounces to $22^{3/4}$ ounces. It was a situation that some were to believe had infected the game of cricket. Writing about the phenomenon of slow play in the English game in 1952, Neville Cardus would state, 'Life in this country is rationed. Can we blame Bloggs of Blankshire if in a four hour innings he lets us know that his strokes are rationed?'

Bernard, like every other recruit, would have been encouraged to participate in football, rugby, boxing, cricket and athletics. A photograph that survives from this period is of an athletics meet at the station. One of the many flat fields sheltered by trees bearing their summer clothes was the venue. The track was a stretch of overgrown grass bordered by small white posts connected by rope; a rural 'red' carpet for runners. A limited crowd of mainly men observe with rolled up sleeves that betray the warm temperatures, some of them clutching programmes, all of them following the progress of the athletes down the course. Bernard is on the far right of the photograph, head as still as a hawk, arm and opposite knee pointing skywards as he accelerates towards the finishing line. The other men appear, by comparison, to be in various stages of murdering their own race. Their faces contorted with pain and effort, they are straining every sinew to get on level terms with the aircraftman who is in the lead. My guess is that they were not successful. Bernard was showing what had already been noted by others who watched him. He was a natural athlete who could compete across a wide range of sports. His big chance in the RAF would come during the summer of 1948.

In May he was invited to RAF Henlow for an RAF cricket trial under officer-in-charge, Flight Lieutenant Tony Shirreff, who had been a Cambridge Blue before the war, and then enjoyed a county career with Hampshire, Kent and Somerset. The latter only lasted for two appearances after he fell out with Somerset captain Maurice Tremlett, but continued his career in the RAF, becoming a Squadron Leader. Peter, Bernard's brother, remembers being introduced to him at one of the county games in the early 1950s. 'He was a lovely man', he recalled. He would captain the side that season in a team that also had Alan Rayment, who subsequently played for Hampshire.

Bernard was selected to play for the 'B' team but must have made an impression because he appeared for the RAF in two fixtures that summer. One was a great experience; the other became significant for his future as a first-class cricketer. On 23 and 24 July, the RAF lined up against the Royal Navy at Lord's. This was the first time Bernard had played at the home of cricket and it must have been quite an occasion for the valleys boy.

The match ended in a draw, with hundreds in the first innings for Ian Lumsden of the RAF who was also a Scottish rugby international and John Manners of the Navy, who went on to enjoy a limited first-class career with Hampshire. Bernard supported Lumsden for a little while, scoring 30. Batting at five for the Navy was an 18-year-old Charterhouse schoolboy who was inconsequential to the outcome of the game. His future, though, was to be somewhat more than inconsequential. His name was Peter May.

From London, the RAF team travelled up to Newcastle for their game against the Minor Counties which began on 28 July. The sun was shining and the batting track was true and quick paced. One of the local papers described it as 'a batsman's paradise.' Minor Counties, batting first, registered a score of 438 with Yorkshire's Freddie Jakeman making 102. The RAF finished the day on 78-1, with Bernard coming in at number three, 34 not out.

Day two was another beautiful day. In London, George V and Queen Mary were opening the 1948 Olympic Games. Ernest Bevin, the Foreign Secretary, was warning Parliament of the strain on military services as a result of the Berlin airlift. He explained that 'men who in accordance with the release programmes would have been eligible for release from the RAF in August would have to be retained for a period after the date laid down as it was necessary to make good the gaps in certain trades.' This decision would directly affect Bernard's immediate future but he did not let that news detract from his batting. The *Newcastle Evening Chronicle* would report, that evening, under the headline 'Aircraftman Brilliant Bat' a hundred that came in quick time. The team made 147 before lunch, with Bernard building partnerships with Lumsden and Rayment. He was bowled by a player who had already experienced first-class cricket that season with Lancashire as well as the excitement of a match against a touring side, in the shape of Bradman's Australians. Malcolm Hilton would feature in Bernard's early career far too often for Bernard's liking. However, on this day, 'the boy who had bowled Bradman' twice for scores under 50, had to be thankful to take Bernard's wicket for 143.

The scorecard for day two was kept by Peter Hedges for over 60 years. The RAF side is shown, on the card, in order of seniority. Flight Lieutenant A.C. Shirreff was named at number one, Squadron leader W.E.G. Payton at number two and so on. At number eleven, just before the name of the 12th man, was 'Aircraftsman R. Hedges'. They had managed to get Bernard's initial wrong. Above the advert that solicited spectators to 'Drink Ringtons Tea' and reminded them that refreshments would be served in the canteen, the card outlined the details of the RAF first innings. As they had been bowled out, every player had a score against their name. It only looked odd when you noticed that R. Hedges, going in at number eleven, had scored 143!

This was an innings that reverberated way beyond the pavilion of the County Ground in Jesmond. Back in Wales, despite the fact that the side was involved in a successful bid for the County Championship title, this confident and fluent batting display was being noted by George Lavis and Wilf Wooller. The young man from 'Ponty' was to remain on their radar for the rest of this season and the next. It was also an innings that the young batsman was particularly keen to brag about. Russell Robbins, soon to be a playing partner of Bernard's at Pontypridd rugby club, remembers him talking about the innings with a mutual friend:

> 'I remember Bernard watching with Wally Hoskins down in Cardiff. There was a table and on the table was a hose pipe. Wally told him he'd done well at Jesmond. Bernard picked up the hose pipe. 'I could have got them with this', he said, as he waved it about.'

Bernard finished the limited services season on top of the RAF averages due primarily to that innings at Jesmond but also with three not-outs to his credit. Overall, he scored 251 runs from only seven innings at an average of 62.7.

In the meantime, Ernest Bevin's words had their impact. Working in the logistics section of RAF Halton, Bernard's National Service was extended as a result of the Airlift. On 24 June 1948 all freight and passenger traffic to Berlin by road, rail and inland waterway was closed by the Soviet Union followed by a ban on supplies from East Germany. Two and a half million people faced ultimate starvation. The airlift began two days later and would last until May of 1949. An estimated 2,325,808 tons of supplies were delivered with 195,530 trips or sorties. Hundreds of pilots and thousands of technicians, ground crews and logistics officers like Bernard contributed to the success of the airlift. It is unlikely that any of them expected reward for their efforts. It would, nevertheless, have surprised them that their participation was not recognised in a world where Anglo-Soviet relations were deemed more important than their hard efforts. In Great Britain, an effort to award them a medal was scotched by an Air Ministry memo that pointed out that such an award would give the airlift a 'military' and perhaps even an aggressive character.

George Lavis (© Glamorgan CCC)

Bernard finished his National Service and returned to Wales in scarch of work. Within a year he would have an offer that any young man in his position would find impossible to refuse, a professional contract to play cricket for his county, Glamorgan.

4

Rugby with 'Ponty' and the All Whites

'The best full back in Wales'

Rugby was king after the war in Wales and people flocked in their thousands to see the victorious international team competing in the newly established Five Nations Championship. Pontypridd was no exception to this surge in popular support for the game, with 10,000 turning out at Ynysangharad Park to watch a Welsh trial match in 1946.

Pontypridd had battled throughout the inter-war period to be seen as a first-class club. Whilst there was no official league, the *Western Mail* was seen as providing an unofficial list of the top teams in Welsh rugby. In 1945, the list ran as follows: Aberavon, Abertillery, Bridgend, Cardiff, Cross Keys, Llanelli, Maesteg, Neath, Newbridge, Newport, Penarth, Pontypool, Pontypridd and Swansea. Glamorgan Wanderers, Ebbw Vale and Tredegar soon joined this list. Pontypridd's fortunes in this unofficial league were not great but showed improvement as the 1940s gave way to the 1950s, with the club rising from 14th place in 1947-48 to fourth spot in 1950-51.

However, the financial situation facing the rugby club was tight. Wartime austerity and rationing meant that money and facilities were both in short supply. The club had to appeal to supporters to donate some of their clothing coupons so they could purchase kit. A full kit of jersey, shorts, socks and boots would cost 14 coupons. The club's total allocation from the Welsh Rugby Union (WRU) was 22. The ground, too, fell rather short of the facilities you might expect at a first-class club – the teams changed in the swimming baths several hundred metres from the pitch and there were only two showers, and no bath. The 'grandstand' was known locally as the pigeon loft, painted in the clubs colours of black and white.

One solution proposed to this problem was the amalgamation of Cilfynydd rugby club with Pontypridd. The idea was not welcomed by supporters of either club. Under headlines of 'Village Birthright Given Away' and 'Plan Doomed to Failure' it knocked discussion of the General Election off the front page of the *Pontypridd Observer* as people vented their passionately held views.

Rather than my country, it was my village right or wrong. In the words of the historian of Pontypridd RFC the proposal was a 'bit like the Catholic Church deciding to amalgamate with the Communist Party.'

Amalgamations aside, there were more immediate matters pressing on the officials at the club that were apparent for all to see at home games. The hedge which separated the cricket ground from the rugby pitch at Ynysangharad Park had been trimmed so low that anyone could watch the games for free from outside the ground. Some weeks saw well over a hundred spectators up against the fence. According to reports, the standard of rugby played by Pontypridd at that time was so poor that most drifted quickly away.

On 3 May 1947, the 19-year-old Bernard made his debut for Pontypridd against Aberavon. At the end of that first season, the name B. Hedges appears on the scorers' sheet with one conversion, against Ebbw Vale. They were 3-0 ahead with ten minutes to play when Dickie Watkins crossed for the try that Bernard converted. Right at the death, Ilian Evans dropped a goal to make the final score 9-3 to 'Ponty'. Bernard appeared mainly as fly half as Glyn Davies was still on duty in the Army. But as Russell Robins recalls, there were positional changes that affected Bernard:

> 'I always remember, we were down at Maesteg, who were a very powerful side in those days and Bernard was playing at outside half. We were struggling a little bit. I forget who was captain; Des Jones maybe. Bernard was moved to full back, the full back went to centre and the centre moved to fly half. They kicked off and it went straight into Bernard's hands and he was through them like a dose of salts. Different problems were presented to him and he handled the ones at full back more easily.'

The position of full back in the closely fought games that favoured kicking was primarily a defensive one. You needed to read the game well, catch well and kick well. If the opposition's kicking was good, you would also need to be brave as you would invariably end up at the bottom of a ruck under some pretty heavy and sadistic forwards who liked nothing more than an opportunity to flatten the opposition full back. Bernard proved himself more than capable in all these departments but he also had, in his game, the unusual and sometimes devastating skill of the counter attack. Maurice Stallworthy, when asked about Bernard as a rugby player, praised him for his positioning and:

> 'Anticipating where the ball is going to be. Full backs were required to catch the bloody thing. It always amazes me that full backs today knock on. They simply need to turn to the side so that if they drop it

the ball goes behind them. I can't ever remember Bernard knocking on.'

His footballing skills were used to good effect in some situations, as Maurice recalls,' I saw him dribble the ball round a forward before picking it up.'

Russell summed up Bernard's ability on the field in the following way: 'I think he was the best full back in Wales at the time. He was a magnificent full back. He was never out of position. He could kick the ball. He could run with the ball. He was marvellous.' His National Service interrupted his rugby in the following two seasons as the club wrestled with itself over its position in the hierarchy of south Wales rugby. Viv Jenkins, writing before the start of the 1948-49 season, stated that the town should have a rugby side that should be visiting the likes of Cardiff, Swansea and Llanelli but that to achieve such a side 'we must train and train hard.' On his return to the side at 21, Bernard was referred to as an 'old stager'. The WRU, concerned at the influence of Rugby League over the amateur game, issued an 11-point plan to counter the intrusion from 'the North'. The points included encouraging players to adhere to the true spirit of the game and to abolish the 'win at all costs' mentality, to purge teams of players guilty of 'roughness' or 'shady tactics' and to curb the activities of wing forwards. Despite such advice, club rugby remained an uncompromising and, at times, brutal affair. Bernard was often caught up in,

Pontypridd Rugby Club photographed before the 1950/51 season. Russell Robins is standing (eighth from left). Bernard is in a suit (standing fifth from left) (© Hedges family)

or witness to, some less than sporting acts. He remembered as an old man an incident where a maul had formed near the touchline. From amidst the knot of players came the cry 'He's got my ear. He's bit my ear!' As the players separated, one could be clearly seen with blood gushing from a wound. The culprit, although well known for such tactics, was not seen in the act and so went unpunished.

Russell remembered a game at the beginning of the 1950-51 season, 'Maesteg had gone the whole of the previous season without being beaten, except in a friendly. Pontypridd were the first side to beat them the following season. Bernard was knocked out in that game. They gave him a right going over. 'There was nothing illegal here, but the Maesteg pack made sure they had left their mark on the Pontypridd full back. 'Ponty' had its own fair share of tough forwards. Stan 'Horse' Owen was one of the hardest. He turned professional on the eve of his Welsh trial, playing for Leigh in the Northern League.

One thing that may have affected opposition team's attitude to Bernard was his size. He had taken over the full back role and had played with great distinction throughout the previous season. The Club's official history retells, 'he was brilliant in every phase of the game and although short in stature his kicking was long and well-judged and his catching was flawless'. His height was something that many who admired his abilities commented on. In cricket it was a fact that could be worked around; a factor rather than a barrier. In rugby, it was undoubtedly an impediment and although in the years to come Wales were to produce such miniature geniuses as Cliff Morgan, Phil Bennett, Gerald Davies and Shane Williams. For Bernard, in his position, in his time, size could have really mattered. Stan Thomas, a wing three-quarter and contemporary of Bernard's at Pontypridd remembered him as a player who punched well above his weight, 'which was about that of your average jockey!' Russell and Maurice's reflections are clear on this matter. 'John Llewellyn was the first choice full back for the school. He played for Cardiff. He wasn't in the same league as Bernard but he was big. If Bernard had been six inches taller and a stone heavier he would have walked into any side in Wales and played for his country too.'

At the end of the 1949-50 season, the club toured Cornwall where a young Russell Robbins, fresh from captaining the Welsh Secondary Schools XV, made his debut in a black and white jersey. Russell was born in Cilfynydd in February 1932. His father was a brilliant mechanic but could not get any work and liked his drink a bit too much. Russell remembers, 'If it wasn't for my mother and my brother, the family would have disintegrated.' His mother was a Geordie who had moved down to south Wales. She had two brothers who were professional footballers, playing for Wolves and Blackpool. Russell remembered the story of one of them going off to fight in the First World War aged 15. His trajectory as a sportsman was very similar to Bernard's with first the County School and then the forces being his training grounds.

'I went to the County School in the middle of the war. There was no other winter sport at the County School except a little bit of cross country. We played inter-form rugby. When it got to form five, I went straight into the 1st XV. Then, after two years, I played for the Welsh Secondary Schools XV. I went into the Army and had a couple of fantastic years playing rugby. I played for Yorkshire and won the County Championship.'

After his debut, press reports described him as 'thick set and sturdy with plenty of zip and great stamina.' He was named player of the season at the end of the 1950-51 season and was already being thought of as a future Welsh International. This was Pontypridd's most successful campaign since the war, with only six defeats and 29 victories leaving them fourth in the league. Russell's first trial for Wales was remembered by him for some of the wrong reasons. As with many players, he found the attitude of some of the WRU officials less than helpful.

'I was selected for a trial. I had come down to play on leave. I had to pay for my ticket home. As I walked to the bus stop to go to Cardiff I bumped into a Welsh selector. He came up to me and said, "Eric Evans knows you're home." He was trying to say I couldn't put in a claim for the fare from Catterick. We played the game and were having a high tea. Eric Evans came round. He came to me, walked round the back of me. He never gave me a penny. One shilling and 10 pence it was to get from 'Ponty' to Cardiff. I never got a bit of it back.'

His first International match was against Scotland at Murrayfield in 1953. J.G.B. Thomas, writing in the *Western Mail*, described his selection as 'a great surprise and experiment.' In front of 70,000 spectators, the experiment appeared to work as Wales won 12-0 with Bleddyn Williams scoring two tries and 'the greatest praise' being reserved for the pack for playing a possession game that placed a great deal on their collective shoulders. Russell was promptly dropped. He went on to have 13 caps in total, in the middle of which he was selected as a British Lion in 1955.

'There was a rumour flying about that I might be chosen for the Lions. I went home one day and there was a letter that had arrived. It was my invitation to play. Now that was something. I played more games than anyone on that tour. I played in all four tests and, of course, in the side there were players I'd played with in the Army, Johnny Evans, Reg Higgins, the England player, and Vic Harding who was up at Catterick with me. A wonderful side, dazzling. They could all play. I picked things up easily. I didn't go out there as a number eight; I went out as a second row. I played number eight and played there for the rest of my life. I read books on how to play.'

Such versatility is almost unheard of in the modern game. Russell's frame matched most of the forwards of his day at 6ft and 14st 4lbs. Such a frame would barely get him onto a rugby pitch these days. Russell captained Pontypridd for three seasons from 1955 to 1958 before ending his career playing rugby league for Leeds. As a schoolboy, Russell's greatest love had been for cricket. He had pretended being Walter Hammond in his impromptu games with friends and had loved watching Peter May, Fred Trueman and Brian Close over the years at the Arms Park. 'We used to go to Cardiff to watch the cricket and everyone would crowd behind the sight screens to try and watch the ball moving. At tea time, we would walk out into the middle and have a look at the wicket. When Surrey played I remember looking at Alec Bedser's bowlers footsteps. They had taken a huge chunk out of the wicket.'

The 1950-51 season saw Pontypridd being captained by Des Jones and ex-Cardiff player Roy Roberts. On 27 September, the rugby pitch played host to a comeback fight by the great Tommy Farr, now bankrupt and forced back into fighting to make a living. Over 30,000 watched him defeat Jan Klein of the Netherlands. The pitch was left in a 'morass' and would not recover for the rest of the season. There were stories around the club that Bernard, now a professional county cricketer, was being 'instructed' to give up playing rugby by Glamorgan. This pressure could only have come from one place and that was Wilf Wooller. However, given Wilf's past as a rugby international himself and given the number of other players in the team who were dual sports players, it seems unlikely that there was any such instruction.

There has always been mistrust between the valley clubs and those involved in rugby or other sports that appear to come 'from the capital'. In modern times, Lynn Howells, Pontypridd and Warriors coach, couched this mistrust in categorical terms in the first sentence of his autobiography 'Despite the Knock backs'. The sentence was two words long and questioned the parentage of the individuals he believed were responsible for killing valleys rugby. The mistrust was there just after the Second World War. Pontypridd Club Secretary Des Jones commented that the Cardiff RFC programme should carry, each week, on its front page, the words of the 21st Psalm: 'I shall lift up mine eyes to the hills from where cometh my strength.'

It also extended to the cricket club. The minutes of the committee from 22 November 1945 state, 'After discussion, the practice of the Glamorgan CCC calling upon players to take part in county games at short notice – depriving the club of their services, and causing much inconvenience – was allowed, after a free exchange of views, to drop.'

That free exchange may or may not have contained Lynn Howell's choice of words to describe the faceless administrators of county cricket but the inference is clear. There was a prevailing common conception that 'Ponty' came second to Cardiff in the whole great scheme of things and people were quick to believe that the sportsmen of the town were being unduly influenced by those on the coast.

The truth, in Bernard's case, appears far less controversial. There was no evidence that Glamorgan placed any pressure on him. Rather, he had in very old fashioned terms, come under the influence of something far stronger than a captain's advice or committee's instruction. He had fallen in love. He had met an 18-year-old girl, Margaret Jean Davies, and they had agreed to see more of each other. The only problem was, she lived in Brynhyfryd, Swansea. So Bernard made the first gallant sacrifice of their courtship, and arranged digs in the town. Playing for 'Ponty' would not be possible. Playing for Swansea RFC, the All Whites, beckoned.

Jean remembers when they first met after a game at the Arms Park:

'We went inside The Angel Hotel. The first thing Bernard ever said to me was 'what would you like to drink?' Well, in those days, drink was only brought out in our homes at Christmas time. My friend's mother was a publican and she always had liqueurs and nice drinks on the side board. "I'll have a Tia Maria," she said, and I asked for a cherry brandy. Bernard always maintained that it was a week's wages that he spent that evening.'

That Bernard was conflicted about the decision to finish playing for 'Ponty' is clear from the fact that he first announced his retirement from rugby in February 1951 but was persuaded to return and play for the club in the first half of the 1951-52 season. Before that announcement, on 3 February, he had one of his most notable games for the club. The club's history records; 'Bernard Hedges was the hero of the moment against Pontypool, having to step in for Des Jones at the last minute. Bernard played in borrowed boots two sizes too big, gave a faultless display in defence and capped it all by scoring the only points with a dropped goal.' Russell remembered another game where boots were a factor: 'He was a devil sometimes. We went up to Mountain Ash to play and Bernard comes out in his cricket boots. He was funny. '

Bernard and future wife Jean during a rare taste of the high life at the Pigalle nightclub in London's West End, 1953. (© Mrs M.J. Hedges)

Bernard was Swansea's regular full back for the All Whites in 1952-53. After defeats to Neath and Cardiff, there was a recovery with a 'spanking win' against Leicester in which Swansea played some champagne rugby. Bernard was mentioned by local sportswriters alongside the half back pairing of Viv Davies and Des Bater and young forwards Dudley Thomas and John Leleu as giving hope for the future of the team.

On 4 November 1950, Bernard had featured in a final Welsh trial at Pontypridd's ground. Bernard played in the white of the Possibles against the Probables, kitted out in red. Of the 30 players who played that day, only nine went on to achieve full caps and only four earned more than three caps. Russell Robbins summed up Bernard's performance in the trial in the following terms:

'He messed it up a bit really. I'm not saying he was to blame. Some of his supporters encouraged him to run and the circumstances were not quite right for that type of game.'

Welsh Rugby Union

Dear Sir,

Trial Match at Pontypridd

You have been selected to play/reserve in the above match on Saturday, November 4th 1950.

Jerseys will be provided.

Players and Committee will travel by private buses:-

From the West — Mr.Ivor Jones in charge

Leave			
Police Station, Alexandra Road, Swansea	—	10. 15 a.m.	
Angel Hotel, Neath	—	10. 30 a.m.	
Grand Hotel, Port Talbot	—	10. 45 a.m.	
Wyndham Hotel, Bridgend	—	11. 15 a.m.	
Arrive — Arms Park, Cardiff	—	12. 25 p.m.	
(Lunch — Queen's Hotel, Cardiff)	—	12. 30 p.m. sharp	
Arms Park, Cardiff for Pontypridd	—	1. 15 p.m. sharp	

From the East — Mr.David Jones in charge

Leave			
Clarence Hotel, Pontypool	—	10. 45 a.m.	
Main Road, Crumlin	—	11. 10 a.m.	
Beulah, Newbridge	—	11. 20 a.m.	
Western Welsh Depot, Cross Keys	—	11. 35 a.m.	
Railway Station, Risca	—	11. 40 a.m.	
Railway Station, Newport	—	12. 00 noon	
Arrive — Arms Park, Cardiff	—	12. 25 p.m.	
(Lunch — Queen's Hotel, Cardiff)	—	12. 30 p.m. sharp	
Arms Park, Cardiff for Pontypridd	—	1. 15 p.m. sharp	

Players, please let me know at once —

1. Whether you can attend.
2. Where you will join the bus.
3. What your minor expenses (with details) will be.

N.B. Third Class rail-fare or bus fare, and essential meals (Lunch 5/- , Tea or supper 3/-) only will be allowed. Unless I receive a statement of your expenses by Thursday morning, 2nd November, they cannot be paid.
(A stamped addressed envelope is enclosed for the above purpose)

The Committee, teams, and reserves will dine at the New Inn, Pontypridd, at 5.30 sharp.

The homeward journeys will be by private buses, leaving Pontypridd at 6.45 p.m.

Yours faithfully,

Secretary.

The letter inviting Bernard to his Welsh trial. (© Peter Hedges)

It was the only trial that Bernard ever had. All that remains in the Hedges household of that day was a photocopy of the match programme and a battered and faded invitation to the trial. The purple typewritten text was a 'Dear Sir' letter. The opening sentence gave the office staff a delete as appropriate option saying that the recipient had been selected to 'play / reserve'. Almost exclusively, the rest of the letter comprised the details of transport to the game either from the West, calling at Swansea, Neath, Port Talbot and Bridgend or from the East calling at Pontypool, Newbridge, Cross Keys, Newport and Cardiff. Underlined near the bottom was a line familiar to many who attended trials before and since, 'Unless I receive a statement of your expenses by Thursday morning, 2 November (two days before the trial) they cannot be paid.' The signatory was WRU secretary Eric Evans who sadly died less than five years later.

The valleys being what they were, this part of Bernard's story could not be told without its share of tragedy. During the international season of 1950, 80 Welshmen opted to fly over to Belfast to see Wales take on the Irish in the Five Nations. After watching a 6-3 victory, the 80 supporters headed back to Llandow Airport near Cardiff on an Avro 689 Tudor V aeroplane. It experienced difficulties when coming in to land and then stalled and crashed as the crew tried to deal with those problems. Of the 83 people on board, only three survived. It was, at the time, the world's worst air disaster. David Smith and Gareth Williams, in their official history of the Welsh Rugby Union *Fields of Praise* wrote of those for whom the eventual grounding of the Tudor V came too late:

> 'too late for those towns and villages in Monmouthshire from which half its victims came. Too late for Abercarn whose club lost its captain, its coach and its star three-quarter; for Newbridge, where a 75-year-old widow lost her three sons; for Llantarnam, where a house lost three menfolk; for Pontypridd, where four children were abruptly orphaned; for Alltwen, where two brothers and their next door neighbour never came home; for Glynneath, Risca, Nelson and the Amman valley, where fathers, sons and daughters were mourned by communities that lived in ever present dread of disaster beneath the ground, but not above it. 'There is shadow across the sun in south Wales', noted the Belfast Telegraph the next day.'

The children from Pontypridd were given the news by one of the committee who was called to go down and identify a body. It was that of Ilian Evans, the player whose drop goal had confirmed that victory against Ebbw Vale the season before. His last game for 'Ponty' had been on 3 March, the week before the international.

ON TRIAL: Remember this fine body of players? They were the Possibles XV from a Welsh trial staged at Pontypridd in November, 1950. Standing from the left are T J Griffiths, (Crynant), R Hurd, (Bargoed), W O Williams, (Swansea), S Judd, (Cardiff), A Morris, (Swansea), and T Davies, (Maesteg). Sitting are V Callow, (Maesteg), G Rees, (Cross Keys), W D Williams, (Maesteg, capt), C Meredith and E Thomas, (Neath). In front are D H Jones, (Maesteg), H Greville, (Llanelli), B Hedges, (Pontypridd), and B Williams, (Newport).

A cutting from the Pontypridd Observer recalling the Possibles team that played in the final Welsh trial at Ynysangharad Park in 1950. (© Pontypridd Observer)

Another 'Ponty' player was to lose his life in tragic circumstances at Aberfan in 1966. Dai Beynon, described in the club's history as 'a wing forward with pace and good hands' had appeared on that Pontypridd scorers list for 1946-47 alongside Glyn and Wynford Davies. He trained as a teacher and ended up as deputy head at the Pantglas Junior School in Aberfan. He was there on 21 October 1966 when tragedy bulldozed its way through the school in the form of a landslide from the local colliery spoil tip. As one commentary recorded, 'As a filthy black river of death swept all before it, 144 people – 116 of them being children – lost their lives. The body of deputy head Dai Beynon was later found still clutching grimly to the bodies of five youngsters he'd tried to protect in brave, if futile, desperation.'

Some things are far more important than what happens on a rugby pitch or a cricket field. However, in Wales, tragedy and sporting triumph, in results at least, appear the same. They unite the community, holding us together and provide the evidence and confirmation that we will endure. Tragedy and triumph, the two unexpected guests, whose arrival illuminates us and whose departure leaves us believing in something bigger and better than ourselves. For Bernard, as a Welsh sportsman, there was an unwritten and unspoken expectation that he would produce something that would 'illuminate' his countrymen. The tragedy of Aberfan lay in the future, in the winter before his final season as a professional cricketer. For now, his opportunities for sporting triumph would exist exclusively in the arena of first-class cricket.

5

The Early Years with Glamorgan

'The tallest of the shortest.'

The minutes of the Glamorgan CCC Finance sub-committee meeting held on 30 December 1949 noted that George Lavis had reported, as the club's coach, that 'Hedges could be released (from National Service) for 22 weeks the following summer.' It was decided to offer him a summer contract for £6 10s a week for those 22 weeks.

News of his signing became public at the end of the following month as the *Pontypridd Observer*, on Saturday 28 January 1950, during its report of an upcoming Pontypridd rugby fixture, commented that: 'Bernard Hedges will again be on the side-lines. All will be pleased to learn that he has been enlisted to the club and ground staff of the Glamorgan CCC and his many friends wish him every success in this new sphere. He played in most of the 2nd XI games last summer. If enthusiasm counts, Bernard will go a long way in the game.'

If he arrived for the pre-season nets at Cardiff Arms Park expecting to meet a number of specialist cricketers, talented in only that sport, then he was much mistaken, as the majority of the playing staff in 1950 excelled in other sports too. Haydn Davies, the county's long-serving wicketkeeper, was a skilful and effective squash player. He played at Cardiff Squash Club which had been established during the mid-1930s by Maurice Turnbull, the Glamorgan captain, who himself had been a fine all-round sportsman and an international for Wales at both squash and rugby.

Several of the other batsmen also shone in other sports. Willie Jones, the left-handed batsman from Carmarthen, had also been chosen as a fly half in the Welsh rugby side for a wartime international and played club rugby for Llanelli, Neath and Gloucester. Stan Montgomery also mixed professional cricket with professional football, appearing as a centre-half for Hull, Southend United, Cardiff City and Newport County. Gilbert Parkhouse had played rugby for Swansea besides representing Wales at hockey, whilst Jim Pleass might have become a footballer with Cardiff City had it not been for the war. Allan Watkins was a true all-rounder who, in 1948, was the first Glamorgan cricketer

Haydn Davies, longstanding wicketkeeper with Glamorgan and a talented squash player. (© Glamorgan CCC)

to appear in an Ashes Test, having also played football for Plymouth Argyle and Cardiff City. Several of the bowlers had also been talented footballers, with Don Shepherd, then a fast bowler, having a trial with Leeds United alongside John Charles, whilst fellow spinner Stan Trick had won schoolboy caps for Wales. But perhaps the best footballer in the bowling department was spinner Jim McConnon who had opted to play professionally for Glamorgan after a career which began at Aston Villa and ended with Newport County.

But all of these talented sportsmen's experiences pale into insignificance alongside the sporting record of the Glamorgan captain, Wilf Wooller. Like Maurice Turnbull, he had been a member in 1932-33 of the first Wales rugby side to defeat England at Twickenham, before going on to play a key role in the victorious Welsh XV that defeated the All Blacks in 1935. Wilf was also a Welsh international squash player and a Cardiff City footballer. Add to this his achievement of leading Glamorgan to their first ever County Championship in 1948 and it is no surprise that Wooller's biographer, Andrew Hignell, could refer to this list of achievements as something 'a hero out of a *Boy's Own* novel would be proud of.'

Dubbed by the press during his rugby playing days as 'The Dragon of Wales' he was a colossus of Welsh sport whose success in the sporting arena gave him great influence and credibility off it. He had been identified by Johnnie Clay in 1946 as the man to fill the void left by Maurice Turnbull's tragic death, and the Cambridge graduate duly acted as both the county's captain and secretary.

After coming down from Cambridge during the mid-1930s, Wilf had worked in the coal trade and mixed rugby and cricket, plus a few guest appearances for Cardiff City, with the all-rounder playing as an amateur. However, his cheery smile, happy-go-lucky attitude and bonhomie towards opponents was replaced, after the Second World War, by a cold and steely determination with Wilf, known to all his colleagues as 'The Skipper', adopting a more gimlet-eyed approach on the field, with success, at whatever cost, being paramount. This change to Wilf's outlook followed the physical deprivation and mental trauma he suffered during three years as a prisoner of war in Japanese hands and undertaking manual labour in searing heat and dreadful conditions on the notorious Death Railway. For Wilf, his time in Changi, and on the Burma-Siam Railway was literally a case of life and death, and one which had left an indelible mark on his character.

Wilf also had a real physical presence, with his good friend and fellow journalist J.B.G. Thomas likening him to Australia's Warwick Armstrong, 'a mountain of a man who was successful, imposing, commanding and frightening,' and someone who 'symbolized cricket power and dominance; the desire to win at all costs within the laws of the game, never to yield, never to submit, to play hard at all times and maintain pressure upon the opposition.' Wilf's physical and psychological presence was something that both teammates and opponents alike had to learn to live with.

As a cricketer, Wilf was a formidable all-rounder, amassing 13,593 first-class runs, claiming 958 first-class wickets and taking 412 catches. He was well-known and highly regarded as one of the finest and bravest of fielders close to the bat on the leg-side, and players with far inferior records went on to win England caps. This honour eluded Wilf but his tactical nous and judgement of a player saw him serve for seven years as a Test match selector. As a captain, he always led from the front, taking the new ball when necessary and opening the batting during the mid-1950s. Ossie Wheatley, describing that period, commented that Wilf 'made sides that survived'. He was seen by many outside Glamorgan as representing the county itself and he welcomed this role, placing himself at the forefront of any confrontation. He famously faced up to the ferocious speed of Frank Tyson, being hit in the chest. When the England and Northamptonshire pace bowler enquired after his health he barked back, 'Bugger off Tyson, you're not fast enough to hurt me!'

Alan Jones was to arrive a few years after Bernard on the Glamorgan staff, and he well remembers how great an influence Wilf was on all the players:

'I could go to the indoor school in Neath and have a net, and our coach Phil Clift was there, who was good with discipline. You would have a couple of players chatting whilst you were having the net but Wilf would walk in and you could hear a pin drop. Everything went quiet. Nobody said a word. That's the respect that they had for him. He was in charge.'

Wilf's influence stretched beyond the Arms Park and St. Helen's, reaching some places that left the young Jones speechless. Doing his two year National Service and faced with the prospect of a posting to Benghazi, he was called into the office of Major Stephenson, his commanding officer, and had the following conversation:

'Jones. You play cricket?'

'Yes Sir.'

'You're on the Glamorgan staff?'

'Yes Sir, I am.'

'And you're on draft to go to Benghazi?'

'Yes Sir, I am.'

'Do you want to go?'

'Yes Sir, I do.'

'Well I've had Mr Wooller on the phone and he doesn't want you to go to Benghazi.'

'I wouldn't know anything about that, Sir.'

'Well Jones. I'm taking you off draft and you can play for the Army and Combined Services and if you don't do well, we'll send you to Benghazi at the end of the summer.'

Wilf's intervention had kept Alan at home. It was an act of cricketing pragmatism, of course, but also one of kindness and compassion. It made a huge impact on Alan: 'He kept me in Cardiff for two years. Amazing. Very powerful man. He was good to me.'

The Glamorgan team in 1950. Back row (from left): Bernard, Phil Clift, Norman Hever, Jim McConnon, Gilbert Parkhouse, Allan Watkins. Front Row (from left): Willie Jones, Haydn Davies, Wilf Wooller, Emrys Davies, Len Muncer. (© Glamorgan CCC)

A photograph from this period (seen below) shows Bernard and Wilf together. 'The Skipper' relaxed and assured in county blazer and white neckerchief, stares nonchalantly back at the camera as if posing for a picture was no less important to him than breathing or eating. This is the amateur, confident of his own place in the team and comfortable with the interest that his position brings. Bernard shows the awkwardness and clear-eyed keenness of the new player. Smiling uncertainly, he reveals his front teeth that look like a fractured chess board. Indeed, Robin Marlar, the Sussex captain of the 1950s described Bernard in a telephone conversation with me as 'A lovely man ... terrible teeth.' There are few better images that sum up the relationship between the amateur and the professional. The middle class captain and the working class professional. Both inhabiting very different worlds and with experiences that only the world of cricket could throw together. Here they were: master and apprentice, both marching behind the same banner but both having taken very different routes to the battlefield. Wilf, who took his commitment to developing cricket and cricketers in Wales very seriously, was to be an important steadying influence on Bernard during the early years of his career.

Bernard's first-class debut came at Cardiff Arms Park against Somerset on 3 June 1950. Injuries to both Allan Watkins and Wooller himself meant

Bernard photographed with Wilf. The amateur 'master' and his professional 'apprentice'.
(© Mrs M.J. Hedges)

that there was a vacancy in the batting line-up and having played well in 2nd XI games, a message was sent to Bernard who was on tour in South Devon with the Glamorgan Nomads. He duly travelled on a late evening train from Plymouth and reached Cardiff during the early hours of the morning – not the most ideal preparation for a Championship debut.

The game itself proved to be quite an eventful one. Len Muncer posted his maiden century as he scored 114 in Glamorgan's first innings total of 308, whilst Gilbert Parkhouse – who was in a purple patch of form – equalled the club record of making a century in each innings, with scores of 121 and 148. The latter came as stand-in captain Emrys Davies set-up a run-chase on the final afternoon for the visitors, leaving them a target of 281. Behind the stumps, Haydn Davies equalled his own record of claiming seven victims in a match, but for Bernard, his debut was a very low key event, with a first innings score of three. He was not required in the second innings with 'Nomad' of the *Western Mail* commenting how, 'newcomer Hedges was out to a quick catch just when he appeared to be accepting his 'baptism' with commendable calm.'

For Bernard, it was a start that must have felt slightly overwhelming: three hundreds for Glamorgan in the game, a finish that almost went down to the wire and the opportunity to see up close the great Harold Gimblett who the England selectors would recall during the summer for the series against the West Indies, eleven years after his last Test match. There was certainly plenty for Bernard to tell his proud family about each night after travelling home by bus from the Arms Park. There was more for the young professional to talk about, and to listen to, as he sat in the changing room and pavilion as the following match against the Combined Services was washed out.

He retained his place for the next batch of Championship matches, against Northamptonshire at Ebbw Vale and Sussex at Chichester. The latter was Wilf's first game back from his hand injury and with Norman Hever and Ken Lewis sharing the new ball duties, he operated below full pace as a change bowler. After Sussex made 280 with Norman Hever taking 6-59, Glamorgan's top-order found life difficult against the Sussex attack, with wickets tumbling at regular intervals. Bernard came to the wicket to join Len Muncer with the score on 77-5. The youngster duly turned the tables on the Sussex side when he arrived at the wicket, and as 'Nomad' reported: 'By the time he left, three and a half hours later, he had hit 103 (with 13 fours and one six) and helped to push the Glamorgan total past Sussex ... With skipper Wilf Wooller he featured in a seventh wicket stand of 153.'

The home bowlers would not have seen the fresh-faced youngster before, nor his favourite stroke, which he frequently deployed and was described as 'a Compton-like sweep to leg'. Any comparison with the 'Brylcream Boy' of English cricket was the greatest of compliments. With the Welsh cricketing enthusiasts eager to know a little bit more about this young new 'star', the newspapers dutifully contained a few vignettes – 'Among the Glamorgan team he is regarded as the tallest of the shortest players,' said the *Western Mail*. 'He stands 5ft 5 and a half inches with Jim Pleass 5ft 5in., and Willie Jones just reaching 5ft 4 and a half inches.' In contrast, the *Daily Express*, described him, as being 5ft 7 inches, and his height duly became a matter of some dispute that was to outlive his cricket career. He and his wife, Jean, disagreed on his height long into their old age, Bernard claiming he was 5ft 8in and Jean saying it was more like 5ft 6. Whatever height he was, he was remembered by those who saw him as small, diminutive or little.

Telegrams flooded in to the Chichester cricket ground praising his maiden first-class century. He received congratulatory messages from Pontypridd Rugby Club, the Grammar School and all his friends and relatives. There was also one from Johnnie Clay, the grand old man of Glamorgan Cricket who had been there at the birth of the club in the first-class world in 1921 and who had taken the final wicket of the Club's Championship-winning summer in 1948. Now in retirement, Johnnie was so pleased to see one of the Club's bright young things achieve success in the Championship. Friends from 'Ponty' were just as delighted for Bernard. Alan Oliver said, 'I'll never forget reading about Bernard getting his first century (for Glamorgan). I was in the RAF and I remember showing my mates the paper and saying "Look! I know him!"'

Reading all the messages of goodwill was an uplifting feeling for the young batsman who had announced himself on the professional stage. The match itself petered out into a draw despite Glamorgan having secured a modest first innings lead. Little did Bernard know that it would be almost three years to the day before he would score his next hundred. His efforts against Sussex meant he retained a place in the line-up as Glamorgan finished in 11th place in the Championship table, and his experiences during the second half of the 1950 season, further added to his cricketing education.

He played against the touring West Indian side at Swansea and in front of what at the time was the largest crowd he had ever experienced. He watched Willie Jones get 105, before being completely outshone by a scintillating 147 from Everton Weekes in under two hours. Weekes, in addition to scoring 338 Test runs that season amassed 2,310 first-class runs on the tour, and Glamorgan could count themselves fortunate that he did not go on to add to his tally of five double hundreds whilst on British soil that summer.

Bernard ended the 1950 season with a tally of 322 runs at an average of 23 – a very respectable aggregate given that he was batting at number six or seven. But his debut season was more than just these bare numbers – it was about learning and watching his professional colleagues. In many ways, he could have had no finer role model than opening batsman Emrys Davies, whose

From left: Willie Jones, Gilbert Parkhouse and Wilf Wooller. Jones was, like Bernard, rather diminutive but was capable of playing some sparkling innings. (© Glamorgan CCC)

county career had started in 1924, a full three years before Bernard was born. Emrys had certainly tasted the highs and lows of life in the Glamorgan side. It had taken him eight seasons of sweat and toil before posting his maiden century but after moving up the order to become Arnold Dyson's opening partner Emrys had not looked back. In 1939 he posted an unbeaten 287 against Gloucestershire at Newport with his efforts remaining as the county's highest individual innings until the year 2000. Then, in Glamorgan's Championship-winning year of 1948, Emrys shared a record third wicket stand of 313 with Willie Jones against Essex in Brentwood, with the pair confounding the Essex fielders by calling to each other in Welsh. With a solid and compact style, like several left-handers who subsequently followed him, and a calm and composed disposition, Emrys was – quite fittingly described by Stephen Chalke as being – 'more like a chapel minister than a professional sportsman. Time and again he lived up to his nickname of the 'Rock of Glamorgan' by holding together a faltering innings.

By the time Bernard appeared on the county circuit, Gilbert Parkhouse was Emrys' regular partner, and when the Swansea-born batsman was called up by England, it was Phil Clift who moved up to open the innings. During the late 1930s,

Phil had been one of several promising young players from Monmouthshire to shine at first-class level, and like much of Glamorgan Cricket at the time, his rise from Usk schoolboy to Glamorgan cricketer stemmed from the management decisions of Maurice Turnbull and Johnnie Clay, with the pair overseeing the merger of Glamorgan with Monmouthshire in 1934, allowing Glamorgan to field a 2nd XI in Monmouthshire's place in the Minor County Championship. For Phil it proved a superb training ground and together with Allan Watkins, his good friend from Usk, the pair went on to enjoy success with Glamorgan.

Indeed, in 1948, Don Bradman rated the free-scoring Phil as one of the finest young batsmen he had seen in the country. Sadly Phil's career was curtailed by illness, and he was forced to retire in 1955, but he maintained his links with the club until 1982, serving as assistant to Wilf, as well as coach, scorer and manager. Inadvertently, he highlighted the homespun nature of the county as others were moving at full speed into the professional age. A minuted item in the meeting of the Finance and General Purposes sub-committee in March 1965 noted that, 'it was agreed to replace the blazer of Phil Clift which had now been used for more than ten years.'

Allan Watkins was the star turn in the middle-order which also contained Willie Jones, Len Muncer and The Skipper himself. Allan had made his Test debut in Bradman's last Test at The Oval in 1948, and with his free-flowing stroke-play, solid defence and alert fielding in the leg trap, he had been a vital element in Glamorgan's Championship-winning team in 1948.

Willie too had played a major part in Glamorgan's Championship success, striking a pair of double hundreds in the space of a fortnight, with 207 against Kent at Gravesend followed by 212 against Essex at Brentwood. But he was a more complex character than others in the batting line-up, and was renowned for his lack of confidence in his own abilities – a circumstance that, at times, was made no better by his domineering captain. Willie duly scored over 1,000 runs in a season on no less than seven occasions, but despite this success, he was in a constant state of anxiety over his form. Don Shepherd once remarked that 'in the evening, when he'd had a couple of drinks, he became a much better player.'

There were therefore many role models for Bernard to follow, but he proved to be his own man, and continued the more phlegmatic approach which had stood him in good stead whilst at school and for the various military teams. He duly approached the vagaries of the cricket season in quite a philosophical way, and did not get as visibly stressed as Willie sometimes did. To those

Phil Clift. A great servant of Glamorgan, on and off the field. (© Glamorgan CCC)

around him, Bernard seemed to accept and balance the success that came with his ability as well as recognising its limits. His approach could be summed up in the phrase that he used often when discussing the game or other aspects of life. 'It happens' he would say. His pithiness was no accident. He was a man who did not relish social occasions and was never one to regale friends and family with stories or verbal embellishment. It was a fatalistic outlook combined with a verbal brevity that he needed to rely on frequently in those early seasons when his outings for Glamorgan became more significant for the bowlers that claimed his wicket rather than the runs he scored.

In the final game of the 1950 season against Hampshire he had the opportunity to bat against Derek Shackleton, the great medium-pace bowler, but Bernard's lesson was cut short by the wily bowler as Bernard became one of the 2,857 first-class wickets he claimed during an outstanding career. In the match against Warwickshire at Edgbaston in July 1951, Bernard also had plenty of time to experience the bowling of Eric Hollies, the England spinner who had claimed the wicket of Don Bradman for a duck in the great Australian's final Test match innings at The Oval in 1948. Hollies was a faster than usual leg-spinner, and it was a relatively new experience for Bernard to face a leg-spinner who used variations in pace, as well as a loquacious humour, rather than the googly as his main weapon. Towards the end of the 1951 season, when Surrey met Glamorgan at the Arms Park, Bernard also faced the Bedser twins, Eric and Alec, plus the wily spin of Jim Laker and Tony Lock as the Welsh county faced an attack that was to win seven consecutive Championship titles. It was a steep learning curve for the Pontypridd youngster, who was Bedsered twice in the game – departing to Eric in the first innings and Alec in the second, but not before he had posted a fluent 50 first time around and sharing in a partnership of 90 with Wilf Wooller.

For a batsman making his way in the first-class game, there could have been no finer array of experienced county bowlers, England regulars or fringe Test match performers against whom to hone your technique. Given this glittering array of talent it was quite surprising, therefore, that over the years his nemesis was Malcolm Hilton, the slow left-arm bowler from Lancashire. In Bernard's first five seasons as a professional cricketer, Hilton claimed his wicket on eight of the 14 times he was dismissed by a Lancashire bowler. In 1951 Hilton bowled him twice at the Arms Park in early August before two weeks later having him caught at Old Trafford. Hilton had burst onto the first-class scene after the war and became widely known as 'the boy who bowled Bradman' when he took the great man's wicket twice in the Australians' match against Lancashire in 1948. 'Fame caught up with him overnight' was the shrewd conclusion of *Wisden's* correspondent when Hilton belatedly became one of their Cricketers of the Year for 1957.

Hilton would often quote Harry Makepeace, the coach at Old Trafford, who would say, 'On the bad days, think of the good, on the good days think of the bad.' Bernard had more than his fair share of bad days facing Hilton but there must have been something in those experiences that he used to his own betterment. He was to become, in the words of no finer a judge than Wilf Wooller, 'one of the best Welsh players of slow spin bowling.'

His progress in first-class cricket was briefly halted during 1953 by kidney stones. In all, he only appeared in four first-class games and during May went into hospital for an operation to remove the painful obstructions which besides being an agony to live with, were set to trouble him for the rest of his life. As his wife Jean remembered, several multi-coloured stones were removed and it was not until August before Bernard was fit and able to return to county cricket.

After a winter working for the Atlas Sprinkler Company in Swansea, Bernard duly made up for lost time during the summer of 1954, but not before joining the rest of the Glamorgan players at a break from pre-season training by visiting the shoe shop owned by W.B. Penhale in St. Helen's Road, just a short distance away from the Swansea cricket ground. Long before kit and cars were thought of as items for player sponsorship, his patent leather shoes represented the players' sole piece of merchandise in addition to their wages from the club. 'Expertly fitted with the latest X-ray equipment', all the players were delighted as they posed in 1954 for a publicity photograph. But that situation did not prevail; a couple of years later as the Club forgot to arrange the photocall and Mr Penhale angrily withdrew his offer. There was another example of Bernard's affirmation as a regular in the side as he managed to appear in a Dai and Ianto cartoon in the *Western Mail*. The Glamorgan team was depicted posing for a team photo along with the cartoon characters and there was Bernard, standing in the back row, complete with broken teeth.

The 1954 season began inauspiciously for Bernard, who after impressing with his solid defence and unflappable temperament had been earmarked as a potential replacement for Emrys Davies at the top of the order. Bernard duly occupied the number three spot for the summer, but the season began with a pair against Lancashire at Old Trafford. Wooller and the selection panel were adamant that Bernard had a role to play higher up the order than where he had languished in previous seasons, and he repaid their confidence with a disciplined half-century against Northamptonshire at the Arms Park.

Bernard then enjoyed what J.B.G. Thomas later described in the *Playfair Annual* as 'one glorious month' in June, when he rattled up the following sequence of 83, 89, 4, 103, 125, 10, 0 and 129, and had the match against Middlesex at Swansea not seen two days rained off, his tally might have been even more impressive. Nevertheless, he was the third highest run-scorer in the country during the month, with only Tom Graveney (700) and Peter May (677) having a

SOUTH WALES FOOTBALL ECHO & EXPRESS, SATURDAY, APRIL 24, 1954
DAI AND IANTO

The 1954 Glamorgan team as depicted in cartoon form. Bernard, on the far right and back row, has the defining characteristics of an ex-rugby player; a bent nose and broken teeth! (© Peter Hedges)

higher first-class tally than Bernard's 629, and his average for the month of 52.41 was better than that of Denis Compton, Don Kenyon or David Sheppard.

Ossie Wheatley, Glamorgan captain from 1961 to 1966, describes what must have faced those bowlers in 1954:

'Bernard had an unusual technique. Short of stature; not a great driver. Cutter. Puller. Whacker. When he was in form, and he was a guy who played in purple patches, he was very difficult to bowl at. He played shots. He was quick on his feet. He would cut close to his body. He would get runs quickly. He got on with the game. Unorthodox you would say. If I was bowling at him, I would have pitched it up to him. I wouldn't have bothered bowling short to him because he'd murder you if he was in form. It was short arm stuff. Boom! boom! boom! (he mimes three consecutive cut shots) I regarded him as a guy who would always move you on in a game into a position of strength. You gave yourself a chance to win games with players like that in the side.'

So there was a collective benefit, not just a personal one, for Glamorgan's new number three as his efforts during June helped to set up several exciting run chases. The first came in the game against Derbyshire, as Glamorgan were set a formidable target of 381 to win – a huge total by anybody's standards even in the modern era of four-day cricket – but together with Willie Jones, Bernard helped to add 195 for the third wicket, and after both men had recorded centuries a collapse set in, leaving Glamorgan's last pair to score ten more to secure a famous victory. They could only manage four, but Bernard's free-scoring abilities had set down a marker and at Trent Bridge his 129 helped to turn the game. A stand of 164 with Allan Watkins laid the foundations for a 40-run victory over a strong Nottinghamshire side.

In July, Bernard also opened the batting for the very first time for Glamorgan, and where better than in the hallowed surroundings of Lord's. His elevation to open with Wilf in the second innings, stemmed from the fact that Gilbert Parkhouse, after scoring an immaculate 182 in the first innings was indisposed. The pair duly added 89 before Bernard was dismissed by Fred Titmus, but his efforts were not in vain as Middlesex, after being set 252 to win, were dismissed for 229 with Wilf claiming 7-65 as Glamorgan recorded only their second victory at the home of cricket.

His purple patch did not continue for the remainder of the season as he failed to register another century and only scored two more 50s in 26 further innings. It's a truism that top-class players can deliver consistently over the entire course of a season, but for Bernard – in his first season at the top of the order – there was much to look fondly back on at the end of the summer, and few would have disputed *Wisden's* comment that Bernard was 'a much improved player'.

Fittingly, he was awarded his county cap during June whilst Glamorgan were meeting Warwickshire at Llanelli. Telegrams came in from friends and relatives but there was one in particular which Bernard cherished. It simply said 'Sincere Congratulations. I am very proud of you.' It came from George Lavis, who had invested such a great deal of time and thought into the development of the young player from Pontypridd, and had become a regular visitor to the Hedges household, monitoring Bernard's progress through his National Service. As Peter Hedges remembered 'George Lavis was a smashing man. I remember many times he'd come around to the back door and he would spend ages at the house. He did a lot for Bernard when he was at the County School.' Arriving at the back door was a significant sign in valleys houses. It meant you saw yourself as a friend of the family, not a formal 'caller' at the house. George's was a friendship Bernard would never forget.

Two years later, and close to a premature and tragic death, Lavis wrote to Don Shepherd after he had become the quickest bowler to reach 100 victims in a season at Kettering. In it he said, 'Please tell Bernie I was going to write to him too, but I am afraid this is it for today. That 40 was worth 100 any time. Make him get stuck in Don – he is a fine player.' It was in fact 41 that Bernard

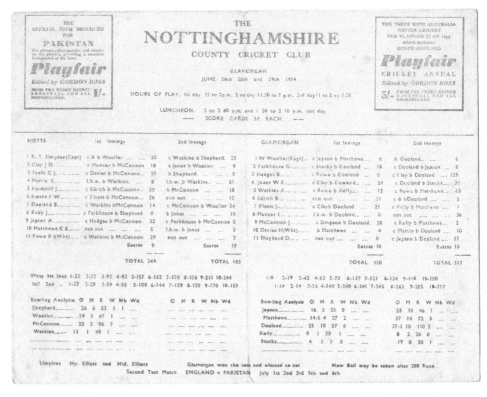

The scorecard from the county match against Nottinghamshire, June 1954. Bernard's match-winning 129 was made against great Australian spinner Bruce Dooland. (© Peter Hedges)

had scored and was run out chasing quick runs and a declaration. Glamorgan won the match with Wilf Wooller taking a five-wicket haul.

Sadly, within two weeks of writing this letter George was dead, yet Bernard never forgot the man who was his first – and in many ways most important – mentor. Searching through the house after Bernard's death, we came across a small pewter mug with the engraving 'George Lavis – 1950'. It was from his Testimonial. Bernard had no trophies or memorabilia from his own cricketing days. There were no framed photos or cricket balls or bats or anything indicating a career in cricket and yet this pewter mug was still in situ. Jean said that she had once suggested that they use it as a pen and pencil holder. 'If you do', came the reply from Bernard, 'it will be divorce.' It was a joke but it demonstrated how strongly he felt about George. In many ways he was a similar man – quiet, dedicated and deeply respectful of all those around him – and he could not have hoped for a better man to see him through those early years of his career.

Don Shepherd, then a raw fast bowler and the man who roomed regularly over the course of the next two decades on away trips with Bernard, was another to benefit from George's wise counsel. As Don remembered:

'I was very fond of George. He was the sort of guy who was brilliant in the nets but couldn't replicate it in the middle. That sort of person for whom it had been hard work had a lot more to offer than someone for whom it had all come easily. He was very understanding. '

Looking now at that Dai and Ianto cartoon which was published at the beginning of the 1954 season, it is clear that the cartoonist's skill, of exaggerating the peculiarities of a person, had been well executed. Jon, of the *South Wales Echo*, had got it spot on with the key member of that Glamorgan team. Wilf Wooller was depicted sitting centre stage, taking up the space of two or three men and jovially manhandling the eponymous duo. He was, in no uncertain terms, the King of the Castle. Everyone playing for the county had to learn to live with the way he played the game. Bernard was no exception.

The Glamorgan team in 1954. L to R back row: Bernard Hedges, Jim Pressdee, Jim McConnon, Don Shepherd, Gilbert Parkhouse, Jim Pleass, Don Ward. L to R front row: Phil Clift, Haydn Davies, Wilf Wooller, Allan Watkins, Willie Jones. (© Glamorgan CCC)

6

The Wooller Way

'By all means play cricket the hard way. But play it the fair way Wilfred.'

The 1950s may have started with Bernard as a callow youth in the Glamorgan set-up. The decade ended with him being a well-established and well-regarded member of the team. The late 1950s also saw Wilf Wooller's glittering playing career gradually draw to a close, with 'The Skipper' handing over the reins at the end of the 1960 season to Warwickshire seam bowler Ossie Wheatley.

During these years Bernard had experienced every aspect of the county circuit, including the ribald comments of bowlers out to claim his wicket and desperate to 'get inside his head.' He remembered a game against Essex where he was having a shaky start and had edged the ball several times down through the slip cordon off Trevor Bailey. The future radio commentator, after one such edge, looked at him and said, for all to hear, 'They gave you the right name didn't they!' If such verbal jousts usually had a light hearted centre to them, with Wilf they often became blunt, to the point and repeated, losing some of their humour as a result. County cricket was certainly a far quieter place after Wilf retired. He had been a ruthless and, at times, very outspoken captain, leading from the front and never afraid to ask anyone to do anything that he would not think twice about doing himself. Indeed, Wilf was ready to do anything in the side's best interest, whether it was opening the batting, bowling for hour after hour as a stock bowler, or fearlessly standing at short-leg, letting the opposition batsmen know what he thought of them! He lived and breathed Glamorgan Cricket, and many of his critics rather misunderstood his intentions, not realising that everything Wilf did was, at the end of the day, what he believed to be in the best interests of Glamorgan CCC.

How you viewed Wilf often depended on how close or how far away from him you were. To strangers or those who did not play with him, he would appear brusque and rude. To the Glamorgan team, he may have been that but a lot more besides. The view of the outsider, even a renowned one, could often be one dimensional and simplistic. The award-winning sports journalist

Frank Keating, in a *Guardian* article of 2011, remembered how Wilf appeared to him as a player. 'He seemed to dominate his Welshmen like a galley-slave skipper.' Alternatively, Jim Pleass recalled:

'Wilf Wooller was a colossus among captains, with the ability to lead by example; to drag up by their bootlaces a side of average talent so that each individual on occasion could play above himself; all of these things, but, at the same time, stubborn, domineering, and distinctly lacking in tact; a person whose word was law, and who did not take kindly to anyone contradicting his opinion. '

Jim mentions two other players, in addition to himself, who crossed swords with 'The Skipper'. They were Stan Montgomery and Jim Pressdee. He believed that, but for the clash of personalities, these two players would have had longer careers in the first-class game. A note from the Selection Committee minutes from May 1956 hints at Wilf's relationship with Jim Pressdee. 'Mr Wooller reported that he had had occasion to take him to task on his bowling at the St. Fagan's game. Pressdee had not been receptive to the suggestions made to him.'

Those familiar with the industrial rather than Parliamentary language that would be used on the cricket field at the time and, certainly, those familiar with Wilf's vocabulary when communicating with his players will have read this note in a slightly more colourful way.

There were two occasions when Wilf's zealous approach to playing the game led him and Bernard into some tricky spots. The first came in May 1956 against Sussex at Hove after Wilf had inserted Sussex on what he thought would be a wicket that would cause problems for the batsmen. There had also been a few previous occasions where Wilf had locked horns with Robin Marler, the Sussex captain, so this time, Wilf hoped that by bowling first he would have the bragging rights.

But to Wilf's chagrin, Alan Oakman and Don Smith added 241 for the first wicket and Sussex cantered to a decent total of 379. Smith then followed up his hundred with career-best figures of 6-29 as Glamorgan were bowled out for 64 half way through day two. Forced to follow-on, Wooller ordered his team 'not to play a shot' in their second innings on pain of being sent straight back to Cardiff. Leading from the front, Wooller opened with Gilbert Parkhouse and they proceeded to take the rest of the day to painstakingly accrue 143 runs. By the evening, the Sussex crowd had become so incensed by Glamorgan's tactics, and Wilf's approach in particular, that they barracked the 'go-slow' performance before slow-hand clapping an over that saw Wilf stoutly defend a series of gentle deliveries from one of the Sussex bowlers.

With the clapping getting louder, Wilf responded by sitting down and play was held up for two minutes until the barracking subsided. The following day, Wilf responded loudly to some of the comments he received from Sussex members as he prepared to bat by saying to them on his way out from the pavilion, 'Good morning, gentlemen. See you at the end of the session!'

These were prophetic words as Wilf remained unbeaten as Glamorgan ended on 200-1 from no less than 138 overs with Bernard also playing to orders after Gilbert Parkhouse had committed the heinous crime of getting out whilst attempting a drive. It was hard going for the number three batsman whose inclinations were to sweep, cut or pull any loose deliveries. There were certainly plenty of these as Marlar let everyone in his side have a bowl, but Wilf had decreed that defence should be their approach, and who was Bernard to play any differently? Just like he had learnt in the Armed Forces, a good soldier follows instructions and he duly helped Wilf save the game.

Many of the Glamorgan players still have vivid memories of the match – Don Shepherd remembers having to leave in taxis via the rear of the ground to avoid the incandescent Sussex supporters. Peter Walker remembers the dressing room emptying when Gilbert walked back in for the fear of 'Wilf's wrath' coming down on him and Wilf's subsequent words to Gilbert when coming back into the pavilion – 'I knew it would be you!'

Glamorgan's approach met with plenty of adverse comments from the London media, several of whom had been waiting for the day when they could have a pop at the Glamorgan captain. But when asked about his approach by a *posse* of pressmen after the game, Wooller remained as defiant as he had been out in the middle with bat in hand. 'When a team cannot win, the object should be not to lose,' he explained and tactfully – for once – did not draw too much attention to the fact that some of the Sussex supporters had thrown cushions and other items at the two Glamorgan batsmen when they left the field. Nevertheless, the newspapers the following morning, Saturday 19 May, were almost unequivocal in their criticism: 'Go Slow' announced the *Daily Mirror*, whilst the *Daily Express* exclaimed 'Slowest Ever Glamorgan Get the Bird', drawing attention to a statistic that it was the slowest scoring rate in a County Championship match. As far as Robin Marlar was concerned, he attaches little blame to Wilf for the outcome of the game at Hove:

'The incident with the 1956 Glamorgan team at Hove was all sounding brass and tinkling cymbals. Much more was made of it than there actually was. Wilf's mistake was to put Sussex in on the opening day and that coloured his thinking for the rest of the game. We made a big score and then bowled Glamorgan out cheaply on the second day. They got the conditions that we should have had. But there was also previous history with Wilf. He had bowled underarm in a previous game in annoyance at our slow scoring rate. We simply could not get them out, that was the problem.'

The second incident involved Peter May, who at the time was the captain of England. Batting at The Oval in the second game of the 1957 season, he chipped the ball low to mid-on where Bernard was stationed. To May and many others, the Glamorgan fielder appeared to clutch the ball just above the surface, so the batsman, believing a catch had been taken, started to walk to the pavilion. Bernard though, always placed honesty above all other values on a cricket pitch and he immediately turned towards the umpire and intimated that he thought the ball had not quite carried to him. Wooller, quick as a flash, called for the ball from Bernard and noticing that May was yards out of his ground, he threw the ball to Haydn Davies who removed the bails, and the appeal for run out was upheld by the umpire.

This left Surrey somewhat precariously poised on 48-4, but they recovered to reach 259 before their spin-twins of Tony Lock and Jim Laker scythed through the Glamorgan line-up as the Welsh county were dismissed for just 62 and 31. It had been an outstanding display of spin bowling but for the sizeable contingent of pressmen the real story for them was the May dismissal and they used it to decry some aspects, they believed, were creeping into the game. Pat Marshall of the *Daily Express* described the running out of May as 'an act of premeditated gamesmanship' – a charge which these days would be equivalent to ball tampering or match-fixing. Marshall finished his article with an open letter addressed to Wilf saying: 'By all means play cricket the hard way. But play it the fair way Wilfred.'

No blame whatsoever was attached to Bernard in what had taken place. Wilf was a tough and bloody-minded captain with a steely resolve and a determination to win that sometimes rubbed up against the spirit, if not the laws, of the game. Bernard had served a long apprenticeship and was fully aware of Wilf's foibles. He was also now an established professional and seen as a key member of the team. He was certainly not in the anti-Wooller lobby and as he had learnt on National Service, he let those charged with leadership carry on undertaking the decision-making. Wilf's acts may have been wrong, but Bernard was certainly not going to rock the boat by saying so.

But not everyone within the Glamorgan camp thought the same, and as at Hove, Wilf's actions at The Oval led to a lot of chatter within the committee room. At least the Surrey committee did not follow the example of the Sussex administrators who, after the incident at Hove in 1956, wrote a terse letter of complaint to their Glamorgan counterparts but, even so, there was a lobby on the Glamorgan committee who had been embarrassed by Wilf's actions in 1956 and 1957, and things came to a head during 1958.

Wilf had several enemies in the corridors of power and the furore which these incidents engendered became part of the ammunition used against the club's captain, as a faction of the committee questioned whether Wooller was the right man still to lead the club. Wilf, though, had the last laugh as the bid to mount a palace coup ended with egg on the face of his detractors. In 1958, A.C. 'Tolly' Burnett, a housemaster from Eton, who had not played first-class cricket for eight years was given a six-week trial as a future Glamorgan captain, all without the knowledge of Wooller. Given his modest record at

The Glamorgan team leaving the field at New Road, Worcester, in 1956. Wilf's leadership of the club was to be challenged in 1958. A challenge he saw off to reassert his influence. (© Glamorgan CCC)

first-class level, Burnett proved to be way out of his depth. His ability on the field was questionable, whilst his tactical ability as a captain was never really tested given Glamorgan's poor form and they were never really in a position to force a victory.

Several of the Glamorgan players felt that Burnett was also acting as a spy for the committee, and this was far from conducive to delivering good performances. Two matches reflected the potential of the team and the paucity of its state at that time. They both resulted in records of a kind: one that Bernard and his opening partner Gilbert Parkhouse might treasure, and another that the team would rather forget.

At the end of June, against Middlesex, Glamorgan replied to Middlesex's first innings total of 258 with a mammoth 427, including a Parkhouse and Hedges opening stand of 181, which remains a club record against a London-based side. Five weeks later, Burnett made his Championship debut against Lancashire, who posted a

A.C. 'Tolly' Burnett (© Glamorgan CCC)

decent first innings total of 351. What followed from the Welsh county can only be described as a 'horror show' as Glamorgan were bowled out for 26; their third lowest score in the County Championship. Last man in, Peter Gatehouse, was top scorer with eight, as Lancashire only used two bowlers, Brian Statham and Roy Tattersall.

With a highest score of 17, and a record of one win from eight games in charge, Burnett returned to his scholastic duties at the end of the summer, leaving Wilf to resume the leadership and in a stronger position than at the start of the season.

7

'Shep'

'One more over'

Cricket is a team game but it has, at its heart, individual performances and relationships. There were two players with whom Bernard would build a strong relationship. One lay in the future, his opening batting partner Gilbert Parkhouse. The other had been there right at the beginning of his career and would still be there right at the end of it. His name was Don Shepherd.

Don Shepherd wearing the daffodil he so proudly carried through his 22 seasons with Glamorgan. (© Glamorgan CCC)

'Shep' and Bernard roomed together for almost 20 years, with the pair becoming akin to Glamorgan's Morecambe and Wise, such was their close affiliation. The two professionals had many things in common – both had made their first-class debuts during 1950, neither of them ever won higher honours, and both were highly regarded by colleagues and opponents alike. But there were several differences as well, not least the fact that Don was a bowler – initially fast, before converting to off-cutters, and had an attitude to batting that was a polar opposite to Bernard's more textbook approach. They say that opposites attract, and together, from 1950 until 1967, the master bowler, and top-class batsman lived, breathed and slept Glamorgan cricket.

Don's career continued until 1972 by which time he had amassed a Club record of 2,174 first-class wickets. Only a handful of legendary English bowlers including Fred Trueman, Fred Titmus and Derek Shackleton took more wickets in the post-war era. No less an astute observer of the game than John Arlott included Don in his best England XI alongside Shackleton and Brian Statham, 'the three Ss' as he nicknamed them. A true legend of the club, he helped Glamorgan to the Championship in 1969, and fittingly took the final wicket as the Welsh county defeated Worcestershire to secure the title. In the modern world, where bowlers often set a target of 50 wickets a season, Shepherd's career statistics are truly remarkable – he claimed 100 wickets or more in a season on a dozen occasions and it is still quite baffling that given his success, year in year out, he never played for England. Yet, he was never bitter or disillusioned about his lot, and as reliable as the rain showers that dogged Glamorgan on their home grounds each summer; he was rarely taken apart, acting as the anchor of the county's bowling attack across three decades.

His first-class career began, like Bernard's, in 1950 and the pair were in the Glamorgan side at the Arms Park in early July when 'Shep', then a strapping young fast bowler, claimed his first five-wicket haul. It came in some style as well, as he removed three of the top four in Middlesex's illustrious line-up and helped to set up a Glamorgan victory by 86 runs. It was the first time that 'Shep' had hit the cricketing headlines with his bowling, and it was quite fitting that he had achieved the feat against Middlesex, as two years previously he had spent the summer on the MCC ground staff at Lord's, and had been one of the battery of net bowlers who wheeled away for hour after hour against MCC members, visiting batsmen and the Middlesex players.

His time at Lord's in that daffodil-golden summer of 1948 was not the result of the Gower-born youngster having taken a stack of wickets in club cricket in south Wales. In fact, in his youth Don had barely played any organised cricket and his rise to prominence stemmed for his time on National Service, as well as plenty of luck. Stationed at an RAF base in Worcestershire, he was spotted in a service game by one of the county's selectors, and noises were made about going to New Road for a trial. Word of his prowess soon reached the ears of Wilf Wooller, and whilst 'The Skipper' was leading his men to the 1948 title, Don undertook his cricketing apprenticeship at the St. John's Wood ground.

Whilst lady luck had favoured 'Shep', some of the other Glamorgan debutants in 1950 were less fortunate. Four others – Ken Lewis, Jim McConnon, Roy Davies and Bill Watkins – also made their debuts that summer, but in Roy and Bill's case, it was their one and only appearance for Glamorgan. Roy was Haydn Davies' brother and was a late call-up into the side for the match against Somerset at Weston-Super-Mare. Bill was also a late addition when Glamorgan were struck by an injury crisis shortly before the start of their match against Hampshire at Swansea. He had a fine record in club cricket and answered the SOS, but despite continuing to churn out the runs at club level, he never got another chance to wear the daffodil sweater.

Ken and Jim, like Don and Bernard, both had longer careers with Glamorgan, though Ken's – like several other fast bowlers – was dogged by injury. All these new players had to feel their way into the side and that meant not just on the pitch but socially as well. One of the more basic decisions to be made was where you would sleep. As a professional cricketer you would find yourself away from home and, for many of the players, this meant staying in hotels for the first time. As Don recalls:

'Once we (Bernard and I) were both selected for the first XI, there was the issue of who to room with. Jimmy McConnon had moved in with Willie Jones whilst Allan Watkins was always with Phil Clift. Haydn Davies or Emrys Davies, as senior pro, might have had a room to themselves. We would have been the two youngest in the team.'

Like many of the decisions made at that time, who you roomed with was based on practicalities. Don again:

'Neither of us smoked which was a happy coincidence. In those days, everybody smoked: in the changing rooms, in the bedrooms, everywhere. When I mentioned it to Bernard later that that was the reason we roomed together he said he had hoped it had been a bit more than that and I think it was. When we were together it just felt natural. We were both pretty easy going and we got on together. I was also tee-total and Bernard did not drink much. '

Bernard and Don were to remain room-mates for the rest of Bernard's time as a county cricketer, and during their 18 years together they developed a more relaxed attitude to alcohol, Don taking to a pint and Bernard to a little bit of brandy. For the Glamorgan team in later years, denying the players access to alcohol was regarded as a legitimate part of team management. Roger Davis remembers, after a poor team performance, being booked into a temperance hotel on the Hagley Road in Birmingham for the next away fixture against Warwickshire. However, in those early days, there was a lot more for Bernard and Don to worry about than whether or not the hotel had a bar. Don again:

'As 12th man we would have to make sure the bags got on and off the train and then to the hotel. We became experts on the train timetable, knowing which ones would get us back to Cardiff or across the country from Swansea. There was always an early finish on the final day if we had to travel a long way for the next match. The other thing about hotels was that there were no luxuries. We had to take our own soap and our own towels, and the toilets were on the corridors.'

When Glamorgan were playing at home, Don and Bernard would often stay at each other's family homes to save on expenses:

'When we were coming back to Wales from a long way away, I stayed at Bernard's house and he stayed with my family. It saved a hell of a lot of money. It was a small house. Bernard's mother worked a miracle. It was all organised. Once or twice we stayed with Allan and Molly Watkins in Usk. They had a dairy. Usk was on the main road to London. The lorries used to come thundering through all night. They were great people. The morning after we would make our way down to Cardiff for a home game.'

Bernard's brother Peter also remembers those days. 'There were so many bloody people here. There were people eating out in the kitchen almost all the time. Don used to visit the house and Jim Pressdee too, as well as Allan Watkins.' All the players' families would therefore grow up with an unusual collection of uncles, fellow cricketers who would stay for one or two nights every so often, with giant bags full of their kit and filling the house with talk of the day's play and what lay ahead tomorrow. In those early years, Bernard was still playing rugby for the All Whites. Don would go down to watch him play, as he recalls. "I saw Bernard play full back at the recreation ground end. He followed a high ball kicked into the in goal area, caught it and fell down the trench that lay behind the pitch. I thought we would never see him again!"

Another huge difference in life on the county circuit during the 1950s compared with today was the prevalence of three-day matches. There were no limited-overs games, bar the occasional exhibition or benefit match against a club side plus, in Glamorgan's case, two matches each year against the touring teams. This stemmed from the fact that when Glamorgan became the 17th side in the County Championship, all of the other teams had lucrative local derbies across the Whitsun and August Bank Holiday weekends. Glamorgan were therefore the only county who were free to accept challenges against the tourists, so for no other reason than this, the Arms Park hosted the international teams at Whitsun, whilst in August, the touring side headed to Swansea to play Glamorgan again in a match dubbed 'the Test match against Wales!'

Peter Hedges remembers going to a number of these fixtures: 'Two West Indian games and an Australian game in 1964. It was absolutely packed on

Bernard and Don glued to the screen as players watch some sport after the close of play.
(© Glamorgan CCC)

the Saturday. It was like a rugby international.' The financial imperative of making money out of these opportunities was made obvious to Don:

> 'Glamorgan have beaten all the major touring sides twice. When I scored a quick 50 against the 1961 Australians, Wilf told me I'd saved the gate. That was important because it was the entrance gate that was part of being able to pay the wages! There were 60,000 spectators over three days. Huge crowds around the field. There was a school of thought to play the tourists twice at Swansea because it was a bigger venue. Throughout the 1950s, on a Saturday, you'd be disappointed if there were not 8 to 10,000. Going to Pontypridd or Ebbw Vale, you were guaranteed a big gate because it was the only first-class cricket they would see. We felt like we were spreading the gospel.'

Despite the big crowds and the intensity of the cricket at the out-grounds, the game was still played with a laxity that would turn the modern player wide-eyed in disbelief. An example came at Dudley against Worcestershire that marked the beginning, at that time, of Bernard's best three weeks as a professional. It followed a particularly wet spell of weather which besides playing havoc with the county schedule had washed out the opening day of the Lord's Test against Pakistan. The encounter with Worcestershire also looked like being badly affected by rain but, in between the showers, Bernard made an unbeaten 64 to see Glamorgan to 163-3. 'Shep' can still recall what followed:

> 'After rain restricted play Wilf declared. In the end, thanks to Bernard, we had a competitive total. I think, if I remember, there was a marquee by the pitch and there was another shower. The Worcester boys had a few jugs because they thought that they wouldn't be playing again. How wrong they were. They had to come out and bat on a drying wicket, which is hard enough at the best of times without having a couple of pints of beer. I hit somebody on the head and he still went on to get 99.'

That somebody was Laddie Outschoorn, the elegant Sri Lankan batsman who made over 15,000 runs during a 13-year career at Worcester. He may or may not have partaken in the drinking but his team made a creditable 218 fuelled by whatever they had imbibed in that marquee. Bernard added 89 in the second innings, but the loss of time – or possibly a few hangovers in the home side – prevented a positive outcome being reached as the game ended in a draw.

Don was a shrewd observer of the batsmen in his own team as well as those of the opposition. His keen-eyed analysis identified their strengths and weaknesses, including their predilections. He saw Bernard as a predominantly back-foot player, guiding and pushing the ball, cutting and pulling. Although he would take the game to the bowlers at times, his demeanour was more defensive than Gilbert Parkhouse. As 'Shep' still recalls, 'Dennis Brookes of Northamptonshire, Jack Robertson of Middlesex and Reg Simpson of Nottinghamshire were the same. They just stood up and played into the ball and made it look so easy. The ball went with all the velocity that was necessary through the covers. Gilbert would have a go at the quickies too. And on a slow turner, he would pick out the sweep, which he had developed to cope with those sort of wickets.'

Don recognised that batting was not like an 'off the peg' suit with one style suiting all. It was more complicated than that. To see batsmen altering their strategies for scoring on wickets that could vary dramatically from ground to ground and from day to day during a match was enthralling for the spectator. Each strategy represented a challenge to the bowler, as 'Shep' recalled:

'Each batsman worked out what was best for them. I knew I could get Reg Simpson out hooking. I also knew that if I deliberately fired it down leg stump he'd get me away. There were others such as John Jameson and Rohan Kanhai. Just give them a little bit of room and they would get you away. Some of them were compulsive hookers. And with boundaries in those days being generally smaller, it was an encouragement to batsmen to play the pull and the hook. I remember Jeff Jones bowling to Tom Graveney. I told him to bounce him first ball because Tom used to pull off the front foot. We got him out caught at long leg. He laughed afterwards. He said he knew it was coming but he couldn't stop himself!'

As Don and Bernard moved into their second decade as Glamorgan players, they naturally found themselves given more authority in the team. In 1960, with Gilbert injured and Allan preferring not to take command, Don found himself captaining the side against Lancashire at Aigburth in Liverpool. After early victories in the season, Glamorgan's form had faltered and they were without a win in nine games and had no away win all season. Lancashire, on the other hand, were riding high in the Championship table and challenging Yorkshire for the title. With Bob Barber and Geoff Pullar, they could boast a pair of Test batsmen and with Statham and Higgs opening the attack they were likely to prove formidable opponents. Don won the toss and elected to bat. Glamorgan were soon floundering at 26-5, with Bernard the only recognised batsman remaining, but as Don vividly recalls, the game remarkably swung back in the Welsh county's favour: 'We were able to set a declaration. The pitch was quite wet. It was a great effort. Bernard did really well. He got 83 out of a total of 158. It was a proper professional innings.'

Given the context of this innings, many contemporary observers of Glamorgan cricket regarded this as Bernard's finest and most important knock for Glamorgan, with long-serving journalist Basil Easterbrook calling it an effort which 'stands supreme in his career'. In all, he batted for three and a quarter hours, striking eleven fours and shared a century stand with Don Ward, the off-spin bowler from Trealaw in the Rhondda. Bernard's sensible approach and protection of the tail allowed Glamorgan to reach a decent total. In what turned out to be a low-scoring game, every run was crucial and the all-round performance of the team vital to the outcome. 'Shep' took five wickets in the Lancashire first innings, Allan Watkins made a battling 66 and Bernard another 38 in Glamorgan's second innings. Then Peter Walker weighed in with four wickets as Lancashire were left with a target of 190. They fell 50 runs short with Bernard taking two great catches on the boundary. It was the first away win of the season against a top side. Don was naturally pleased as punch:

Glamorgan players photographed at Colwyn Bay in 1959. Don, Bernard and Jim Pressdee are joined by a very young looking Peter Walker. (© Glamorgan CCC)

'I remember afterwards being so pleased with the way the team had played. I got on the phone to Cardiff hoping to keep us together for the next game but I got a flea in my ear from Wilf and six of them were dropped. It was exceptional, and there were huge crowds. When you get that sort of effort from everybody it makes it all worthwhile.'

That was how it went sometimes at Glamorgan. Wilf made the bulk of the cricketing decisions and, as so often, he got it right, with Glamorgan winning the game against Northamptonshire by nine wickets. Despite these wholesale changes, there was no animosity and, as Don recalls, few of the professionals questioned Wilf's methods:

'Wilf ran the show. You did what was required of you. It was still in the days of professional and amateur. Whatever the amateur says goes. We were used to being given orders. Quite a lot of the captains had been through the war and had been officers. Wilf was a prisoner of war in Changi. That meant something to all of us who played under him. All the years Bernard and I played, we had three captains and three wicket-keepers. Now they seem to chop and change so much.'

As time went by and both Don and Bernard established their presence in the team, they relaxed into their respective roles and allowed themselves a little self-expression. Roger Davis remembers once arriving in the dressing room and, amongst other things, discovering the two senior pros having a laugh and joke at their own expense 'Don and Bernard were like Morecombe and Wise. They were so funny together. They would take the mickey out of one another.'

During their playing careers with Glamorgan, Bernard and Don moved from being young men onto the cusp of middle age, with the pair appearing in a combined total of 1,069 matches. Don holds the club record for the most appearances – 647 – with the longevity of his career stemming from his decision during the second half of 1955 to switch to off-cutters. Bernard was a passenger in the car when Haydn Davies first persuaded 'Shep' to switch from fast bowling. He was also there when the stalwart wicketkeeper first discussed the idea of him standing back to Don's bowling in order to cope with the new restrictions on leg-side field placings.

They shared the highs and lows of each other's playing careers, with 'Shep' being a delighted colleague when Bernard played his man-of-the-match innings against Somerset in 1963 at the Arms Park in Glamorgan's first ever Gillette Cup game. As befitted a loyal friend, he also helped Bernard from the field when he was struck a painful blow in the mouth whilst fielding at gully against the West Indians as well as being around in the changing rooms or the hotels on away trips when Bernard was struggling with his kidney stones.

For Bernard's young sons, Uncle Don was, most importantly, the man whose family owned the shop that sold ice cream on the way down to the beaches of the Gower. Many journeys to the beach were broken by a stop at Shepherds of Parkmill. We knew next to nothing about Glamorgan or Lord's or Aigburth or any of that. Our lives were only complicated by the problem of whether to have chocolate or strawberry, and Uncle Don was the man whose shop would supply it.

As time went by, the decisions facing both men took them in different directions. In 1967 Bernard left cricket and began another career outside of sport. Don played on until the end of 1972 and then found great pleasure in being a commentator, coach and pundit. Their choices were made in good faith with a generosity and a concern for their family's wishes. As old age gently swept over them like the tide on Swansea Bay, their two paths crossed each other once more, this time not as room-mates but as neighbours in the Mumbles. Cricket remained their language of choice. It is a game that they both loved to play and to reflect on. It was not just a profession that they shared; it was a pastime that allowed them the best moments of their lives.

As Bernard lay in bed during the last few weeks of his life, it was Don's visits that brought relief in the reminiscences of two old comrades. Cricket was at the forefront of their discussions; grounds they had played at, cricketers they had played with, and characters they had known. The conversation turned to Roscoe Howells, a long-time supporter of Glamorgan and President of the St. Helen's Balconiers. He had died in recent days. Don and Bernard smiled as they recalled the 'generous hospitality' made available at Roscoe's house in Amroth. Behind the smiles and the stories, there were some things that were left unsaid. It was cricket

Don Shepherd – the Glamorgan bowling legend. (© Glamorgan CCC)

that assisted even here. As Don climbed the stairs to speak to his old friend, Bernard could be heard quietly saying 'One more over, 'Shep'.'

8

Opening Partner #1: Gilbert Parkhouse

Showing 'more zest and attacking ability.'

The distinction between club cricket and county cricket is a significant one and the gulf in class between an ordinary club cricketer and a county professional is obvious even to the most inexperienced of observers. County batsmen appear to have all the time in the world to play their shots, often waiting at the crease for the ball to arrive before stroking it with ease through the arc between wide mid-on and mid-off or cutting and hooking with the venom of a swatter who knows he's just too quick for the flies. County bowlers, if scrutinised, are able to exert a level of control over the movement and pitching of the ball that appears miraculous to those of us who have never picked up a ball or been perplexed by how to propel it from wicket to wicket.

Gilbert Parkhouse, with John Evans the club's physiotherapist, at Leicester in 1956. To many of his Glamorgan contemporaries, Parkhouse was 'a class apart'. (© Glamorgan CCC)

The step up from county to Test cricket is, in its own way, just as significant. An element of luck or bias can creep into the process, with selection sometimes being rather fortuitous, based on the exigencies of the moment rather than the ability of the player. Even so, a Test-class player is unmistakably superior in the eyes of his peers. Such was the case with Gilbert Parkhouse, the man who became Bernard's first regular opening partner and the player who helped Bernard become such a success at county level.

Born in Swansea in 1925, he was fortunate to have been coached at St. Helen's by Billy

Bancroft, the Welsh county's first home-grown professional and, despite his paid status as a cricketer, a Welsh rugby international and a star of Swansea RFC. There were many occasions during the 1930s when there was a gleam in the eyes of old Billy as he threw balls to the young batsman in the nets at St. Helen's, the ground near to where he and his father had lived for so many years, tending the wicket and playing area at the ground overlooking Swansea Bay.

By the time young Gilbert made his first appearances in senior cricket for Swansea, and later for Glamorgan, Billy was in charge of the player's gate at the foot of the long flight of steps back up the embankment to the St. Helen's pavilion. It allowed him to pass on a few personal words of congratulation seconds before the crowd rose to show their collective appreciation of Gilbert's graceful batting. Indeed, players and supporters alike were captivated by his batting style that, at once, appeared a thing of beauty yet was full of destructive power.

There is an oft-quoted description of Don Bradman by the famous journalist and former county cricketer R.C. Robertson-Glasgow, who wrote of the Australian batsman, 'Poetry and murder lived in him together. He would slice the bowling to ribbons and dance without pity on the corpse'. Parkhouse may not have been as prolific or as ruthless as Bradman but when he was in full flow there was the same air of cultivated annihilation about his batting. Contemporaries such as Don Shepherd described him as 'a class apart' whilst Tony Lewis described his batting to me in the following glowing terms:

'A very special player. He would take the ball late and run it off. I grew up as a kid watching him play in 1948 with his flowing drives. He was a class performer. The way he played Tyson was beautiful because he could hook. Gilbert had amazing timing and footwork. He was one of those players who never slogged the ball ... it just went. Colin Cowdrey used to get a hundred at Canterbury and you never heard the ball on the bat all afternoon. Gilbert was similar. He was top-class.'

Countless numbers of Welsh schoolboys called themselves Parkhouse when they played their games of street cricket. Joan Rees, a Glamorgan supporter who was to later marry Tom Cartwright of Warwickshire and England fame, had called her first cat Compton, but when he ran away, she duly named his replacement Parkhouse, such was her adoration of Gilbert's batting. Her husband was also a huge fan, appreciating how easy on the eye Gilbert's batting could be:

'We had beautiful ball players ... with touch and with a lovely balance that goes with it ... Arthur Milton: Arthur cloth-bat they called him because there was no sound on the bat. George Emmett, Joe Hardstaff, Dennis Brookes, Gilbert Parkhouse. There was a craft, a caress about the way they played. There was something gentle and pure right through from the way they looked so well turned out.'

That gentleness, purity and separateness from other players expressed itself in other ways than on the cricket field. Parkhouse was a Welshman, but he spoke with a cultured English accent. This was a lasting legacy from his days at Wycliffe College, a public school in the Cotswolds, much in favour at the time for the sons of the well-to-do and *nouveaux riches* of south Wales. Inevitably he incorporated, into his lifestyle, some of the more cultured aspects of day-to-day living of those he was educated alongside. As Joan Rees remembers: 'I never told him that I called the cat after him. Gilbert was a bit distant. There was a Berni Inn in the High Street in Swansea. I went in with my friend after a game and there was Gilbert on his own with a glass of red wine. We didn't know anybody that drank red wine then. We were so impressed. I think we bowed. It was so embarrassing.'

National Service meant that Gilbert did not make his debut for Glamorgan until 1948, but he swiftly made up for lost time by scoring over 1,000 runs in his debut season, a feat he was to repeat another 14 times consecutively until his career finished in 1962, by which time he had amassed a grand total

Gilbert Parkhouse turning a ball to leg and beating the leg-side trap against Nottinghamshire in 1958. (© Glamorgan CCC)

of 23,508 runs. This tally still places him fourth in the all-time run scorers list for Glamorgan.

Three years later, in 1950, Gilbert's England career began and as Bernard was making his maiden hundred at Sussex, Gilbert was fighting a rearguard action with Cyril Washbrook as England battled to save the Second Test at Lord's. They failed and West Indies won their first ever Test on English soil by 326 runs, thanks mainly to 'those two little pals of mine', Ramhadin and Valentine.

Gilbert's England career continued through the winter as he was chosen on the MCC tour to Australia and New Zealand. But it proved a disappointment for Gilbert, marred by injury and disagreements with senior figures in the England line-up and, as a result, his next taste of Test cricket did not come until eight years later, by which time he and Bernard were experiencing their best season as an opening pair, averaging 46.12 for the first wicket in first-class games during the 1959 season.

In all, Parkhouse played only seven times for England, a number many on the Welsh side of Offa's Dyke feel was an injustice. However, he was not alone in having only a brief international career at a time when England were blessed with a fine array of batting talent, with George Emmett and Dennis Brookes, both of whom scored more first-class runs than Gilbert, only being selected to play for England on one occasion.

But England's loss was Bernard's gain as he had plenty of opportunities to open the batting with the gifted stroke maker and to continue the fine tradition of opening batsmen which Emrys Davies had established either side of the Second World War.

Bernard and Gilbert first opened together in July 1955 at St. Helen's when Surrey visited the Swansea ground with Jim Laker and the Bedser twins on top form. They duly claimed all the wickets, Laker finishing with match figures of 10-121. Glamorgan had Jim McConnon and Wilf Wooller injured so the side had an unfamiliar and inexperienced look with Don Ward, Hugh Davies and George Shaw all included.

The first season where Parkhouse and Hedges were the regular openers was 1957, with the pair joining forces at the top of the order for the match against Leicestershire at Coalville which started on 5 June. Bernard made 128 in the first innings as Glamorgan romped to a victory by an innings and 52 runs, and based on their success – both collectively and individually – the selection committee (or Wilf really!) decided to continue with the pairing for the rest of the season. In July, against Nottinghamshire at Stradey Park, they notched up 156 with Bernard going on to make 139 and completely master the spin bowling of Australian Test player Bruce Dooland.

The leg-spinner had been the ace in Notts pack for several seasons and Reg Simpson, the visiting captain, has gone on record in more recent times to claim that Dooland was 'the best leg-break bowler in the history of cricket; better than Shane Warne. He had far more variety. His top spinner was an absolute devil.' At Stradey Park, on that day in 1957, he was overheard remarking to one of the tanner bank supporters: 'This wicket is as good as Trent Bridge.' He might well have said, of the openers, that these two were as good as Jimmy Gray and Roy Marshall of Hampshire or Young and Emmett of Gloucestershire. Their stand of 156 came in over a run a minute and helped Glamorgan to 387-8, their highest total of the season to that point. It laid the foundations for another sizeable victory, this time by an innings and 120 runs. How Wilf Wooller must have smiled as he watched from the pavilion as the team of his most consistent rival in county cricket, Reg Simpson, were completely outplayed.

There were other useful partnerships against Hampshire at Portsmouth (78 in the second innings), Northants at Northampton (75 in the first innings) and Derbyshire at Pontypridd (77 in the first innings). In the final match of the season Glamorgan played Yorkshire. The Tykes were to finish third after beating Glamorgan but it was a close run thing. Set 173 runs to win in a low scoring game, Parkhouse and Hedges put on 95 before Ray Illingworth and Bob Appleyard initiated a dramatic collapse as Glamorgan fell just five runs short of their target.

In all, Parkhouse and Hedges amassed 897 runs that summer, with one 100 and five 50 partnerships, but there were two rather more significant events to come after the end of the season. The first was Bernard's marriage to Jean on 6 September at Manselton Church in Swansea. Gilbert and Don Shepherd were in attendance, with Don acting as best man. It had been a seven year courtship that had contained moments when Bernard had proven his ardour in most gallant ways. Jean recalls:

'We'd been to see this film; it was about the RAF. The actor, I can't remember who it was, had his collar up and was smoking a pipe, blowing out the smoke. When we were going home I said 'I do like men with an overcoat and the collar up and smoking a pipe but you don't smoke do you?' Not long after, Bernard came up to Penvylia Road, where I was living with my mum and low and behold, I opened the door and there he was with his collar up with this lovely Lovett blue double-breasted overcoat. He came inside; I took his coat and put it on the hall stand. He came into my mother's living room, sat down and out of his pocket he takes a pipe and tobacco. He asked my mother if she minded him smoking and after she said no, he lit up. After a couple of puffs he was turning green. 'Put it out' my mother said. 'The boy doesn't like smoking.' He never smoked a cigarette or pipe again!'

Gilbert, on the other hand, was an inveterate smoker. So much so that Jim Pleass used to refer to Gilbert and Bernard as 'Benson and Hedges!' Bernard also showed a persistent kindness that made a great impression on his future wife.

'He was a very generous boy. None of us had any money in those days but he always brought a record that we played on our Sobell table model radiogram. My brother bought it in 'J's Furniture's' on hire purchase. He went to New Zealand and left my mum to pay for it. The records he bought were lovely. Frank Sinatra ... and always very sentimental tunes. I was smoking in those days and he used to bring me Benson and Hedges cigarettes. I always used to like seeing him because I knew there would always be cigarettes and a record for me.'

Whilst still living in Pontypridd, Bernard had been asked to take part in the BBC Radio programme *Down Your Way* which visited different towns and villages throughout the UK, asking local people about their lives and getting them to recommend records. Sadly, I have been unable to track down a copy of the

Bernard and Jean on their wedding day. Don Shepherd is in attendance as best man.
(© Mrs M.J. Hedges)

recording. However, all of Bernard's family and his friends in 'Ponty' remember the programme, not because of what Bernard said to Richard Dimbleby the interviewer, but because of the song he asked to be played. It was the voice of tenor Jussi Bjorling singing a song that most of us who do not dabble in anything other than popular culture will know from the 1990 football World Cup in Italy. *Nessun Dorma*, the aria from Puccini's opera *Turandot* was what he requested. Jean has a memory of her and Bernard seeing Bjorling sing at the Brangwyn Hall in Swansea. There were recordings of it available at the time so Bernard may even have bought it. Either way, it came as a surprise to everyone in 'Ponty'. They must have been expecting something from the valleys not from the operatic stages of New York or Milan. Whether it was the result of a grammar school education or rubbing up against some of the more cultured members of the Glamorgan team, this love of opera stayed with Bernard for the rest of his life. He loved, especially, listening to Pontypridd born tenor Stuart Burrows and he would develop his own particular style of semi-operatic delivery whilst he was doing the dishes.

Once married to a county cricketer, there were lots of things for Jean to get used to:

'We had a flat in Wimmerfield Avenue, Killay in Swansea. It was three guineas a week plus £330 a year ground rent. We didn't have a car so I let the garage and we were being paid £3 guineas a month for the rental. I was working; Bernard was doing the indoor school in the winter and playing in the summer. Once they started training, the Neath indoor school would stop. He was there five days a week. He'd leave about lunch time and I wouldn't see him until 11-11:30pm at night. He'd have a bus from Neath to Swansea and then in the bus garage he'd come down on the last bus to Killay. It was hard work. Very tiring. Sometimes he would be away with Glamorgan for ten days and then he would come home with a bag full of smelly, sweaty socks and jumpers. They were allocated one long sleeve jumper and one sleeveless pullover besides their trousers and shirts. Being a new bride and never having washed wool before, I asked my mum how to do it. 'Tepid water and lots of swills. Gentle washing.' I didn't have a washing machine so I had to do it all by hand. Sadly, his cable jumper was shrunk until he was going out to bat with his arms like this (*arms outstretched like a scarecrow*). I'd be stretching the arms to get them wider. In the end, I rolled it in a towel and lay it out flat to dry. I got the hang of it just as his career was over!'

The second major event came just six weeks after his wedding. It was the death of his father Jack. Like many former miners, Jack's lungs had an inherent weakness and he succumbed to an outbreak of flu which had spread though the factories on the Treforest Industrial Estate where he worked. Things were so bad that some units faced closure, such was the scale of the manpower shortage. On 2 November, an anti-flu vaccine arrived in the town but it was too late for Jack. He had died on 19 October with a short obituary in the local newspaper reporting, 'Popular Cricketer Bereaved.'

This was a very difficult time for Bernard. As the eldest son, he needed to support his mother and sisters. Only he and his brother John attended the funeral. The younger boys, Peter and Gerald were too young, by tradition, to attend and his mother and all his sisters waited at Chestnut Road. Jack had been a figurehead for them all and would be sorely missed. His workmates at Johnson and Jorgenson had drawn lots to decide who would attend the funeral as so many of them wanted to go.

The autumn of 1957 had been an emotional roller-coaster for Bernard, experiencing the highs and lows of life associated with marriage and death. If there was one positive to be gleaned from the sad weeks leading up to the Christmas period, it was that Jack had passed away at the end of the cricket season, with Bernard being able to give his fullest attention to looking after his mother and sisters at such a sad time, without the distraction of matches and net practice.

The 1958 season proved to be a poor one for Glamorgan, with the county slumping back to 15th place in the Championship table. Performances and morale were each affected by the on-going battle between Wilf and the committee, with the players being treated like pawns. Not surprisingly, the players were not sorry to see the back of the season but they were not, however, glad to see the back of Haydn Davies or Willie Jones who both retired, each a little weary and frustrated by the back-biting and carping. They had played a key role for many years in the Glamorgan side, and with both having Championship honours to their name, they were well-respected by their fellow professionals. In fact Haydn, for several years, had acted as an unofficial shop steward, acting as an arbiter between the county and its professional players. For example, in 1957, he wrote to the finance committee on behalf of the players, requesting a pay rise. The financial remunerations at that time at Glamorgan were not the best but they were certainly not the worst. In summary, they consisted of:

- capped players received a weekly wage of £10 10s a week for 52 weeks.
- £4 per match for capped players.
- £5 for all players playing in winning side.
- £2 10 shillings per night for matches played out of Wales.
- Talent money bonus paid at the end of the season depending on performance.

- After ten years as a capped player, a Benefit Year which could bring in as much as £4,000 tax free.

Comparisons are difficult to make between sportsmen and other walks of life but most cricketers would say that, at the time, they did not earn much for what they did. In football, the maximum wage was still in effect in 1955; the average club footballer would earn around £8 a week plus bonuses. Factory workers could earn somewhere in the region of £11 a week, but were arguably much better off when considering the modest pay and uncertain career prospects facing most professional sportsmen. Despite the government of the day reassuring everyone that 'our people have never had it so good' the specifics pertaining to the working life of a professional cricketer were bound to make them feel less than secure. John Arlott, writing as early as 1949, pointed out some of these conditions in an article, for the purposes of which, he created a 'mythical' county professional:

'He has no trade union. He can be dismissed with no reason on personal grounds. He can be denied a benefit which he has morally earned but which he has no right to claim. There is no guarantee of his security should he be injured or ill for any appreciable period beyond the end of his contract. He can draw crowds running into thousands and fill the headlines of the press of an empire yet be living on the wages of a good artisan. His career is over before he is 50 and he must make his own provision for his subsequent years.'

Haydn, in his letter to the committee, voiced his concern that the conditions of his teammates had deteriorated during the 1950s: 'Whereas a cricketer had a good middle-class income before the war, he now has to struggle for a living.'

Before the beginning of the 1959 season, the Glamorgan membership and publicity committee met to discuss the decline in membership. Overall membership had fallen from 6,154 in 1953 to 3,137 in 1958. The first reasons given in the committee's discussion were that the post-war boom in interest in sport had passed and that the public were generally apathetic about seeing all sport. There were also diverse counter attractions that included TV and other leisure pursuits that were now more easily available. Also, money was tighter, there were unattractive touring sides and poor weather. The remedies put forward were more attractive cricket and a winning side, ground improvements and a need to try harder with recruitment. These discussions were reflected up and down the country with the MCC insisting on the need for 'brighter cricket.' The long term decline in attendance at county games would form the background, in several years time, to the abolition of amateur status and the introduction of one-day cricket.

After all the arguing and grumpiness of the previous season, it was a blessing that 1959 proved to be a long, hot and largely dry summer. Rather than sitting around in damp changing rooms muttering darkly about their lot, or wondering who would be their next captain, the players were out and about in the sunshine, and letting their cricketing skills do the talking. For batsmen, the fine weather meant wickets were hard and flat. The result was lots of runs, with 23 players scoring over 2,000 runs, and there were 337 centuries scored in the first-class season compared to 146 in 1958. Don Shepherd recalls: '1959 was the toughest season I ever played in. I can't remember losing a day's cricket. It was deep into August before I got 100 wickets.' In all, he took 107 wickets that summer and managed to take ten wickets in a match on three occasions. Only in 1956, when he bowled more than 1,200 overs, did he better this statistic.

With harmony having replaced the hatred, Glamorgan rose back up to sixth place in the county table, and they could have finished second if they had beaten Middlesex on the final day of the season. *Wisden's* correspondent outlined a series of other factors behind their renaissance – the will to win engendered by Wilf, fast scoring at the top of the order by Gilbert and Bernard, the consistent support from Allan Watkins and Jim Pressdee in the middle-order, the deadly off-breaks of Don and Jim McConnon, plus the excellent fielding, particularly by Peter Walker, who took 64 catches, mainly in the leg-trap, as he became the leading fielder of the season.

The first win came against Worcestershire at St. Helens in mid-May, and prompted a *Western Mail* headline of 'Crocks Crack Way to Fine Win.' Bernard batted the whole of his second innings with a runner after pulling a groin muscle on the first day. Gilbert had strained the muscles in one leg and badly bruised the other. Wilf did not play either because of a leg injury, so Allan Watkins captained the side. Set 263 to win, Gilbert and Bernard created the platform for victory with a 170-run opening partnership. Gilbert stayed at the crease for five and a half hours for his 111 whilst Bernard, despite his injury, struck nine boundaries in his 79.

Not for the last time that season, prominent in the report of the victory at Swansea were the words of John Evans, the Glamorgan physiotherapist. In the game against Gloucestershire at Cheltenham in August, Wilf would play with painkilling injections plus supports on both his arm and leg, and take three wickets to win the match, prompting Evans, talking about the Skipper to the Press, to say, 'If he took off the strapping, his leg would fall off.'

The opening pair shared another century stand against Derbyshire in late May with Gilbert scoring a chanceless 154 and Bernard a fine 56 as their side posted a five-wicket victory. At the beginning of June, Glamorgan chased down 230 to win against Northants. Parkhouse and Hedges set the tone with lively and confident 50s, with one reporter, perhaps competing with a colleague to demonstrate the best use of a pun in a match report referring to Gilbert's batting as being 'as safe as Parkhouses!'

Glamorgan's performances were becoming good enough for another match report to finish with the comment that 'The only trouble about this latest Glamorgan triumph is the standard it has set for success.' Not content with puns, John Billot of the *Western Mail* decided to mix some metaphors after the win against Gloucestershire at St. Helen's. Opening stands of 41 and 59 by Gilbert and Bernard had helped propel Glamorgan towards a 119-run victory, their seventh home win in succession. Billot, perhaps letting the moment carry him away somewhat, described the team thus: 'unlike lightning, which never strikes in the same place twice, Glamorgan have kept on striking, cobra-like and with as deadly an effect.' Lightning they were used to in Swansea, cobras, not so much. The two of them together? Never. But the team were obviously playing with a tenacity that was allowing them to attack and beat other teams, particularly on the third day of a game.

The 1959 season had started, like several before it, with concerns over the way many matches were becoming dull to watch, with batsmen doing their best to protect their averages, and captains being too defensive to avoid the criticism often brought about by defeat. Warwickshire were one of the counties who were concerned by this negativity and in their annual report, they stated: 'If cricket is to continue as a spectacle to interest a public and provide them with entertainment, the great majority of players will have to show far more zest and attacking ability.' Neville Cardus, the great cricket writer eloquently summed up the situation with the following: 'The word cricket is rapidly becoming a synonym for all that is boring and ungallant in sport.'

There were discussions about how to improve the public perception of cricket: weekend matches, one-day cricket and changes to the regulations to promote a more exciting game had all either been tried or mooted. In 1959, a London-based newspaper intervened in the debate by offering a 500 guinea prize to the team to hit the fastest 200 in its first innings of a County Championship game. Parkhouse and Hedges were to set the pace in this race during June. At Dartford, after being put in by Kent, they hit 207 for the first wicket in five minutes under three hours.

The 'sizzling speed' of their batting at 4.26 runs an over matched the soaring temperatures. Bernard had to be treated for cramp at the wicket after getting his hundred, eventually being out for 129. The report in *The Times* mentioned that the start of play had been delayed for ten minutes while covers were drawn across 'offending car windscreens glinting in the sun', an operation that had to be repeated later in the day. The outfield reminded the reporter of 'a sheet of glass' with the two batsmen placing their shots so well that it seemed like 'all the Kent players in the field were standing in the wrong positions.'

Despite scoring 371 in the first innings Glamorgan lost the game, with Kent winning on the final evening of a match which saw over 1,100 runs scored – if this did not represent 'more zest and attacking ability' then I am not sure what would.

Bernard and Gilbert followed this performance with a scintillating effort during the next game at the Arms Park against Essex. Replying to an Essex total of 367, they raced to 140 in an hour and 45 minutes, and in the process recorded their fourth century stand of the season before their colleagues upped the scoring rate as they reached 200 in even quicker time than previously.

Gilbert and Bernard – Parkhouse and Hedges.
(© Glamorgan CCC)

The weather, constantly warm and occasionally blisteringly hot, highlighted another contrast between Bernard and Gilbert. Many remarked how Gilbert would often return to the dressing room after a long innings without a bead of sweat on him, as if his graceful batting rejected such an ungraceful process as perspiration. Bernard, on the other hand, always looked like he had been working at something more equivalent to manual labour as he went about his batting bathed in sweat. Batting was hard work and Bernard approached it in that light. He was the artisan to Gilbert's artist, the perfect battling foil to the clean rapier of the Test batsman. The two gained a great reputation for their running between the wickets, putting pressure on the fielding side and constantly forcing bowlers to readjust their line of attack. Their contrasting efforts in swiftly seeing Glamorgan to the 200-mark in June had put them in with a decent chance of winning the 500 guinea prize, but the cash was eventually won by Middlesex who got to 200 in even quicker time against Nottinghamshire during late August.

The boys had come very close to bagging the prize. Only two other opening pairs in the country would better Bernard and Gilbert's 207. They were Martyn Young and Arthur Milton of Gloucestershire, who added 226 against Somerset at Bristol, and Hampshire's Roy Marshall and Jimmy Gray, who amassed 214 against Gloucestershire. The Glamorgan duo were hindered from achieving more when Gilbert was recalled to the England team. He played in the Tests at Headingley and Old Trafford and consequently missed four Glamorgan games. Bernard scored a hundred in one of them, against Warwickshire at Neath, but who knows how much more they could have accomplished together in the game at The Gnoll.

The net result at the end of a hot and tiring summer was that Glamorgan were only nine points away from finishing second and 26 points behind eventual champions Yorkshire. Another couple of wins inspired by the immaculate Parkhouse could have made it very close, even for the title, though Wilf had a different take on things as, when reflecting on the season, he said, 'We would have won the Championship if we had possessed pace bowlers.'

Parkhouse and Hedges were the best opening partnership in the County Championship in 1959, yet there was never any consideration of Bernard as a potential Test player. The pair had scored nearly twice as many runs as Bryan Stott and Ken Taylor of County Champions Yorkshire, and had amassed a higher average partnership than all the openers in the top five teams, despite having played more games together. They stood head and shoulders above the likes of Arthur Milton and Martin Young of Gloucestershire, the young John Edrich and Mickey Stewart at Surrey, and Bob Barber and Alan Wharton at Lancashire. So why did Gilbert, after eight years out of the England team, get another chance to open for England and not Bernard?

The first and obvious answer is runs. Bernard's haul for the season was a more than decent 1,521 but in a scorching summer of hard wickets there were many top batsmen who outscored him. Arthur Milton (1,984), Geoff Pullar (2,647), Raman Subba Row (1,917) and Gilbert himself (2,243) all opened for England that season. Even John Edrich, then aged just 21, scored 1,799 but at an average of over 50 compared to Bernard's 30.42 (Edrich had an unbelievable 11 not-outs to his name as an opener, courtesy of the outstanding Surrey bowling attack). Add to that, the fact that Pullar and Subba Row both made runs on their introduction to the team and you see how Bernard never made enough runs at the right time and against the right opponents to come into the reckoning (Pullar made 137, batting at number three, eight days before the third Test, while Bernard missed the game against the tourists at Cardiff).

The second is less obvious and the subject of supposition. England had experienced a very disappointing winter, losing the Ashes series 4-0 and were attempting to rebuild. They had an opportunity with a touring Indian side to try new options for the top of the order that had failed so significantly Down Under. This went in Bernard's favour. His comfort against spin and his willingness to attack the bowling would have been important considerations. However, by their own admission, the selectors - Gubby Allen, Herbert Sutcliffe, Doug Insole and Glamorgan's own Wilf Wooller - were embarking on a three-year plan aimed at producing a side capable of regaining the Ashes in

Jeff Jones, who made his debut in 1960, was one of the fastest bowlers in English cricket during the early 1960s. (© Glamorgan CCC)

1961, so Bernard's vulnerability to top class pace would have counted against him.

There was, also, that nagging feeling that Bernard did not fit the profile of an English Test opener. A working class boy from the valleys did not have the same attraction for England's selectors as the public school background of both Parkhouse and Subba Row. Without what Derek Birley called 'easy access to the magic circle', only an avalanche of runs would have brought Bernard's name into the equation. 1959 may have been the closest he ever came to a Test call-up but the dream of playing for England remained, for him, just that.

Given their return to form during 1959, and the profligacy of their batsmen, hopes were high for 1960. Their optimism did not look misplaced as Glamorgan began with victories against Worcestershire and Leicestershire at Ynysangharad Park and St. Helen's. The second of these was by an innings and 144 runs which saw Gilbert and Bernard add 137 for the first wicket. Remarkably, only 24 of these were contributed by Bernard, as Gilbert was busy combining poetry and murder whilst his partner quietly looked on from the other end.

But after this fine start, Glamorgan ended up 11th in the table, and experienced a very mixed bag of results. This was despite the efforts of the opening pair as Bernard and Gilbert rattled up 1,207 runs at an average of 29.07. A series of injuries, notably to Wilf himself, meant that on occasions a quite inexperienced bowling unit took to the field. One of the new fresh faces was 18-year-old Jeff Jones, a left-handed fast bowler and his raw but hostile pace could only have brought a twinkle to the eye of The Skipper after his reflections of the previous summer.

How comforting it must have been as well for Bernard and Gilbert, who had faced uncomplainingly for so many years, the quicks from other counties, to know that Glamorgan now had an outstanding prospect to add fire and pace to their attack. Although Jeff was a left-armer, and Fred Trueman bowled right-arm, comparisons were made in terms of pace with England's Fiery Fred, the man whose hostility, plus a few barbed comments, were the dearth of countless teams at county and international level.

Every leading batsman at that time had a story about facing Fred, and Bernard was no different. There were very few stories that Bernard would tell about his time playing time. Perhaps, for him, those stories were for sharing with a more sympathetic and understanding audience of ex-players. More likely was that he was a moderate, modest man who never wished to attract attention to himself or what he had done. Stories were perhaps too much like ostentation; a puffing and a preening which as he grew older became more alien to his character, but the one involving Fred was, with coaxing, the one he would tell and retell.

Some of its details became hazy but the core of it remained true to its origins. The venue is not certain, though it could have been Scarborough. It certainly was not Headingley. Glamorgan were batting first; with Gilbert taking strike and Bernard at the bowler's end. Fred was to bowl the opening over of the match. His first ball was a full toss outside off-stump which was elegantly dispatched for four by Gilbert. Fred returned to his mark with a grunt and a groan before steaming in, putting a little extra into the second delivery. Another full toss outside off-stump just as elegantly dispatched as the last. Another boundary. Fred turned around, a little perplexed. 'Must be something to do with the wicket' said Bernard, trying to make light of the situation.

Sadly, for a bowler as conceited as Fred, this made absolute sense. In what world could Fred Trueman have bowled two consecutive full tosses? He seized upon Bernard's explanation. 'Do yer kna what Bernard. Aye think thas right.' There followed a formal request to the umpires to bring out the 'chains' to measure the length of the wicket. A delay of several minutes ensued whilst the groundstaff dragged the chains out to the square and measured the length of the wicket in front of the whole of the Yorkshire fielders plus the two Glamorgan openers. The result? An immaculately measured pitch measuring exactly 22 yards. Glamorgan were 8 for 0 and play continued, with one fiery fast bowler seething with embarrassment!

Bernard and Gilbert enjoyed one more meaningful season together, in 1961, before Alan Jones moved up to replace Gilbert who, by 1962, was in the twilight of his illustrious career. Ossie Wheatley had arrived as captain at the beginning of the 1961 season. He remains, even today, rather shocked at what happened to Gilbert:

'Gilbert's was the fastest deterioration I have ever seen in an athlete. He reached the stage when he was 36 when he couldn't hit the ball off the square. He'd play a perfect shot but it wouldn't go anywhere and he used to hobble between the wickets. He looked immaculate but his legs had gone.'

Having learnt his trade, like Bernard, lower in the order, before going on to enjoy rich success as an opening batsman, Alan is in a good position to assess the merits of 'Hedges and Parkhouse', and their standing alongside other great Glamorgan opening partnerships of the modern era, especially those of recent times who enjoyed, unlike Bernard and Gilbert, life on covered wickets. Alan's illustrious career straddled the period of uncovered and covered wickets, and, in his own words:

'Moving from uncovered to covered wickets was a huge change. They talk about wanting to play exciting cricket. I think what would make it exciting? Why don't they give it a go for a couple

Arnold Dyson (left) and Emrys Davies. Glamorgan's most prolific opening pair, with 32 opening stands of a hundred or more. (© Glamorgan CCC)

of years playing on uncovered wickets? Then you'd separate the good players from the bad players. Technically you would see how good they are. We couldn't trust the wicket in our day. You could play at St. Helen's or Cardiff and you could be playing on two different wickets, one half dry and one half wet. If you didn't have a good technique you would struggle.'

Conversely, of course, this initiation and development of your technique on slow pitches meant that you were ill-prepared to play on the faster wickets that you would meet elsewhere. Tony Lewis again:

'We were brought up on slow turning club wickets. That's why we struggled on bouncing green tops like Chesterfield and Trent Bridge where there was a lot of movement and bounce. Trueman and Brian Statham would never have got the number of wickets on Welsh wickets.'

The other factor affecting opening batsmen in particular and alluded to by Tony, was the battery of top-class swing and seam bowlers that you would face right across the county scene. Trueman of Yorkshire and Statham of Lancashire were two but you could add Tyson and Larter of Northants, Loader and Bedser of Surrey, Jackson and Gladwin of Derbyshire, Pritchard of Warwickshire, Shackleton and White of Hampshire, Moss of Middlesex, Flavell and Coldwell of Worcestershire, Thomson of Sussex, Halfyard of Kent, Smith of Gloucestershire. Openers would be the ones to face this battery of accurate and hostile bowling, very often at the end of a hard day in the field, facing fast bowlers armed with a hard and shiny new ball. The quality of the home-grown opening attacks during the 1950s and 1960s was probably never surpassed before or after. It may only have been challenged in terms of speed, not overall quality, with the influx of fast bowlers, especially those from overseas but in terms of guile and exploiting wickets in damp or overcast conditions, the bowlers who Bernard and Gilbert faced were masters of their art, and making runs as an opening batsman may have been more difficult at that time than in any other in the history of the County Championship.

It is difficult to compare generations, but it is against this backdrop that their opening pairing needs to be assessed. They cannot compete with the sheer weight of runs amassed by Emrys Davies and Arnold Dyson. They scored over 12,000 runs in 389 appearances together, almost twice as many games as Bernard and Gilbert's tally of 200. Perhaps, if both had not been as injury prone and perhaps if Bernard had matured more quickly into an opening batsman, they might have proved to be Glamorgan's most prolific opening pair.

There are too many 'if onlys' to contemplate, but it is certain that whilst they were together, Parkhouse and Hedges provided Glamorgan fans with some great memories of hot, hazy summers with run chases that defied not only The Skipper's trenchant 'don't lose first' philosophy but also, sometimes, the record books as well. They went about their cricket with a purpose and panache that brought a smile to many cricket supporters across the county scene. In a period when professionals were being derided by those who ran

Opening partners, Parkhouse and Hedges, at Dartford, Kent, in June 1959. (© Press Association)

the game, they did their best, along with other paid performers, to deliver entertainment. In their own way, they were appealing to a general public being tempted away from spending their money on a day at the cricket by watching TV or spending it on the increasingly wide range of consumer durables on the market.

Like these machines, they occasionally broke down, but Gilbert and Bernard were practical cricket professionals. They played according to the conditions and to the quality of the opposition bowling. When conditions were in their favour they could take on the most formidable of new ball attacks, and in the words of the *Western Mail*, could 'blaze a trail'. But perhaps the most fitting assessment of their contribution comes from a man who spent many years looking on from his place further down the order. Tony Lewis very neatly summed up their contribution thus:

'Gilbert and Bernard together were great. They got on together. They were both brave. They ran between the wickets wonderfully well. They made a lovely partnership ... the perfect mix, though you could try Martini!'

9

2,000 Runs in 1961

'The finest characteristics of a professional cricketer'

The calendar year of 1961 saw many notable events in the world of international cricket, the most notable being the first tied game in Test match history. Australia and the West Indies ended level in front of a world-record crowd of 90,000 at the Melbourne Cricket Ground. At county level, there were some notable performances as well, and for Glamorgan, it was a season to note purely because it was the first since 1946 without Wilf Wooller, as 'The Skipper' had finally called it a day at the end of the previous summer.

His replacement, Ossie Wheatley, had limited experience of captaincy but had performed well against Glamorgan the previous year and was an amateur. Maintaining the tradition of having an amateur as captain was an important principle for the Glamorgan committee. The only other amateur at the club was Tony Lewis. However, his studies at Cambridge University ruled him out of consideration for the captaincy before an injury on the rugby field ended his involvement that season.

Ossie recalls discussing his impending move to Wales with some of his Warwickshire teammates:

'Glamorgan wickets were different. They were made generally for spin. When I was in the Warwickshire dressing room and said I was going to leave we had Hitchcock and Bannister and all these people and they said 'Where are you going? I said I was retiring. I'm going down to Glamorgan for a couple of years. I'm working down there. You're going where? You must be bonkers! They don't even play two seamers. They play one seamer and four spinners. You won't get a bowl.'

To that, Ossie had the ultimate response. 'But I'm captain.' Tony Lewis would remember that Ossie 'straightened out some of the pitches.' but that this 'wonderful medium slow bowler couldn't get wickets either.' There was something of a culture shock for Ossie when he arrived in Cardiff before the season began:

'I came from Edgbaston and Warwickshire. I was very fortunate because it was run by Leslie Ekins who was without doubt the best secretary in the country. He built Edgbaston from a county ground into a major Test ground with help from a very good lottery which they ran. He ran the thing on oiled wheels. Nets were available anytime you wanted them. Coaches were there, everything was there. I remember visiting Wilf in his little two room office up three flights of rickety stairs at no. 6 High Street and I thought gosh, this is a bit different from Edgbaston where everything was laid out in palatial circumstances but I thought it was all rather charming.'

There were more revelations awaiting Ossie in his first few months in Wales:

'Then you came to the season of course and there were no nets to speak of. How they produced cricketers of any worth is one of the miracles of life. It was a bit of a scene change for me but it was like playing club cricket which I was used to. It was great fun but it wasn't run like a professional operation. They picked players from the clubs, supported them and played them and survived. Wilf had a lot to do with it. He knew a lot about cricket, picked good players and knew a lot about the game in those terms. He made sides that survived. Generally they were a Welsh side.'

For Bernard, 1961 was to be the high watermark in his playing career as he amassed 2,026 runs and became only the second batsman in the club's history, following Gilbert Parkhouse in 1959, to reach the landmark. The season began in quite unremarkable fashion for both Bernard and Glamorgan with draws against Essex, Lancashire and Sussex, followed by defeat to Yorkshire at Swansea. The first victory of the summer came against Oxford University before the Whitsun Bank Holiday encounter against the Australians at the Arms Park which

Ossie Wheatley, Glamorgan's new captain in 1961. His brisk medium pace and positive approach to captaincy brought new opportunities to the club. (© Glamorgan CCC)

ended in a draw. Glamorgan began their winning ways for this season during the last game in May, against Derbyshire at Chesterfield. It was a notable game for Bernard, who made 96 in the first innings, and went past the landmark of 10,000 runs in first-class cricket in the process. As a team man, he was more delighted by the fact that they had won an exciting game by 14 runs.

Glamorgan were still at the bottom of the Championship table at the end of May, and in the newspapers there was a string of articles trying to pinpoint the reason for Glamorgan's lack of success. To make matters worse, Allan Watkins announced that he was intending to retire at the end of the season. Increasingly troubled by asthma and a stomach complaint, he decided to accept the offer of a warder's post at Usk Borstal. In South Africa, during the 1948-49 season, he had become Glamorgan's first centurion in Test cricket, and throughout the 1950s had delivered some stellar performances with bat and ball. He certainly had not let anyone down, but his body had broken down under the relentless onslaught of first-class cricket. What certainly had not broken him was the pressure of being captained by Wilf. As one player has remarked, 'Allan used to threaten Wilf on a daily basis'. Wilf, despite their confrontations, must have thought a great deal of Allan as he played a key role in Allan subsequently becoming cricket coach at Oundle School.

Those who were starting to doubt Glamorgan and their new leader were silenced as early June saw a series of further victories for the Welsh county and a truly outstanding bowling performance from Don Shepherd. It came on the second day of the match against Nottinghamshire at Newport. On the first evening 'Shep' had conceded five runs off his five overs but when he came back the following morning he took the wickets of Clay, Poole, Winfield, Springall, Millman and Davison all without conceding another run. He finished with the remarkable figures of 16 overs, 14 maidens, six for five, as the visitors were bundled out for 86. It was a blow from which they could not return and Glamorgan ran out winners of the game by 155 runs.

By the middle of June, Bernard had 500 runs to his name, whilst Hampshire's Roy Marshall and the Nawab of Pataudi, who played for Sussex, had already reached the 1,000 run mark. He knew that he would need to find some inspiration from somewhere if he was going to emulate their achievements. That inspiration was waiting for him at Old Trafford in mid-June after Lancashire set Glamorgan a target of 192 in 135 minutes. As the *Western Mail* reported, 'just when it seemed there was to be no real bid to accept the Lancashire challenge, Hedges slammed successive balls to the rails and the big thrash was on.' Parkhouse and Hedges ran a 'succession of brilliantly judged twos and singles.'

Bernard was out for 40 trying to despatch Ken Grieves out of the ground, but Gilbert went on to make 85 as Glamorgan fell just short of their target with one wicket still standing. It was not so much the result that was important but the way the batsmen had chased the game that ignited something in Bernard and the Glamorgan top order. It had provided all those watching with a thrilling climax that, as the newspaper stated, 'should be described chronologically in order that the mounting tension that burst into a wild crescendo of excitement can be properly savoured.'

The following game at Trent Bridge followed a similar pattern with the home side setting a target of 235. On day one, Ossie Wheatley had been so dissatisfied with the team's performance that he had marched them back onto the field of play for net practise. They had slumped from 44-0 to 76-6. Allan Watkins, travelling with the team and asked to comment said 'They (the batsmen) have got so used to trouble that they are looking for it even when it is not there.' However, on the final day, with a hundred from Gilbert and an undefeated 48 from Jim Pressdee, the county romped home to a six-wicket victory. Bernard had batted on despite being hit in the stomach by a delivery from Ian Davison. Now the batting unit was trying to get to grips with the situation.

The next match was away to Northamptonshire who boasted batsman Colin Milburn plus pace bowler David Larter in their ranks. After the home side had made a reasonable 229, Glamorgan slipped to 46-4 by the close of the first day's play. Bernard remained unbeaten on 17, and after adding a slow and difficult 28 in the following morning session, he raced to a century. He struck eight successive boundaries to take him to his hundred as he shared a match-changing stand of 206 in even time with Jim Pressdee. Glamorgan declared at 315 for 6 with Bernard 134 not out, five short of his career best-score. But in the context of the match, even better was to follow in the second innings. Bernard and Gilbert shared an opening stand of 165 in just an hour and a quarter to put their side well on the way of reaching their target of 214 in two and a quarter hours.

Gilbert raced to what still is one of the fastest authentic hundreds in the club's history, reached in just 70 minutes and when he departed, Bernard duly saw Glamorgan through to victory with Alan Rees. The *Wisden* report said that 'Glamorgan concluded the match in a whirlwind fashion.' Bernard remained unbeaten on 95 and was quite satisfied to push a single past the bowler to see his side home rather than smashing a six to reach three figures. That was typical of Bernard. He had no real interest in personal goals. All his efforts were bent towards making the team more successful and with an unbeaten tally of 229 runs in a match during which he had been on the field throughout. He returned home very proud of his efforts after a monumental feat of concentration, endurance and no amount of skill. It was to silence any critics amongst the members or Glamorgan committee and was to act as a launch-pad for the rest of the season.

Worcestershire were up next and Glamorgan's opening pair carried on where they had left off at Northampton, as they completed their third consecutive hundred partnership and brought their tally that glorious week to 614 runs. The profligacy continued in early July with Bernard and Alan Jones adding 112 for the second wicket against Middlesex at Lord's, but it was not enough to secure a first innings lead, and after Alan Moss claimed eight wickets, the home side eased to a nine-wicket victory. But after this defeat to a North London side, Glamorgan romped to a five-wicket victory over a side to the south of the Thames as they chased down the target of 249 in 170 minutes set by Surrey at Ebbw Vale. After a first innings score of 86, Bernard launched the run chase with a crisp 40 as he shared an opening stand of 94 with Gilbert, and in the process passed 1,000 runs for the season. The *Western Mail* hailed the win with the headline 'The Magnificent Glamorgan Eleven!'

His purple patch continued with a superb 141 in 226 minutes, against Kent at St. Helen's, before Glamorgan headed to Dean Park in Bournemouth where in 1948, under Wilf Wooller's leadership, they had clinched their first-ever Championship title by defeating Hampshire by an innings. By a quirk of fate, Dai Davies, the stalwart Glamorgan batsman from the pre-war era who had stood as an umpire in the historic encounter in 1948 was present in the white coat again. This time, it was the home side who were chasing the title and, at first, Glamorgan were made to look like the mid-table side they were. 'Bit different from 1948?' one of the journalists joked with Dai after the second day's play. 'Aye, a different team, too' was his sage like reply, but as if to prove the veteran wrong, Don Shepherd – who had not made his Glamorgan debut until 1950, delivered a match-winning performance of 7-41 as Hampshire were dismissed for a paltry 101. The champions elect had been turned over on their own turf.

By the end of July, further victories had been recorded against Leicestershire and Somerset, and with Bernard top of the Glamorgan averages with 1,334 runs at an average of 33.35, a tally in excess of 2,000 runs was now a real possibility. During the match against Somerset at Weston-Super-Mare he had a new opening partner in 19-year-old Euros Lewis who was making his debut. The pair enjoyed a productive stand of 98 in the second innings, with Bernard leading the way with a fluent 71.

With their form being quite topsy-turvy, captain Ossie Wheatley had commented to the press that his side had 'a lack of concentration, lack of experience, and a lack of application.' Looking back, Ossie felt this was something that set the Welsh county apart. 'I assumed that the Glamorgan side would be very similar to the other county sides I had played against but they weren't. They were quite different in temperament from a traditional English county. They either played out of their skins or they had a bloody awful time. It was up and down.'

Shortly afterwards, Bernard proved his captain wrong by batting for two hours and 50 minutes for a fine 99 against Warwickshire at Edgbaston and shared in a fourth wicket stand of 170 with Jim Pressdee which helped to guarantee a draw.

He built a further series of consistent innings during August, and by the time the side headed off to meet Surrey at The Oval in the closing match of the season, his tally stood 95 runs short of 2,000. Glamorgan arrived looking to secure the double over Surrey for the first time in their history, and even before the first run was scored, the omens were in their favour with the 'Brown Hatters' having their poorest season for 70 years, and languishing in 15th place in the table.

With Euros Lewis continuing to open with Gilbert Parkhouse, Bernard occupied the number four berth and spent the entire first day in the field, wondering when his chance would come to move towards his personal landmark. He didn't have to wait too long as after Surrey limped to 262, he lit up the second day's play with a glittering century. Shortly before reaching three figures, he scored his 2,000th run of a never-to-be-forgotten summer,

The Glamorgan side of 1961 on tour in Ireland, with Bernard standing in the back row, third from the right. Ossie Wheatley said 'they were quite different in temperament from a traditional English county. They either played out of their skins or they had a bloody awful time. (© Glamorgan CCC)

before celebrating both his achievement and reaching three figures by hoisting Tony Lock high over mid-wicket for six. Glamorgan then dismissed Surrey for 142 and after an unbeaten 73 from Euros, Glamorgan eased to an emphatic victory to round off the season in style.

Ossie Wheatley had come with a project that was to build a team capable of winning the Championship again. Although he had some gifted senior players, he felt these would have to go to make way for fresh talent:

'You are never going to win anything with older players. There was room for sentiment but, in hard talk, you have to have a youngish side who are keen. You don't want a lot of old pros who have seen it all before. There is a sort of self defence mechanism. They do enough not to be left out.'

Bernard was 33 years old and 1961 was his 12th season in the side. Ossie regarded him wholeheartedly as a player who could be part of his plan for the county:

'We had to build a side right from the beginning. Bernard was one of a few senior players, a very good team member around which to build a team. The way people build in a team is important and Bernard played a great part in that. He was a great guy to have around because he was very honest with himself and with everybody else. The first year I came he had a great year with over 2,000 runs. I remember Hampshire saying they had never seen him play before and they always wondered how he got runs because he always got out against them. But he got in and started hitting them everywhere, including Shackleton, who didn't give you much room. He could dominate. He was a good guy to have in the dressing room. Always supported the captain.'

Bernard had plenty to look back on with pride as the 1961 season drew to a close and his mind shifted towards his winter work at the indoor school in Neath as well as some DIY on his home. But the latter nearly resulted in Bernard sustaining a career-ending injury as he put his left arm through the window of the back door and came within an eighth of an inch of completely severing the tendons in his arm. He was left with a deep wound which required stitches and these were still in his arm as the 1962 season began.

'You are a lucky man,' said the doctors treating him, but although he was still able to bat, 1962 proved to be an up-and-down year for Bernard. He was dropped down the order and then dropped from the side altogether.

As he himself was quoted, 'There are so many good young players worth a chance in the side that competition is more fierce than I have ever known.' He duly fought his way back after making a pair of hundreds in the match against Somerset 2nd XI, plus a career-best 144 against Pakistan. He averaged 118 against the tourists that summer with an unbeaten 81 in the May Bank Holiday fixture at the Arms Park. He also won back his opening spot, before being injured again, duly missing out on the chance of becoming the first, and so far only, Glamorgan player to register 2,000 first-class runs for the second successive season. Bernard finished with 1,851 runs.

The journalist John Billot, again proposing Bernard for *Western Mail*'s Sportsman of the Year award at the end of the 1962 season claimed that, along with Don Shepherd, Bernard had worked so hard once more, making his personal success 'subservient to team needs'. He finished his valedictory article by saying:

'There is room at the top of any Welsh sporting honours list for batsman Hedges and bowler Shepherd, men who typify the finest characteristics of professional cricketers.'

Bernard being congratulated by young fans after his 81 not out against Pakistan at the Arms Park, June 1962. (© Glamorgan CCC)

10

Thirteen men

'I remember sitting as a young lad in Worcester watching and daydreaming. I was thinking I would love to go out there and play a game of cricket.'

Only 13 men scored more first-class runs than Bernard in 1961. Those 13 players were, in the order they appeared in the first-class averages, and with their run total for the season and average in brackets: Ken Barrington of Surrey (2,070 at 59.14), Bill Alley of Somerset (3,019 at 56.96), Roy Marshall of Hampshire (2,607 at 43.45), Geoff Pullar of Lancashire (2,344 at 43.40), M.J.K. Smith of Warwickshire (2,587 at 41.72), Norman Hill of Nottinghamshire (2,239 at 39.98), Maurice Hallam of Leicestershire (2,262 at 39.68), Henry Horton of Hampshire (2,329 at 38.18), Peter Richardson of Kent (2,152 at 37.75), Graham Atkinson of Somerset (2,078 at 37.10), Alan Oakman of Sussex (2,307 at 36.61), Jimmy Gray of Hampshire (2,024 at 32.28) and Ron Headley of Worcestershire (2,040 at 31.87).

Some of them were household names; Test cricketers who were expected to be at the top of their profession. Some of them were grassroots cricketers, like Bernard, whose appearance in the upper echelons of the first-class averages was a rare event. Three of them played for the county champions that year, Hampshire. One of them, Bill Alley, was the last professional to score more than 3,000 runs in a first-class season. When this book came to be written, five of them were no longer living. Of the remaining eight, a further four died during the writing of the book. I was able to speak to three of them, Geoff Pullar, Jimmy Gray and Alan Oakman, before they passed away. Sadly, I missed the opportunity to do the same with Graham Atkinson. I was, however, able to either meet or correspond with the remaining three players. The results of those discussions are recorded here as a snapshot of the game at that time in the early 1960s. These players are representatives of a generation of cricketers that are slowly but surely exiting the stage. They are the living heritage of the game as it once was and provide insightful comparisons against which Bernard's achievements can be assessed.

Geoff Pullar

Geoff played in 28 Tests for England, scoring nearly 2,000 runs at an average of 43.86. His standout year was 1959, when he scored 2,647 runs in all cricket and was named *Wisden* Cricketer of the Year as a result.

Don Shepherd's vernacular description of Geoff at the crease was that: 'he was a dog. You knew he'd stay there.'

It is rather startling to discover that he had never opened the batting in a first-class match before he opened for England and confessed several times to not ever really liking opening. I made contact with him via Lancashire CCC. He left his home telephone number on my answering machine with a brief message in his Lancastrian drawl that was homely and welcoming. 'Phone me back and we'll have a natter'. He remembered Bernard as follows: 'Bernie Hedges ... a little guy, lively on his feet.' Later he would add that 'Bernard reminds me of a guy called Bernie Constable who played for Surrey'. This amused Peter Walker when I told him. 'I remember Bernard being similar in physique to Bernie Constable but that's where the similarity ends. They were at opposite ends of the behaviour spectrum. Bernard was quiet and considered. Bernie was always at loggerheads with Wilf.'

The 1961 season, for Geoff, was remembered for the Ashes series against Australia. He thought England should have won it. Geoff also remembered a game before the Test series had started at Lord's, where Lancashire were playing Middlesex:

'It was ridiculous. I couldn't hit the ball off the square. I told Ken Grieves, "I'm gonna get out. I'm an embarrassment". I was 21 not out after two hours. After lunch I hit everything out of the middle. Ken Grieves said: "You can't get runs in the pavilion".'

When we talked about memories of Glamorgan, Wilf's name was inevitably raised, not his contests on the pitch but rather his determination off it. Rain had prevented play on day one of the match at The Gnoll in 1961. Geoff, looking on from the safety of the pavilion, remembered watching the Glamorgan secretary at work, 'Wilf Wooller helped get the square ready for play'.

Just over a month after my telephone 'natter' with Geoff, he passed away. His obituary in *Wisden* commented:

'He was sociable, droll, gently encouraging to younger players and utterly without malice. Whether it was the era or whether it was the

M.J.K. Smith of Warwickshire and England. In the top 20 run scorers of all time. (© Playfair Cricket Monthly)

game of cricket, it is impossible not to notice the personal qualities that Geoff brought to the world of cricket. He was not just a good cricketer, he was a good man.'

M.J.K. Smith

Mike, or M.J.K. Smith, remains England's last double international to date in major sports (rugby and cricket). He played in 50 Tests, captaining the team in half of them, scoring over two thousand runs at an average of 31.63. In first-class cricket he made 39,832 runs placing him in the top 20 of all time run scorers in the game. 1961 was the fifth in six successive seasons in which he scored 2,000 runs or more.

I met him, with my son, at a crowded Edgbaston on a night of T20 cricket. M.J.K.'s first words were about Bernard. 'As I say, Bernard had the reputation of being a good bloke and that was it. The game was played in a better spirit in those days. I always thought it was better than working.' Our conversation moved first to a Warwickshire teammate, Tom Cartwright:

'Tom bowled at an innocuous pace with two or three close fielders and everyone else saving one, and you thought, "I'm going to give this fella some stick", but that wasn't the way it worked out. Tremendous accuracy with enough movement off the seam.'

Mike's memories of the 1961 season were, like many who played at that time, dominated by the performances and players of Hampshire CCC:

'Hampshire got a lot of publicity through the captain, Colin Ingelby-Mackenzie. Old Etonian ... good bloke. They had another freak bowler in Derek Shackleton. Always looked smart. Rolled up sleeves and took wicket after wicket.'

Our interview also meandered into the area of psychology. Like many of those who play sport, Mike had a vivid, if rather deprecating way of describing what happens to some players when they lose form:

> 'Basil Bridge went between the ears. He went into hospital for a minor muscle tear, came out of hospital and he couldn't bowl again. He was the first spinner to take 100 wickets one year and there were a lot of spinners around then. He was a great loss to us.'

The year was, in fact, 1961.

Norman Hill

Norman had a 15-year career with Nottinghamshire, scoring over 14,000 runs at an average of 29.43. He captained the side for two seasons, 1966 and 1967. What is perhaps amazing about Norman's performances in 1961 is that he achieved them in a losing side. Living now in Switzerland, he commented:

> 'I have very fond memories of that particular season of 1961. The sun shone, the wickets were hard and true and needless to say that the outfields were fast so all in all it was very conducive to batting. However, I am sorry to say that this did not help Nottinghamshire who finished bottom of the County Championship (17th) with Glamorgan finishing 14th.
>
> The success of the season came to Hampshire who won the Championship for the first time in their history. The 1961 season contained eight double-hundreds and seven batsmen getting 100 in each innings. We all tried to catch Bill Alley but he outpaced us, being the first to 2,000 runs and the first to 3,000 runs!
>
> The Australians were the touring side, captained by Richie Benaud, and I think for

Norman Hill.
(© Nottinghamshire CCC)

the first time ever took all *Wisden*'s 'Five Cricketers of the Year' (Benaud, Lawry, Davidson, O'Neill and Bill Alley).

My recollections of Glamorgan were indeed their batting with your father and Gilbert Parkhouse, who were both fine players, leading the way. The bowlers were led by Ossie Wheatley but my nemesis was Don Shepherd, who had to carry the bowling. Indeed, once against Notts he took six wickets without conceding a run.

My own memories of 1961 were my highest score of 201 not-out against Sussex and being the second batsman to 2,000 runs. My purple patch was getting three 100s and a 90 in four consecutive innings (100 in each innings, followed by a 90 and another 100) and 98 against the Australians.'

Peter Richardson

Peter started his career as an amateur with Worcestershire before switching to play for Kent. In all, he scored 26,055 runs at an average of 34.6 with 44 hundreds.

I met Peter at his home in Kent. He recounted his first Test series against the Australians in 1956, in particular the Old Trafford Test and Jim Laker's 19 wickets, with a philosophical shrug of the shoulders. 'It was the most unrecognised hundred in Test cricket,' he said of his innings in that game. One of his fondest memories of Bernard was from the beginning of that series. 'One of the nicest things I remember about him was when I played my first Test match he dropped me a note wishing me luck, which nobody else did.'

Peter could have played for Glamorgan. His grandmother was from Ystradgynlais and the rest of the family resided in Breconshire. However, he ended up playing for Worcestershire and his first game in Wales was at Ebbw Vale:

'It poured with rain and the ground was flooded so we all went to the cinema. Of course, the moment it stopped, the water drained through the slag heap and it was perfect to play on after about an hour. They had to put a message on the screen: 'Will any of the Worcester players please report back to the ground.'

I only sampled a few of Peter's stories about the game but there were two that had a strong Glamorgan flavour. The first concerned batsman turned umpire, Emrys Davies. Officiating at a Test match and reputed to be struggling with his hearing, one of the West Indian batsmen got struck on the pad.

'A big appeal went up from us and he gave it not out. At the end of the over I walked past and said, "Did he get a nick on that one Emrys?" And he said, "No, no. We're going by the clock up on the pavilion." He was a lovely fellow. Everybody liked him.'

The second involved Messrs A.R. Lewis and P.M. Walker. During a rain-delayed match at Pontypridd, they sat down with Peter and began concocting a series of bogus letters that they would send to the revered journalist E.W. 'Jim' Swanton:

'He used to write such twaddle. I wrote one letter to him about the all-round performances of bowlers. This chap we invented played in the South Wales Colliery League. He bowled right arm fast and got 100 wickets for about eight a piece and then he got another 100 bowling slow left arm. He was known in the valleys as Dai Both Ways. He put it in (the paper).'

Alan Oakman

Alan Oakham, as seen on a cigarette card.

Alan also played in the 'Laker Test' of 1956, taking five catches off Jim's bowling. In all, he held 594 catches during his 21-year career for Sussex. As a batsman, he contributed 21,800 runs at an average of 26.17 with 22 first-class hundreds. As a bowler, he took 736 wickets. His best bowling performance was against Glamorgan in 1954 where he took 7 for 39, and ten wickets in the match (one victim was Bernard, who had top scored with 62).

1961 was Alan's best year with the bat. As well as scoring over 2,000 runs, he made a career best of 229 against Nottinghamshire. When Alan returned to the ground some years later with Warwickshire 2nd XI, he was accosted by a local cricket fan who said, 'I remember you smashing a window over there with your double century!'

When I spoke to Alan on the telephone he remembered the Hampshire team and how much they enjoyed their cricket. 'No training. No practice sessions. They would stay up and have a few beers and be up, the next day, ready to play.'

His memories of Glamorgan were overwhelmingly of Wilf. He recalled the confrontation between Wilf and the Reverend David Sheppard. 'Could you stop swearing?' Sheppard asked, slightly peeved at the verbal onslaught. 'You play cricket your way and I'll play it my way!' was Wooller's reply.

Jimmy Gray

Jimmy scored 22,650 runs at an average of 30.73 with 30 centuries for Hampshire. He also bowled medium pace and took 457 wickets but it was as Roy Marshall's opening partner that he was most remembered in 1961, a year when they shared six century partnerships. Together they held the record opening partnership for Hampshire of 249.

I interviewed Jimmy in the house in which he had lived since he started

Jimmy Gray

playing professionally. He spoke first, in his clipped fashion with a dry humour, about his teammates at Hampshire:

'Ingelby Mackenzie was a super chap. I can't believe he was an amateur. He mixed with the upper classes but he was lovely to us. You had to be a bit careful what you said sometimes. Shackleton was brilliant. Never bought a drink but was drinking all evening; just appeared by your side when you were at the bar. He came from Todmorden. What a loss that was to Yorkshire. He moved you all the time. Bowled a good length and diddled it about.'

I was struck by Jimmy's knack of delivering aphorisms. They characterise the outlook of the generation of cricketers, of which Bernard was one:

'One or two people needed to be called Sir. The good captains got people to play for them. They did it by force of their own personality. You need character as well as ability to succeed. If you're not successful, you don't stay in the side. The first thing you had to remember was not to be frightened of the ball – to get in line.'

For Jimmy, these self-evident truths were the essence of good cricket. He recalled one of the coaching staff at Hampshire. 'We had a chap called Jack Newman. He was an old boy. You hung on to what he said. 'Stand a bit closer. Keep your eyes parallel.' That was a season's coaching. Little gems.' His recollections of Glamorgan were not surprising but do bring a smile to your face. 'You don't get friendly with Glamorgan! Wilf was a tough nut. Glamorgan were a very good fielding side; typical Wilf. They had a will to win. Peter Walker was tall and slim. Don't you ever drop a bloody catch, Walker?'

Looking back on 1961 and winning the County Championship, Jimmy could only say one thing. 'It was a marvellous feeling. We were just Hampshire, not Yorkshire or Lancashire or Surrey.'

Ron Headley

He made 21,695 runs at an average of 31.12 with 32 hundreds during his first-class career. Ron had strong memories of Gilbert Parkhouse, but not for his graceful stroke play or quick scoring. It was his fragility against the rising ball, which often happened on the sticky wickets of Worcestershire. 'Gilbert Parkhouse often wouldn't come to Worcester because of our wickets. When he came we would take bets on Parky. Is it going to be the fourth or fifth over that he calls for some tape for his hands!' Bernard reminded him of another Worcestershire player. 'Bernard was like a George Dews. George was solid. Solid as a rock. Never changing and always pleasant.'

Ron was convinced that he should have played a lot more Test cricket and that if he had, 'Freddo and me could have caused some serious damage.' This, of course, was Roy Fredericks, who played for Glamorgan from 1971 to 1973 and opened for the West Indies from 1968 to 1976.

Ron was one of the earliest black players in the County Championship at a time when

Ron Headley acknowledges the applause as he returns to the pavilion. (© Worcestershire CCC)

there were difficulties around the immigration of thousands of people from the Commonwealth, including the West Indies. I asked Ron if he had ever experienced racism. 'There were very few black players. Let me put it to you this way. I believe that racism is used too loosely. There's a thing called institutional class distinction. We have a class society. Where racism is used, we really mean institutional class distinction. It's how you look, how you speak, what car you drive, where you live. Cricket reflects the society.'

For all his roots in West Indies cricket, Ron fell in love with playing the game in England and it was an English scene that was most vivid when he recalled playing:

'I remember sitting as a young lad in Worcester watching and day-dreaming by the 'ladies pavilion' in a deck chair. I was thinking I would love to go out there and play a game of cricket. Grounds like Worcester are everywhere. People don't appreciate how lovely the countryside is. I looked at the cathedral and thought 'how on earth did they build that?'

11

Opening Partner #2 – Alan Jones

'Nothing means more than wearing the daffodil.'

Following Gilbert Parkhouse's retirement, it was Alan Jones who became Bernard's regular opening partner for the remainder of his career. Like Don Shepherd, Alan is a legend of Glamorgan Cricket holding the record for the most runs for the club, and his tally of 34,056 will never be surpassed. He scored nearly 10,000 more runs than Emrys Davies who is next in the club all-time run scorers list and nearly 14,000 more than Mathew Maynard and Gilbert Parkhouse who are third and fourth respectively. Bernard would have needed two careers in the first-class game to reach the total that Alan achieved!

His career spanned the ending of the amateur / professional divide, the end of uncovered wickets and the emergence of one-day cricket as the driving force in the modern game. He went from wearing whites to coloured kits; from caps to helmets. Yet despite these changes, he was 'Mr Consistent,' scoring over 1,000 first-class runs for 23 consecutive seasons, and showed that he could adapt his game to the requirements of limited-overs cricket by becoming Glamorgan's first centurion in the John Player Sunday League.

Like Don Shepherd, Alan never won higher honours with England, and many who played with him as well as those paid to have opinions on such things believe that playing for Glamorgan cost him a serious opportunity at Test level. In the words of Geoff Pullar, who was Gilbert's partner in the 1959 series against India, 'If Jones had played for Surrey or Middlesex, he'd have played for England.'

A young Alan Jones whose first appearance for Glamorgan was wearing all of Bernard's kit.
(© Glamorgan CCC)

The supposed prejudice against players from the less glamorous counties may or may not have been a fact. What is not in doubt is Alan's wholehearted commitment to Glamorgan and Wales. He saw the high points, being part of the Championship-winning side in 1969 and the low points of the late 1970s when the county finished bottom of the competition twice in four seasons from 1976 to 1979. He took over the captaincy briefly and was the senior professional who helped guide many players through the difficult waters of establishing themselves in the professional game.

The beginning of Alan's relationship with Bernard on the cricket field did not involve a ball or a bat. It did not involve a coaching session nor an observation from beyond the boundary rope. Indeed, it had very little to do with cricket but more to do with their inside leg measurement and shoe size! The story highlights the informality that marked out cricket in those days, as well as providing an insight into what motivated cricketers in Wales. As Alan outlines:

'The first time I walked onto a first-class cricket field, Glamorgan were playing Australia in Swansea. I was 17 years of age and I was on the staff but I went down to the ground because I had been given a free ticket by the club to watch the game. I wasn't involved ... just watching. Both Jim Pressdee and Gilbert Parkhouse got injured in the Glamorgan side and they wanted another substitute fielder. Phil Thomas, the assistant secretary came over the tannoy and said 'Is there anybody on the ground from the Glamorgan staff? Could you report to the pavilion.' So I heard that and went to the pavilion. They wanted me to go on and field but I had no kit so they showed me Bernard's kit. We were the only two people in the club who were the same size! So I had his boots and all his kit. The first person that hit a ball to me on the field was Neil Harvey, my hero. That day, it was Bernard's kit I was wearing. When you were a kid, nothing meant more than wearing the daffodil. It meant something to young players. It really was special. What you earnt for playing was nothing compared to what it felt like wearing the daffodil. So when I went on wearing Bernard's kit, it was something very special.'

The match was Glamorgan's game against the 1956 Australians, and it proved to be a quite one-sided contest as the tourists won by an innings and 11 runs, with Ken Mackay and Ron Archer scoring 163 and 148 respectively. Nevertheless, it was great day for the young schoolboy from the Swansea Valley and the pride that Alan had that day; the overwhelming chest-bursting enthusiasm to be able to represent your county, which meant in Wales your

Alan batting against Hampshire at St. Helen's with Euros Lewis at the non-striker's end. The finest batsman never to have played Test cricket for England. (© Glamorgan CCC)

country, still affects him to this day. Even saying the words were not quite enough. He gently patted his chest where his heart was beating and where the embroidered daffodil would have been on his sleeveless sweater.

Whilst a similar representational pride must exist through all the first-class counties, there is something distinct and more powerful about it in Wales. It was something noted by Ossie Wheatley when he arrived in Cardiff in 1961 to take over as captain from Wilf Wooller and it has been noted in more modern times by a string of great overseas players. Owen Shears, the renowned Welsh poet, has crafted lines that talk of sport being the vehicle to create 'moments when the many, through the few, become one.' To play for Glamorgan was not just about personal accomplishment, it was about your family and community sharing an experience that binds you closer. Many communities lay claim to their famous sons, as if their sporting talent is an affirmation of that village or town.

This pride runs much deeper than the personal. It goes, even, beyond the familial and enters the realm of the historical, even mythical. There is a sacrificial element to it. Players are prepared to endure the bad times and the bad experiences. They will tolerate defeats, poor treatment and ridicule as they know that when they join 'the soil, the *tir*, the *pridd* of this land' they will have contributed to a cause 'they were prepared to suffer for'. This is the sort of pride that would stop Alan, Don, Gilbert, Bernard and countless others from considering a move to another county. Wearing the daffodil was an affirmation of your Welsh identity that was as permanent as any tattoo. In contrast, playing for England was like receiving a medal. A great honour to be treasured, but something you could remove from yourself and place in a box marked 'precious'. It would stay with you but it was not part of you.

The Welshness of the team was cultivated by Wilf Wooller, and 'The Skipper' held a dream that one day he would be able to take to the field with an all-Welsh XI. It duly came to pass in August 1955, with Bernard part of it, as Glamorgan met Warwickshire at Neath with their line-up reading: Wooller, Parkhouse, Pressdee, Willie Jones, Watkins, Hedges, Pleass, Tony Lewis, Ward, Haydn Davies, and Shepherd.

The same size boot and shirt collar were not the only things that Alan had in common with Bernard. They were both sons of miners brought up in big families. That experience gave them a moral grounding and code for living that was to shape their approach to playing cricket. A set of honest values that came straight from the chapel pulpit. Writing an obituary of Alun Richards, journalist Meic Stephens, born in Treforest, outlined the qualities of the pit communities as 'loyalty to family and workmates, warm-heartedness, neighbourliness and compassion, a sense of humour in the face of adversity and the absence of deference on grounds of social class.' There was also the patience and understanding of others' needs above those of oneself that came straight from sharing three or more to a room. Hard work and application came straight from the pit. Alan remembered clearly the impression Bernard made on him:

'He was one of the most honest people I've ever met. I've never met anybody as honest as Bernard in playing the game fair and square. He played county cricket and you needn't have had an umpire because if he hit the ball he would have walked. He always walked. I can't remember any umpire giving him out. All the umpires had high respect for him and the way he played the game. If you play and you walk, it makes it easier for the umpire and it gets around the circuit. There were times when you would have an appeal and you would think 'that's close' but because of the way you played, the umpire would give you the benefit of the doubt. In the end, it evens itself out. Anybody that plays, you hate getting out. You get a good decision you get a bad decision that's the way it goes.'

Alan's approach to the game was very similar to Bernard's, but that sportsmanship was not always shared by other players:

'There were a lot of players that didn't walk. You knew the ones that walked and the ones that didn't. It's funny really, I remember playing at Swansea after Bernard had finished. We were playing Yorkshire and we were losing the game but I was still in and got to 99. Fred Trueman took the second new ball with only about an hour of play to go. Fred bowled me this ball and it went through and it hit me there (brushes his upper arm with his hand). They all went up and I was given out. But in that game, Phil Sharpe got 92 or 93, Jack Hampshire got 95. Dusty Rhodes was umpiring and when Jack and Sharpy were out they hit it but never walked. They said openly in

Alan Jones executing an off drive. A study in concentration. (© Glamorgan CCC)

the dressing room, and in the evening, that they had hit the ball but that they were in the 90s so they were never going to walk. I was sitting in the dressing room. You take ages to take your pads off then because you are so disappointed. The door opened and Fred came in. "Alan, I'm terribly sorry, you didn't hit it." Then Dusty Rhodes came in and said: "Alan, can I buy you a drink." He apologised for making a mistake but the reason why he gave me out was because the two Yorkshire batsmen hadn't walked and he thought I was going to do the same. That's the name of the game.'

The cruelty of sport, for Alan was, over time, balanced out by its kindness. This was a principle, an unshakeable conviction that it was important to do the right thing and Alan is quite clear that for him and Bernard and other players like them, this was a personal decision. He related how he had walked in a Currie Cup match in South Africa, playing for Natal against Western Province. They were 70 for no wicket when Alan got a faint nick and walked. When he got back into the changing rooms he had the worst 20 minutes of his life as Vincent van der Bijl, the giant Natal captain, lambasted him for walking. 'When you're playing in Wales, I don't care if you walk but when you're playing for Natal, you don't walk!' Natal lost the game by 19 runs but went on to win the Currie Cup after the following game. If Alan's decision could resist such an onslaught, it was clearly something that, for him, could not be shaken either by the team's position in the game or the point he had reached in his own innings. Allan Lamb, who was in the Western Province side that day told Alan that he would walk but only if he had made his hundred. So there were always players who played it hard and those who stuck to what they regarded as the spirit of the game. But there is still something about the modern game that is rancorous. Alan again:

> 'The game has changed. You play the game for a living and it's win at all costs but I couldn't play the game that way and neither could Bernard. We both got a lot of enjoyment out of playing the game. We got some success out of playing but I would never have played it any other way. I've seen Atherton hitting the ball, Stuart Broad hitting the ball straight to the keeper and being given not out and staying there. Bernard wouldn't have liked that. There were players in the old days who stayed. But now, everybody stays.'

Alan and Bernard first opened together in 1959. Gilbert Parkhouse was up in Headingley waiting to open the innings against India. Glamorgan were at Edgbaston with Bernard and Alan facing a Warwickshire attack which included Roly Thompson, Ossie Wheatley and Tom Cartwright. The home side dismissed Glamorgan for 105, but there was a Celtic fightback in their second innings as Bernard and Alan shared an opening stand of 85 on the second day. Glamorgan duly ended on 421 and with 'Shep' claiming five wickets in Warwickshire's second innings, the home side had to cling on for a draw.

Between 1959 and 1962, Alan and Bernard opened together in six matches, but their rich potential as a first wicket pairing was clear to see, as at St. Helen's during early June 1961 against Hampshire. The visitors duly went on to win the County Championship, but only after the Glamorgan openers had given them a scare. Set a difficult total of 256 to win on the last day, Alan and Bernard set about their task with some gusto, racing to 102 before Bernard was the first one to depart. It proved to be the turning point as a collapse then followed as Hampshire secured victory by 73 runs.

The pairing of Jones and Hedges began on a regular basis on 8 June 1963 against Surrey at St. Helen's and was followed by a quite eventful game against Cambridge University at The Steel Company of Wales' ground at Margam. Bernard made 90 with the student side finding conditions alongside the noisy industrial complex the polar opposite of the tranquil surroundings of Fenner's.

They were not alone as the game was also Tony Cordle's first-class debut for Glamorgan. The Barbadian must also have found the setting for a cricket match quite alien, compared to the sandy beaches and palm-fringed surroundings of the grounds where he had played as a youngster before migrating to look for work in the United Kingdom. When batting, he brought a ray of Caribbean sunshine to proceedings, albeit after Eifion Jones and Brian Evans had fallen victim to successive balls. In the words of the *South Wales Evening Post*, 'the West Indian strode out to bat in his first match with Kirkman on a hat-trick. So Cordle's response was to crack the hat-trick delivery firmly down to the long-on boundary.'

His efforts saw Glamorgan to 298 and after dismissing Cambridge for 104, the county enforced the follow-on. Believing that everything was conspiring against them, the students even appealed to the umpires against the distractions caused by pungent smoke billowing over the ground from the adjacent steelworks. They duly saved the game but the days of first-class cricket at Margam were not so lucky, and it was deleted from the county calendar in 1964.

Alan and Bernard opened the batting in another quite eventful match later that season against Somerset at Glastonbury. The pair added 183 in the first innings, with Bernard falling five runs short of a century. His partner was more fortunate, scoring a century in each innings and being on the field for almost the entire game, yet he should not really have been there in the first place:

'We were playing at Swansea and then travelling down to Somerset. Ossie came to sit by me and said: "Look Alan. We're leaving you out tomorrow. You're doing 12th man. You've got to have a few nets and maybe go back to the 2nd XI and play. Get back into form." We got to Glastonbury and I said to Peter Walker I'd go out in the morning early and have a net. So the next morning came and a couple of the boys came out to bowl and while I was having the net, Ossie Wheatley comes over. "Alan you're playing, Gilbert's not well." So I opened with Bernard and got 187 in the first innings and 105 in the second innings."

Ossie Wheatley remembered the game well:

'Alan Jones played a couple of years when I was there before he got his first hundred. He went in and opened with Bernard and developed into a top-class player. You wonder now whether he would get the same opportunity. We had him in the side and he played and he played and developed to become one of the great Glamorgan servants. The match at Glastonbury against Somerset was his breakthrough moment. He could do it and he was doing it but Glastonbury made him realise he could do it. He never left the field for the whole of the match. That sort of moment is incredibly important in all sport.'

This was a turning point in their opening partnership and it was not long before the duo were making enough runs together to satisfy the selection committee. As Alan outlines, their success was based on many factors:

'We complimented each other really. Bernard used to cut and he used to pull. He was very strong there in that area. I was a driver and, obviously, a left and a right-handed pairing was useful. Because Bernard was cutting and pulling, the bowlers would tend to pitch the ball up and then when I went down the other end they couldn't change their length so I would get a few away. It worked out very well. Not only that, when you are an opening partnership it means that you've got to have a good understanding and Bernard was always very good at running singles. He was quick between the wickets and there was not very often he would refuse a single. A quick call and you would be off.'

1965 was the most productive season they enjoyed as an opening partnership, and included a stand of 201 in just 205 minutes against Warwickshire at Nuneaton in a game in mid-June at a time when Glamorgan were involved in a dog-fight with several other counties for top spot in the county table. Bernard made a handsome 124, with their personal and collective success being greeted in triumphant style amongst the Welsh and national press:

'Glamorgan Geared for Runs' wrote Malcolm Lewis in the *South Wales Echo*, '222 for 1 and still going strong' said the *South Wales Evening Post*, whilst 'Hedges' Great 124' was the headline in the *Sunday Mirror*. It was the third time in ten days that the batting unit had made 300 runs plus and the fifth time in the season. Basil Easterbrook was convinced he knew the reason:

'One does not have to look any further than the opening pair of Alan Jones and Bernard Hedges. These two have become the most effective opening pair in Britain this season with three century partnerships and a fourth, at Bristol, of 99. Not only the most effective but, equally as important in my book, the most attractive ... There was one unforgettable period in which Hedges scored 43 out of 47 and England's leg-spinner Bob Barber bowled five overs, his only five, which cost him 31 runs. England's captain Mike Smith, who began the day fielding at short square-leg, a few yards from the bat, retired to the covers and finally removed himself to the boundary edge, concentrating entirely on containing Glamorgan.'

In addition to his bright attacking batting, Alan also remembers Bernard's courage and steely resolve, as shown by a series of incidents during his Benefit season in 1963:

'We were playing the West Indies at Swansea and he was resting as one of his children was ill in hospital. But he came back. Somebody got injured and Bernard came on. He fielded at gully, but he didn't have the best hands for catching. Willy Rodriguez was batting against Ossie Wheatley and he cuts the ball and it got Bernard straight in the face. It was the second ball he was on the field. Off he goes. It was terrible. They put a call out for a dentist.'

The blow had smashed Bernard's dentures. Jean remembers him being brought home with blood all over his whites and looking like he had been a walk on actor in a Hammer horror film. The *Western Mail*, telling the story in pictures showed, first, Rodriguez cutting, then Pressdee and Shepherd helping Bernard from the field, his head held back to restrict the flow of blood and third, Bernard, his mouth stuffed with cotton wadding preparing to leave the ground. His parting words to the journalist, 'If Glamorgan want me at Northampton, I'll be ready.'

He was duly patched up and included in the side for the match against Northants where he scored a fine 78 on a pacy wicket, as Alan remembers:

'David Larter was in the Northants line-up but Bernard was up to the challenge and played brilliantly on the Saturday. There was no Sunday cricket so we had a rest day. Alan Rees and I went out for a meal. When we came back to the hotel there was Bernard, sitting in the bar with a bottle of whisky. "Boys! Come here. Come and have a whisky!" It was a quick wicket and Larter was a difficult bowler to play against. Despite having stitches in his mouth, he'd had a great day so we joined him and celebrated his bravery with several tots of whisky.'

It proved to be a match-winning innings as Shepherd and Pressdee took five wickets apiece to see Glamorgan to a 98-run victory. Bernard's whisky drinking was quite a rarity and owed as much to the killing the pain from his recent dental surgery as it did to his liking of the spirits. For Bernard, spending time at the bar was an opportunity to talk with other players and not a reason to drink. In later years, he developed a liking for wine and would often open a bottle over Sunday lunch, but his family never saw him the worse for drink. The two Alans though, on that Saturday night at Northampton, had been very privileged to see the rarest of sights ... Bernard Hedges ever so slightly drunk.

Alan enjoyed batting with Bernard and he also appreciated his approach to the game, as highlighted by a series of events in a 2nd XI match at Margam when Bernard was captaining a young Glamorgan side and trying to instil a bit of discipline and order into proceedings. Alan was also in the side and remembers how things unfolded:

'Brian Evans, the young pace bowler, was playing. Brian was 'creating', he was always creating about something. He didn't want to bowl or something so Bernard sent him off the field and we played with ten men until we came off for lunch, Bernard duly had a chat with him so we took him back out after lunch. But he started to create about something again, so Bernard said: "Off you go".'

There was another occasion when Bernard showed his displeasure about the spirit of cricket and the way to play the game when he was batting in 1960 with all-rounder Peter Walker. As Peter recalls:

'Bernard liked to play the game in a particular way and reproached me on two occasions that season. One was when I had the habit of tossing the ball back to him rather than the bowler. He didn't like it and he told me so. The second was in the match against Somerset at Bath. I'd lost form, been left out of the England team and was a little frustrated. I went out and slogged a 60. He came down the wicket and told me I wasn't playing the game correctly when I was on about 15. I hit someone for six over midwicket. I middled it and looked up for his approval. He very deliberately turned his back on me. He didn't think it was right.'

Turning his back on his partner and refusing to talk was very unusual for Bernard. As Peter also recalls: 'Alan Jones was a silent partner. He would just bat and bat and bat. Bernard talked a little more. You could have a conversation with him.'

Alan and Bernard's partnership had begun towards the start of several golden summers for Alan, with 1965 being the first when he came close to amassing 2,000 runs. It was also a period when the left-hander established himself as Glamorgan's premier opener. Bernard experienced breaks through illness and injury, plus a steady decline in form, but Alan learnt much from his more experienced partner. Bernard was always willing to pass on advice, and despite the gap in experience, Bernard saw Alan as an equal, as evidenced by the way the pair would always alternate taking the strike, right from the beginning of their time together at the crease, without Bernard trying to play a senior role and dominate things.

Many seasons would pass. Alan would go on to play many great innings and develop partnerships with a host of other partners. At Basingstoke, in 1980, against Hampshire, he opened the batting with John Hopkins, and occupied the crease throughout the second day, to post an unbeaten 204, his highest ever first-class score. Slumping into his seat in the

Peter Walker. Bernard once took exception to the way he was scoring his runs and showed his displeasure by turning his back on him. (© Glamorgan CCC)

changing rooms at lunch time, Alan looked up to see Bernard, smartly dressed as befitted an area manager of Barclaycard, smiling at him from across the room. He had come to check on how his old teammate was doing. There was no need for borrowed kit or tots of whisky or even that many words. The pride that had brought them together for Glamorgan over so many years in the past was now the unspoken force that drew them back together in the present. The power of the daffodil!

12

One-Day Glory in 1963

'Borne aloft from the field in triumph.'

1963 was some year. It was the year when Martin Luther King Jnr. made his 'I have a dream' speech, when the 'Profumo affair' exposed the hypocrisies at the heart of government and the year when the Beatles brought out their first album. In the world of county cricket, 1963 was the year when the distinction between amateur and professional ended and an inter-county limited-overs competition entered the playing calendar.

Glamorgan's two amateurs at the time, Ossie Wheatley and Tony Lewis, remembered the awkwardness of the everyday differences that amateur status imposed on them:

[Tony] 'I found it difficult to be part of it all being an amateur being treated differently outside of Glamorgan. You could play at Derby. The President and Chairman would meet you and take you through tunnels in the racing stand to where they had laid out a lunch worthy of the Ritz just for the amateurs and the committee. Tie and blazer. They would open wine in the days before wine was drunk. At Old Trafford I walked past all the pros digging into Lancashire Hot Pot to where a waitress met me at the door and said 'would you like a sherry sir?' Well, not now I said. I'm having enough trouble out there with Mr Statham as it is without playing with alcohol inside me.'

[Ossie] 'The professional and amateur divide was never very serious. It was all rather odd. In Lancashire, Bob Barber was put in a different hotel to the players and met them at the ground. It was absurd. I remember going to The Oval and M.J.K. and I changed with Peter May in the one dressing room and ours was the same size as the one where the other 20 'professionals' were changing. We used to dine separately. It was comical really. When we went to Scarborough for the Gents / Players games we would stay in the Grand Hotel with dinner jackets. Then come 10:30pm, we'd leave with the orchestra playing in the background and we'd go over to the hotel over the road where the players were and slip our jackets off and join the party.'

The idea for one-day cricket had first been mooted at an MCC Advisory Committee at Lord's during 1943 but rejected on the grounds that it would be detrimental to the art and character of the game, whilst captains would be drawn not into taking wickets but to keeping runs down. As late as 1961, the Glamorgan selection committee under Wilf had nailed its colours to the mast, stating that they were 'unanimously against one-day cricket as a game and as a substitute to three-day cricket.' But things were moving fast and with the growth of television coverage, the increasing commercialisation of other sports, especially football, and the greater opportunities for sponsorship, the MCC succumbed to what was probably the inevitable and made plans for what became known as the Gillete Cup.

The manufacturers of razor blades and shaving equipment put up £6,500 in sponsorship for the 65-overs-a-side competition and, in their letter to the M.C.C confirming their involvement, they outlined their wish 'to make awards in respect of each of the matches on the basis of 'meritorious individual performances.' It was decided, in addition, that highly experienced England Test cricketers of the past would decide the winner of these man-of-the-match awards and that they would receive a gold medal plus a cheque for £50.

In Wales, Bernard was not worrying too much about the problems of the traditionalists nor the marketing of the new one-day competition. 1963 had been named as his Benefit Year and he, like many other professional cricketers, set out his stall to make as much as he could from the season. John Arlott, writing back in 1949, stated that the benefit's success 'depends upon the players popularity within his own county; popularity is the most certain guarantee of a good return from the local public.'

That was something that Bernard need not have been concerned about. His attacking style and ever-friendly temperament meant that all around the county he had people who wished him well and would be willing to support his Benefit. In Pontypridd, they had set up a Benefit fund committee and on 26 April 1963 they reported the following events or opportunities:

(a)   Athletic Club – 6 May – Film Show 8:30p.m
(b)   Cliff Morgan XI v Cardiff City - 8 July
(c)   15-minute profile on BBC Wales' *Welsh Sports Parade*
(d)   Benefit Brochure now on sale at 2/6

Bernard's Benefit match had already been allocated by the county committee and, fittingly, was the game against Gloucestershire in July at Ynysangharad.

The young Tony Lewis who captained Glamorgan in their first one-day cricket match against Somerset. By all accounts, none of the players knew what to expect or how to play. (© Glamorgan CCC)

Billy Slade. The talented young cricketer from Briton Ferry who played alongside Bernard in the Gillette Cup first round in 1963. (© Glamorgan CCC)

But before any of these things could take place, there was the small job of applying himself to making runs and bringing success to the team. One of the first hurdles to face was the new one-day competition. The first round was to be played on 22 May and Glamorgan were drawn at home against Somerset.

As the priority for Glamorgan was to perform well in the County Championship, the selectors rested Don Shepherd and Ossie Wheatley in order to keep them fresh for the next Championship game. Tony Lewis was captain for the day, with his team having quite an unfamiliar look about it – Alwyn Harris, Alan Jones, Tony Lewis, Bernard Hedges, Jim Pressdee, Alan Rees, Brian Evans, Billy Slade, Eifion Jones, Hamish Miller and Jeff Jones. As Tony Lewis admitted when I spoke to him, this was completely new territory for all the players, 'All I remember about that game in 1963 was that it was the first time we had played in a game like that.' Ossie Wheatley was just as frank with his comments. 'We didn't take the Gillette Cup very seriously. It was intended to be fun cricket like the Cavaliers Sunday cricket. Very swiftly, of course, it turned into a major competition.'

Tony won the toss and elected to bat; his decision caused some surprise. Indeed of the eight matches taking place around the country, Tony was the only captain who made that decision. Four overs in, he was wishing he had not made it as both Alwyn Harris and Alan Jones were back in the pavilion, with Glamorgan 11-2.

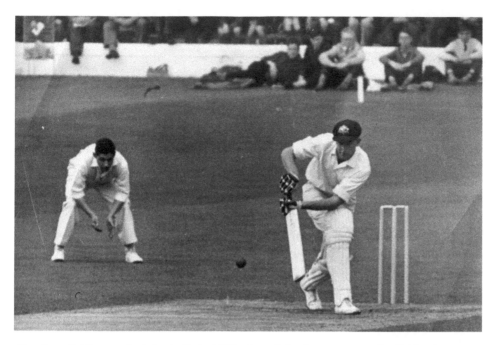

Alan Rees fielding against Australia in 1964. One of the finest cover point fielders in county cricket and a Welsh rugby International. (© Glamorgan CCC)

Tony and Bernard duly found themselves together at the wicket and initially found scoring difficult. There was some dampness in the track and the Somerset new ball pairing of Ken Palmer and Fred Rumsey were finding some assistance for their seamers. Tony found just the right expression to describe the situation. 'We were in deep mire. We had left key players out. 'Shep' and Ossie didn't play because we were saving them for the 'proper matches'. It was dire straits.'

It took Tony nearly half an hour to get off the mark, but gradually, the pair found their way and began to play more forceful cricket. As Tony recalls: 'Bernard and I said 'how do we play this?' One of us has got to stay here while the other one needs to get some runs. I was captain so I said 'I'll tell you what. I'll do you a favour. I'll try and stay here and you play all of your shots.' I thought it was going to be short but it was 65 overs, almost a first-class innings, much longer than we thought. We stayed there. I blocked and we stayed there a long time.'

They had added 100 for the third wicket when Tony drove a ball loftily off David Doughty and was caught at mid-off by Bill Alley. After lunch, Rumsey took the wickets of Pressdee, Rees and Evans in quick succession and was on a hat-trick; Glamorgan had slumped to 152-6. Billy Slade stopped the hat-trick ball but Rumsey finished his allotted 15 overs with figures of 4-24. These were match-winning figures. Palmer soon put paid to Slade so that the home team had now lost four wickets for seven runs. Bernard was caught in that difficult position for a batsman, wanting to accelerate but running out of partners to bat with. He worked his way into the 90s when Eifion Jones, who had made 16 runs in half an hour at the wicket, was out. The match report then reads: 'Miller joined Hedges who in the 64th over (the penultimate of the innings) hooked Greetham for a couple to reach a valuable century after a stay of three hours five minutes and hitting seven fours.'

Glamorgan had made 207-8 in their 65 overs with Bernard becoming the club's first one-day centurion. As Alan remembers, 'Bernard was quite shrewd about batting. We were used to three-day cricket and we thought it was going to be a slog. "It's not, Alan." Bernard said to me. "65 overs is a lot of cricket. You can play your normal game and you can get a hundred." He'd worked out the overs and the pace of the game.'

Jeff Jones took a wicket in his first over but then Graham Atkinson and Peter Wight moved their score along at over three runs an over. Wight was then caught by Bernard at mid-off and Somerset were 28-2. This brought Bill Alley to the wicket. In 1957, Somerset had made several overtures to Alley to bring him to first-class cricket from his exalted and successful position as club professional for Blackpool in the Lancashire League. There, he was as famous as Stanley Matthews and earnt enough, in his words, 'to eat steak several times a week ... and to tip the waiters with an old £5 note.' It was the unwillingness of the Blackpool club to offer him more than a one year contract that brought him to the West Country. Two seasons previously, in 1961, the brash and bullish Australian had destroyed almost every county bowling attack. He described the 1961 season as his 'Indian Summer'. At the age of 42 he had scored 3,019 runs along with taking 62 wickets and 29 catches. He got 11 centuries and ten 50s with an average of 56.96 making two 100s against the touring Australians and only five runs away from completing a third. He was, and will be, the last player to score more than 3,000 runs in a season. The nature of the game today, with fewer championship games and less cricket played altogether make this a feat that is, to all intents and purposes, unrepeatable.

Alley was a left-handed batsman who hit the ball hard. His philosophy was 'if the ball is there to be hit, for Christ's sake hit it.' His straightforward approach, combined with a boxer's physique, led him to bludgeon rather than caress the ball with a limited range of sometimes cross batted strokes. He could play the occasional stylish off drive just to prove he could score in this way too. He brought his straightforward, confident approach to every innings. He was applauded all the way to the wicket by the Welsh crowd. His swashbuckling style had earnt him many admirers around the county circuit and he was seen as someone who was not only capable of a match-winning performance but would also delight in the challenge of trying to prove he was worthy of the cash prize. Alley, along with Atkinson began to score brightly when Tony Lewis introduced his 'secret weapon' into the attack.

'I knew Bernard could bowl because of his work at the indoor school in Neath. He wasn't on the list to bowl but I looked at how the pitch was playing and who we had because we hadn't attempted to put a first-class bowling side out. The ball didn't bounce very much. I knew he could bowl straight. That was the main thing. His bowling in the nets created a bit of a skill for bowling in one-day cricket.' The score when Bernard came on to bowl was 64-2. In his first four overs, he conceded one run and took the wickets of Alley, caught by Alan Jones, and Atkinson, bowled within a run of each other. Somerset were now 65-4. Alan Jones remembers it well: 'He bowled little medium pacers and put it on the spot. He got Graham Atkinson and Bill Alley. He was good.' Bob Barber, recalling his days of playing one-day cricket, described the sort of slow bowling offered up by Bernard as 'phantom medium pace.' His ghostly

The Western Mail's coverage of Bernard's man-of-the-match performance against Somerset. (© Western Mail)

deliveries had captured two of Somerset's key batsmen and put them on the defensive. His finishing figures of 8 overs, 5 maidens, 2 for 17, were a set that any specialist bowler would have been proud of.

Bernard held a steepling catch off the spin bowling of Jim Pressdee from the six-hitting Chris Greetham. This made it six down at 116 and Pressdee followed it up with the wickets of Ken Palmer and Somerset captain and wicketkeeper Harold Stephenson. With 87 runs left to get, Somerset had only three wickets left but Brian Langford, the off-spinner and lower-order batsman, began to connect. With five overs to go, Somerset only required 13 runs, with Langford and Doughty adding 75 for the ninth wicket. However, both holed out to the bowling of Miller and Evans, and Glamorgan had won by ten runs.

The Welsh press were effusive in their praise for the match and Bernard's all-round performance: 'All-Rounder Hedges Hero of Tourney Win'; 'a tremendous cricket match with a storybook finish; 'he achieved the complete performance of a match winning all-rounder'; 'No praise can be too great for Hedges, a modest conscientious cricketer who, in one day, justified his right to take a Benefit'; 'could any player in England have done more?' It is what cricket writer Rob Smyth has called 'the intrinsic charm of improbable success' when a batsman excels at bowling or *vice-versa*. But this was no amusing interlude as when Tony Lewis had to prise the ball from Don Shepherd's hand to come on and take three wickets against Somerset to win a county game. Nor was it an example of the law of unintended consequences as when Tony brought on Alan Jones to bowl against Worcesterhire hoping to prompt a declaration and Alan promptly took his maiden wicket in first-class cricket, that of Ron Headley who had hit the mainstream bowlers for 140. This was a first-class all-round performance born of practice and persistence by a player whose capabilities were well known to the captain. Charming, most definitely. Improbable, perhaps not so much.

Charles Barnett, the former England and Gloucestershire cricketer had been given the job of adjudicating the man-of-the-match award. If he had considered any name other than that of Bernard Hedges it would have created a scandal. As the match report's final paragraph has it: 'The Glamorgan players jumped high with a victory leap as Hedges modestly accepted his prize ... before being carried off the field shoulder high by his colleagues. A marvellous photograph captures the moment, Alwyn Harris and Alan Rees holding Bernard high and him smiling as widely and brightly as he had done all those years earlier when he was camping with his good friend Bernard Cummings.

Gordon Ross, in his history of the Gillette Cup, placed great significance on this moment as representing something more than just the normal elation that characterised the winning team in a tight game of cricket:

'Here was part of the 'new' cricket, carried off the field shoulder high, at a cricket match! Naturally you would have expected it at Cardiff Arms Park if Wales had just beaten England by a late try and enthusiastic Welshmen had borne their hero aloft from the field in triumph. But cup fever at a game of cricket ... this was one of the early indications that the winds of change would sweep away some of the old, and blow in the new.'

Bernard's man-of-the-match gold medal.
(© Stephen Hedges)

Papers on the day of the game had carried a similar photo of someone being carried shoulder high. It was Tommy Doherty, then manager of Chelsea, being chaired by his exuberant team after their 7-0 victory over Portsmouth had put them back in the First Division. Two sports. The same form of celebration. It is almost ritualistic; a tradition that dated back to ancient times. There was a sense of honour and nobility in it. It implied a comradeship and common purpose that was magnified through this one act. It was, in truth, part of 'the old'. The new was yet to come and would involve back slapping, high fiving, hugging and kissing (in football at least). These forms of celebration left Bernard cold. He hated their showiness and he found that they detracted from his enjoyment of the game. They were, in his eyes at least, examples of a new culture that, along with player's hair, clothes and the way they talked, tarnished sport. As the 1970s came with the creation of football's million pound players, Bernard would recoil at what he saw.

He had become the first Glamorgan batsman to score a hundred in one-day cricket. This, at least, was something that no one could ever take away from him. His gold medal would be a permanent reminder of his achievement. Firsts are important landmarks and cricketers, like other sportsmen, hold these achievements close to their heart.

After his heroic deeds in the first game, hopes were high that Bernard, or another Glamorgan player might emulate his achievements in the next round of the competition as the Welsh county met Worcestershire at Neath. But it was not to be Bernard's or Glamorgan's day. Tom Graveney hit an outstanding 93 as the visitors notched up 238 whilst, in reply, only Euros Lewis rose to the challenge with 78 as Glamorgan lost by 46 runs.

Like other counties, Glamorgan undertook a membership campaign during the first part of 1963, and after his heroic performance against Somerset,

Test cricketer Charles Barnett presents Bernard with his gold medal. Both player and schoolboys appear transfixed by its lustre. (© Mrs M.J. Hedges)

Bernard's face was on the literature which was used in the valleys. The Aberdare Leader carried a 'cricket drive' on one of its pages, urging locals to 'Help to Keep the County First-Class'. The membership push was well organised, with Glamorgan, Monmouthshire, Carmarthenshire, Pembrokeshire and Breconshire being divided up into 26 regions, all with their own personal targets. Launching the campaign, David Lockhead, the campaign secretary outlined that it cost £100 a day to run Glamorgan and during 1962 it had made a loss of £5,408. It needed 6,500 new members to 'keep its head above water'. Underneath the article was a signed photo of Bernard and beneath was: 'Support the benefits for players who have been the backbone of the club to help repay them for their loyalty and to show the youngsters who are coming along that being a professional cricketer can be a rewarding career.'

Most cricketers hoped that a Benefit Season would go towards a deposit on a house or would act as a useful 'nest egg' for the days after their retirement from the game. Along with a Benefit tie, the central feature of a player's Benefit season was the brochure. Bernard's was produced by Celtic Press in Pontypridd and went on sale for two shillings and sixpence. In it, there were testimonials and tributes by Judge Rowe Harding, the Chairman of the Club, as well as by sports journalists Basil Easterbrook, J.B.G. Thomas (*Western*

Mail), Ron Griffiths (*South Wales Evening Post*) and Malcolm Lewis (*South Wales Echo*). There were also articles by John Arlott, Trevor Bailey, Ossie Wheatley and former Gloucestershire cricketer Andy Wilson.

Whilst there is no room for a serious analysis of a players technique and style in a Benefit Brochure, there were, in Bernard's, nevertheless a series of comments and statements that are worth recording as they capture his character and his standing as a cricketer at the time. Rowe Harding, in his foreword, focussed on Bernard's personal qualities: 'Bernard Hedges impresses by his modesty, his quiet sense of humour, his cheerfulness and his absolute loyalty.'

Basil Easterbrook, in his tribute, began by making reference to the abolition of amateur status and, by his comments, suggested that for many journalists, the distinction had not been that meaningful: 'B. Hedges – or should that be Hedges, B. – or Mr Hedges?; this changing world of ours is so confusing. Let's forget the protocol. To me he remains what he has long been, Bernard or 'Hedgie' me old butty from Pontypridd.'

He followed this up with a ringing endorsement of not only Bernard but the county cricketer as an entity, saying he, 'represents all that is best in a county cricketer in terms of dedication and endeavour.' This final word implies physical effort, a striving for success. A number of the tributes made mention of Bernard's difficulties in early life and the slow development of his career. He had had to work hard for the position he had achieved in the Glamorgan team. Things had not come easy for him. Easterbrook again: 'There are of course limitations to his talents. Bernard will never be a Hobbs or a Hutton ... but make no mistake, this is a very good player and better yet, a good to watch player.'

J.B.G. Thomas recognised the all-round sporting contribution that Bernard had made and the popularity that brought with it: 'Indeed the work that the people of Pontypridd and especially the rugby club are doing for his Benefit, justifies fully the title of 'Man of Many Parts." Ron Griffiths also noticed the attractiveness of Glamorgan's opening batsman and had a simple theory for this: 'Hedges believes in looking for runs rather than waiting for them to come. There are few more exhilarating sights than Hedges in full cry hooking the quick bowlers off the tip of his chin, driving the spinners in front of the wicket.'

I am not sure some of his teammates would recognise this picture of him as a hooker. It was that short armed pull shot that they all admired and revered. However, Ron's point that here was a player who was attempting to take the game to the bowlers still stands. Malcolm Lewis also saw this, which also encouraged him to use Bernard's example as a means to make a more general point: 'He always tries to master the bowlers before they can master him. To the game he has brought a welcome spirit of aggression. Cricket could do with more players of his like.'

Purchase of the brochure allowed access to Ynysangharad Park for one of the three days of Bernard's Benefit match. If someone had arrived on day one, they may well have turned around and headed back home. Only 20 minutes of play was possible before heavy rain brought proceedings to a halt and wiped out play for the rest of the day. In the run-up to the game, Bernard had accepted the challenge of a local supporter of three pence for every run he scored in the match. It looked as if not only the bet would be off but Bernard could be as much as £500 out of pocket. As the beneficiary, he had to bear all the costs of putting on the game, including the hiring of staff and the travelling and hotel expenses of the Glamorgan players. Insurance, which appears an obvious answer, was not a possibility as, in Bernard's words to the assembled journalists, 'it would have been an uneconomical proposition.'

Jean recalls, 'His match was rained off. All the food had to be paid for. I remember the marquee and the rain pouring down.' Don Shepherd had ended up in the red with his Benefit Match. For such an important part of a cricketer's career, they were, in their own way, a real gamble that depended on factors over which the player had little control. John Arlott again: 'A few years ago a Test match batsman who played for an unimportant county had a benefit at about the same time as the most obscure member of a great county side. The final figure of the Test players benefit was less than a third of that of the other player.'

Bernard was an ordinary player in an unimportant county whose Benefit Match had been rained off. It did not bode well for his final figure. In fact, the total stood at £4,402, over £1,000 more than Don Shepherd had received in 1960 and £3,100 less than the figure Peter Walker received in 1966. This, of course, pales into insignificance alongside the figures raised in the modern era, with Matthew Maynard's Benefit in 1996 raising over £150,000. Bernard's success was down to the many small events and fundraising activity that took place throughout the season. The Pontypridd CC minutes again record that £17 3s worth of tickets had been sold for the Bernard Hedges Benefit cocktail party which was arranged for the evening of the Gloucestershire game. Later, in September, it was recorded that the Benefit dance had raised a profit of £8 and 10s to date. There must have been more ticket money to collect!

1963 turned out to be Glamorgan's best since 1948. They finished second in the table behind Yorkshire, with their success based on three factors: Tony Lewis' availability on a full-time basis for the first time; Alan Jones' emergence as a top-class opening batsman; and Pressdee's rediscovery of his bowling ability. Bernard made 1,406 runs with no centuries, and overcame the facial injury when fielding as a substitute against the West Indians at Swansea. As Tony recalls, 'It was nasty. Blood everywhere. But it didn't break his nerve and he subsequently fielded at short square-leg. You need a lot of guts to field there. Bernard had all the guts but not the reflexes that Peter Walker had. Peter would work out on paper where to turn his body and how to present his back to the ball with his head down. It was a dangerous place to field. Bernard was very good at running around and catching the ball.'

So it would seem. A total of 21 catches for the season would be his best ever haul in first-class cricket. With his Benefit Year complete, Bernard looked forward in hope to help Glamorgan go one step better and win the Championship again. Could he help them achieve it? Could he maintain or improve his form? If he had been inclined to listen to *The Freewheelin' Bob Dylan* album released only days after his Gillette Cup triumph, he would have heard the track *A Hard Rain's a-Gonna Fall*. The song, full of portent about an apocalyptic future, was a warning to many. It could well have been the soundtrack to the years that lay ahead for Bernard. There was certainly more rain than sunshine. He was not to know, but events would not go for him in the following seasons. 1963 would be the last in which he reached 1,000 runs. Though he would play until 1967, this was the beginning of the end.

Bernard presenting an athletics trophy during his Benefit year (1963). (© Mrs M.J. Hedges)

13

The Incident at Llanelli

'The consummate professional caught up in an argument not of his making.'

Bernard would be 37 at the end of 1964. He would have completed 14 seasons in a Glamorgan jumper and whilst not formally a senior player, his experience and longevity put him alongside Don Shepherd in the Glamorgan team. Times were changing but some things never altered. The respect given to the old by the young and the informal hierarchy of professional cricket were part of the Glamorgan dressing room just like any other. Malcolm Nash, who made his debut in 1966, describes turning up for his trial with the club:

Roger Davis. He was in direct competition with Bernard for an opener's position when he joined in 1964. (© Glamorgan CCC)

'There were two changing rooms at the indoor school, one for senior players and one for juniors and others. It really did feel like 'them and us'. There was a mental as well as a physical wall. On my first morning there I was introduced to Mr Wheatley, various Mr Joneses, Mr Shepherd, Mr Hedges. I had no problem with that. We talked for a while before the nets started. On the first day, I bowled all day. I was knackered. On the Tuesday I got a bat first up. At the end of Tuesday, Phil Clift told me they would like to take me on for a summer contract.'

Another new player who made his debut in 1964 was Roger Davis, fresh from Blundell's, the public school in Devon which would in time produce Glamorgan's Hugh Morris and Somerset's Vic Marks. Roger was excited to be playing amongst cricketers he had admired from afar but he recognised there was an unspoken factor that lurked just below the surface of the relationship between old and new players:

> 'It was great to play with all your heroes. They made you feel comfortable but as a young player, you are a threat to an older player. Pros will help other pros but only up to a point. The threat is always there.'

Ossie Wheatley reinforced this point for bowlers as well as batsmen when he said, 'Professional sport is a tough environment. It always amuses me when commentators say "and he'll be bringing on this youngster in the side". Will he hell! He'll be making sure he can't bowl for the next five years. Players were decent on the whole but they would be thinking this guy could put me out of a job.'

With the young talent emerging, Bernard knew that he would have to fight to retain his place in the team. Indeed, as an opener, Roger would be in direct competition with Bernard for a slot at the top of the order, but he never saw it quite like that: 'I was not as natural a player as Bernard. I knew what I could do and what I couldn't do. I was a poor man's Bernard Hedges.'

There were, however, two more personal issues that muddied the waters in terms of Bernard's commitment to his cricket. His first son, David, had been born in 1960 and I then followed in 1964. Bernard was now the father of a young family so his attention was, sometimes, somewhere else other than on the field of play. The second issue was his affliction with kidney stones. They returned in the 1964 season and kept him out of the team throughout August. He missed the historic win over the Australians at Swansea and his run tally suffered. These were a recurring medical problem and one that prompted the only surreal newspaper headline relating to Bernard in the whole of his career. 'Hedges KO'd by Strawberries' read the pink paper. Doctors had apparently informed Bernard that his liking for the soft summer fruit may have been at the root of his complaint, the seeds acting as a nucleus around which the stones could form. Medically, I am not sure how much of this was true but it made its impact on Bernard; he lived for another 50 years but he never ate one more strawberry!

Bernard had attended a meeting of players with the club in July 1964. This had been to put forward their views on their stated request for a rise in basic pay. He was accompanied by Don and Jim Pressdee and they met with four committee members in addition to Wilf as secretary. In the meeting, Bernard had stated that 'the request for an increase in basic pay was based solely on the inadequate guaranteed salary paid. It was not possible to live on it and the rest of the bonus scale was problematical.'

Bernard in the back garden of his home in Swansea with eldest son David. The cap is the festival one he wore during his 1963 match winning innings in the Gillette Cup. (© Mrs M.J. Hedges)

In reply, Wilf stressed his view that bigger salaries meant a better performance from players and less sentiment on retention of those not doing well. It also meant, in his view, good results or the committee would look elsewhere for talent. Senior players were given a rise from £12 10s to £14 10s with an annual basic of £754 at the end of the season. Whether it was enough for the players, it was clear that there was some distance between the committee's view of things and that of the players. At the General committee meeting held on the same day the pay increases were agreed with one member insisting that there was 'too much socialising going on and discipline was slack'.

That committee men might have been coming at this from the wrong angle is clear when you hear Ossie Wheatley, captain at the time, talking about the role of 'socialising' after the day's play:

'We had a rule. The first night of any three-day game when we were at home everyone stayed behind and had a drink with the opposition. That's why very little cheating went on, because you all knew each other. The umpires were there. I would introduce a young player to the umpires so they would know who he was. It wasn't formal but there was a definite etiquette. pretty well all the umpires were ex-players. They were steeped in it. They were beacons. They played their parts. They handled themselves with great dignity and great charm.'

Socialising within the team also had a role beyond just 'having a good time':

'We took 11 players plus a 12th man, a physiotherapist and a scorer and that was that. There was never any question of the coach coming with us. The coach was with the 2nd XI. That was where he was important. The captain and the senior players would sit down in a pub and sort out anybody who was showing a lack of form. We spent evenings talking about it with batsmen and bowlers. It was very professional in a funny sort of way. Nowadays it's quite the reverse. The professionals spend most of their day talking about the game but don't talk about it much in the evenings. That's turned around. We would be deeply involved in the evenings. Now they are not.'

Within the walls of the committee room the concerns about ill-discipline seemed to be focussed on one player. At the selection committee on 30 March, Wilf set out his plan to deal with the situation:

> 'The Secretary stated that there had been considerable trouble with Jim Pressdee last season, but he hoped the new system would simplify this and prevent any unpleasantness.'

The new system was that the captain and senior professional (Don Shepherd) would be the only people responsible for all matters connected with the playing side of the club. Given this description, the meeting about pay attended by Bernard the previous July had not been welcomed by the secretary.

'No Decision Yet on Pressdee' was the headline in the *Western Mail* on Tuesday 27 April 1965. The Glamorgan all-rounder had enjoyed playing in South Africa, and was looking ahead to his future there after playing. He seemed to be saying that he was planning a longer visit. 'I am going to South Africa to coach again this winter and I shall probably stay there with my family.' His decision came as 'news' to Wilf Wooller, with the Glamorgan secretary adding, 'We have had a couple of 'scares' before. We will have to wait and see.' The implication was that Pressdee was using the threat of leaving to extract a better offer from the club in his contract negotiations. The unspoken dispute between Pressdee and the club would hover in the outfield throughout the summer, bursting into life on the last day of the season and engulfing Bernard in the process.

Jim Pressdee was a Swansea boy through and through. He had made his Glamorgan debut aged 16 in 1949 and as a youth had been an exceptional footballer, winning a Welsh schoolboy cap before playing for Swansea Town for two seasons. After establishing a regular place in the Glamorgan side in 1954, he worked on his left-arm spin bowling and became a useful foil to the off-cutters of Don Shepherd and Jim McConnon's off-spin.

None of this was to the detriment of his batting as he scored nearly 2,000 runs in both 1961 and 1962, but Jim lost confidence as a bowler during the late 1950s and took only five wickets between 1959 and 1962. It was whilst playing club cricket in South Africa that he regained his self-belief, and in 1963 Jim did the 'double', taking 104 wickets and scoring 1,435 runs. He also had played a leading role in the victory over the Australians at Swansea in 1964 with figures of 6-58 and 4-65.

1965 saw Jim claim career-best figures of 9-43 against Yorkshire. Ossie Wheatley was to describe him, at the county's AGM in 1966, as amongst 'the six best all-rounders in the world at the present moment' and that 'his best years

Jim Pressdee. A great all-rounder who, at the beginning of the 1965 season was rumoured to be leaving Glamorgan. (© Glamorgan CCC)

were still to come.' But the season proved to be something of a roller-coaster of emotions for both Jim and the Glamorgan supporters. The team alternated from poor defeats to unbelievable victories, whilst they challenged for the Championship almost until the final round of matches.

Commenting on Jim with the benefit of hindsight, both Ossie Wheatley and Peter Walker had similar impressions of him:

'Jim Pressdee was an interesting case. He was a talented guy. He was awkward. He used to upset the other side as much as he upset his own side. He could get everyone going. He would go down the wicket and pat it down way beyond where the bowler was bowling. He would back away when the bowler was in his bowling stride. He was a soccer player. But seriously lacking in self-confidence. When I came he didn't want to bowl at all but he could bowl. He was a very unorthodox bowler. Left arm and a round arm around the wicket. It came from a different direction to anyone else and it came very slowly.'

Peter simply said: 'He was quite a handful.'

In May, Bernard was embarrassed by a dropped catch against Derbyshire. The *Western Mail* recorded, 'the unfortunate Hedges had his turn to drop a dolly and the whole Chesterfield tree-ringed ground echoed to the howl of delight from the crowd.' Bernard's good relationship with umpires assisted him at The Oval when David Gibson bowled a series of short deliveries at him. Again, according to the report, ' he marched down the pitch, tapped the ground a yard in front of Tony Lewis' batting crease and inquired of the umpire whether the light was not rather too dim to expect a batsman to face a battery of intimidatory deliveries.' The umpires took the players off for bad light.

At the end of May, Glamorgan were 11th in the table, yet despite their lowly position, there were some fine individual performances in the following weeks. Tony Lewis struck an outstanding 169 on the opening day against the New Zealanders at the Arms Park, whilst Jim Pressdee and Don Shepherd each claimed nine wickets in an innings in the match with Yorkshire at Swansea, prompting J.B.G. Thomas in the *Western Mail* to suggest that Pressdee should think seriously 'about his future before signing emigration papers'.

Shortly afterwards, Alan and Bernard shared their best-ever opening stand of 201 against Warwickshire at Nuneaton, and on the back of a series of victories, Glamorgan went top of the table on 23 June, leaving a euphoric *Western Mail* to say 'Whether or not they can manage to win the Championship, this side is bringing fresh glory to Welsh sport, and the England selectors could look to the West with advantage.'

Inside the dressing room, there were also those habits and superstitions that sustained players. Tony Lewis has written about Bernard's particular cricketing good luck charm which involved him talking earnestly to his bat and referring to it as Clicky Ba, a comic strip character from *The Hotspur*. It was a cricket bat bound with brass that one of the character's used. Tony Lewis recalls:

'If we were going out to chase runs, he'd say, "C'mon Clicky Ba!" It created a great atmosphere. It was pretty well known by everyone inside the dressing room. Ossie smiled when I reminded him of this. "I do remember Clicky Ba. I don't remember the conversations though." We had a lot of laughs in the dressing room. It was very good fun.'

Bernard was not doing much laughing as June drew to a close. After the game against Sussex he was struck down again with kidney stones. 'He was absolutely in agony with them,' Ossie remembered. 'It was ghastly.' A fortnight later he underwent an operation at Morriston hospital in Swansea. As Glamorgan supporters held their breath and hoped for news about their valiant opening batsman returning to cricket, the rest of the country was transfixed by the escape from prison of the great train robber Ronnie Biggs.

By mid-July Bernard was out of hospital, but rather than speculating about his return to the side, the press spent more time writing about Pressdee's departure, with rumours that he had been offered a three-year contract. They had plenty to write about on-field matters as well, with Glamorgan still in the top three of the Championship table. They routed Leicestershire by an innings and 28 runs with Jeff Jones' phenomenal bowling performance of 8 for 11. Peter Walker's father, who was visiting Britain from South Africa to see his son, stated after watching the game. 'This was worth coming 6,000 miles to see.' Alan Jones has strong memories of this game:

'It was a lovely wicket. Then, after lunch, there was a thunderstorm and Ossie Wheatley declared and we came out to field after tea. As I say, there were no covers. Well, the wicket was like that [Alan bangs the table] and then you had the storm and the top was soft and once she hit the top she just flew and I mean fly! Jeff was quick. I remember Maurice Hallam coming in to bat and the first ball, he got hit. The next ball he backed away and chucked the bat at it. He got an edge. Peter Walker was at first slip. I was at second slip. It went high. Peter caught it, a magnificent catch. Maurice passed us and said, 'I'd rather be a live coward than a dead hero'.

David Constant batted for 72 minutes and remained unbeaten on nine as Leicestershire were bowled out for 40. Tony Lewis described his effort as 'one of the bravest innings I ever saw'.

As Glamorgan focussed on the game against the South Africans at Swansea, supporters and journalists alike reached for their slide-rules to try and calculate the numerous permutations which would determine the outcome of the race for the Championship title. It also saw Bernard's return to the side and after looking in fine fettle, he appeared in the next Championship game against top of the table Northamptonshire at the Arms Park. In front of the largest crowd for a county match for a decade, the two teams fought out a low-scoring game. Glamorgan had a three-run lead on the first innings after Bernard had contributed an invaluable 47, decorated by firm square-cuts and lofted on-drives. After yet another miserly bowling performance by Don Shepherd, Glamorgan were left with a target of 138 to win with the whole of the final day remaining. The pitch, however, had the final say with Glamorgan being bowled out for 120, the wickets falling to Northants off-spinner Brian Crump and medium pacer Albert Lightfoot.

Their victory meant Northants were now 18 points ahead of Glamorgan, but the Welsh county still had three games in hand, and they bounced back by making 167 in 85 minutes on the last day of the match against Somerset to clinch a superb victory. Bernard and Tony shared a stand of 95 in 45 minutes to see Glamorgan to a stunning win – Bernard's 64 was described as a 'remarkable performance' and amongst his 'best efforts for the county'. Glamorgan had scored at nearly six and a half an over, a stunning scoring rate even now in an era of record breaking run chases. It meant that even if Northants won their final match of the summer, Glamorgan could still pip them at the post if they won their four remaining games, three of which were at home.

After a stunning win against Leicestershire, they lost badly to Derbyshire just as Worcestershire put a fine sequence of wins together and, almost from

Alan Jones batting with Bernard, against Kent at Swansea in 1965. (© Glamorgan CCC)

nowhere, went on to deny the East Midlands side their first Championship title. As Ron Headley recalled, there were many reasons which propelled Worcestershire on their title-winning streak:

'In 1964 we had won the Championship. Sir George Dowty was our President. He set the standards and he said he would like to see us win it again. Half way through the season he spoke to us. "In my business, I believe in incentives. I know you're all doing your best but I'd like to give this to you." [Ron could not recall the amount but it was a significant cash sum for each player]. We won 11 out of 12 games from then and won the Championship. It wasn't the money but something changed.'

Glamorgan duly secured their 12th victory of the season against Surrey, but with Worcestershire winning at Hove, the title was settled. All Glamorgan could hope for was joint second place with Northants as they travelled to Stradey Park in Llanelli for their last game of the summer against Essex. It was a difficult game to prepare for. The title race had been decided and the season was, effectively, over. The performance at Stradey was, perhaps predictably, poor. Glamorgan lost in two days to an Essex side that exploited the conditions with leg-spinner Robin Hobbs claiming what at the time was a career-best haul of 6-30 as Essex won by five wickets.

What happened next came to be known, down the years, as the 'incident at Llanelli'. The vagueness of that expression is no accident. All the parties involved had their reasons for wanting to forget about it and move on. The statements taken at the time and the letter that Bernard was to write to the county committee in the weeks after it have not survived. As a result, this account has been written after interviews with players, a reading of the press reports and, most significantly, access to the Glamorgan CCC minutes of the period.

This was the story of a clash between the players and the club's chief administrator that was resolved behind the closed doors of the committee room. The press reports, in truth, reinforced the mystery around the affair by referring to it without describing it in any detail. The fact that it has been remembered by so many connected with the club, for so long, was because it reflected antipathies that went deeper than the incident itself.

At Stradey, there was a small office at the back of the pavilion which players used to reach the car park. The secretary was using this office to count the gate money and said, on this day, that there were 'a great deal of valuables' in it. It was his contention, recorded in the minutes of the selection committee on 7 September 1965, that 'he had stopped players using this room several times.' Bernard, showered and dressed, was the first player to try and exit through the office. The minutes record what Wilf did next: 'The secretary pushed him [Bernard] through the open door and then slammed it behind him, throwing his cricket bag into the corridor.'

Whether Wilf said anything to Bernard at this point is not mentioned. At no point is it said that Bernard either refused to stop or that he said anything to the secretary. From everything we know about Bernard, it is quite impossible to believe that he would have acted in anything other than a professional and respectful way. His respect for Wilf, like many of the players, was beyond question. Peter, Bernard's brother, remembered, significantly, given everything that happened at Llanelli, that, 'He [Bernard] wouldn't have a word said against Wilf Wooller.'

Roger Davis summed up that generation of players. 'Bernard's generation was coming out of the war, National Service, behave yourself, standards, and bring your kids up the right way.' He could have added, 'respect your superiors and do not make a fuss.' Ossie Wheatley attended that meeting on 7 September as the player's rep. After some discussion about whether he could attend, he was allowed to speak and recorded his version of events:

> 'He had been sitting in the dressing room and Bernard Hedges had been prevented from making use of the office as an exit. He later heard some commotion when Pressdee attempted to pursue the same course.'

Jim was a very different man to Bernard. He was only six years younger but he was not afraid of confrontation and sought to challenge perceived injustice wherever he saw it. A news article in the days after the game at Llanelli described him as an 'unofficial shop steward'. It is unlikely that there were three words in the English language more guaranteed to raise the ire of Wilfred Wooller then these. Wilf and Pressdee did not get along and had experienced several run-ins over other issues. On that day, according to another player I spoke to, Pressdee had pushed the secretary up against a wall.

Ossie Wheatley prompted a long discussion at the meeting on the 7th with his concerns about Wilf Wooller making critical comments about the team during his radio and TV commentary. It was clear that the incident had brought a number of issues to the surface. For Pressdee, it may well have been the last straw that made him confirm his future was elsewhere, although everything else tells us that his mind had been made up to leave long before this moment. The press, who always hung around at the end of the game, eagerly responded to Jim's willingness to talk. The following day, the *Western Mail* headline proclaimed 'Jim Pressdee Quits County,' claiming that the player 'did not see eye to eye with the secretary.' There was no mention of the confrontation. *The Mirror*, on the other hand, was keen to play up the incident: 'Rumpus as Pressdee Leaves Glamorgan'. The rumpus was said to be 'involving himself, Wooller and another Glamorgan player.'

The day after the Selection Committee meeting, at which it was agreed to get the players concerned to provide statements, the *Western Mail* carried a commentary piece by Richard Johns entitled, 'What's Wrong With Cricket?' In it he regretted the departure of Pressdee and highlighted the poor wages of the county cricketer. Significantly, it noted that 'too much should not be read into the incident at Llanelli'. Jim Pressdee's main gripe in the piece was not about the behaviour of the Secretary but that cricketers were not valued enough:

> 'Cricketers are paid labourers wages. If you walk down the street you'll find 100 labourers but how many cricketers? County cricket is a skilled occupation with a hard apprenticeship behind it.'

Ex-players, Allan Watkins and Jim McConnon, were willing to go on the record criticising the secretary comments as a broadcaster and his over involvement in team affairs. 'The committee should not allow him to do it. His place is in the office, and that's that,' said Allan. 'One does leave oneself open to criticism by doing that when you are also secretary,' commented Jim.

It was not so much the critical comments that were the issue for some of the players, it was the fact that they were coming from someone who had a privileged position, knowing precisely what was going on inside the club. Not all players felt this way, however. Alan Jones, for example:

> 'Wilf often criticised the players on TV but he would say "Forget about it." All he wanted to do was to get the best for Welsh cricket. When a coach tells you off, some of us could take it. Some of us couldn't take it.'

Whilst all this was taking place, Bernard was in Ireland on a brief end-of-season tour with most of the rest of the team. Commenting to the press about the previous night's selection committee meeting on the same day as the Johns article, Wilf said, 'I have no comment to make. It was a routine meeting at which all matters connected with the club including the troubles at Llanelli were discussed. They will be referred to the general committee which meets at the end of the month.' This is the first point at which Bernard makes any comment to the press. As the article says; 'Bernard Hedges anticipated an apology and that unless it is forthcoming he will take the matter further, presumably to the general committee.'

That Bernard was prepared to say this shows how much the situation had affected him. He was a proud man and Wooller had damaged that pride. An apology would go some way to redressing the balance. Wilf, for his part, was not about to apologise. He had seen what he regarded as a deterioration in discipline since the 1964 season, resulting in what he called 'the disgraceful incident in Llanelly [sic].' There was too much at stake to leave this to the general committee to decide. Despite his comments to the press, Wilf decided the finance and general purposes committee, on 27 September, would be the arena at which to lance this boil.

His Honour the Judge Rowe Harding's comments, as he opened the meeting, were to wonder 'whether any useful purpose would be served by pursuing this matter to a disciplinary end?' Recorded in the minutes were the points made in the ensuing discussion:

(i)   There had been an increasing lack of discipline *visa vis* the players and the committee represented by the secretary.
(ii) This had grown into a trial of strength between the two.

(iii) The actions of the secretary should receive the full support of the committee.

(iv) Certain players and, in particular, J. Pressdee, had deliberately gone out of their way to provoke incidents, bait the secretary, and stir up trouble generally in the club.

It is clear from these minutes that the Llanelli incident was the tip of a perceived iceberg of indiscipline. This was to be where the ice was to be smashed. Wilf wanted the unanimous backing of the committee to discipline the players, sending a clear message about future behaviour. The committee obliged. The proposal was that the two players should be fined, Pressdee two weeks wages and Hedges one week, the extra week for Jim as he'd spoken to the press.

The chairman stated that 'Hedges ought to be allowed to state his case personally.' Bernard was a team man who had struggled back from his hospital bed to join the fight for the championship. Some of this may have ameliorated the committee's view of his involvement. Wooller's response was revealing. He 'thought this unwise and would lead to further adverse publicity. He would again be placed in the position of defendant and subjected to a great deal of unwarranted embarrassment and the matter would drag on unnecessarily.'

The shadow of 1958, when the then committee had tried to oust Wilf and when his behaviour on and off the field had come under intense scrutiny, still hung over him. It was as if he feared having to defend his actions and that he would again be portrayed negatively. Wilf now sat on every committee and oversaw every aspect of Glamorgan's activity. His position was now incomparably stronger than that in 1958. Ossie Wheatley's personal view supports this:

'Wilf had handpicked the committee. They were nice enough people but they had never been in positions of influence before and Wilf handled them easily and that was a problem for quite some time. That was my perspective.'

This strength was, paradoxically, his weakness. He was constantly trying to intervene in team affairs and this caused friction throughout his time as secretary. He agreed, in Bernard's case, to a 'strong letter warning him of his behaviour.' He saw no real distinction between Bernard's and Jim Pressdee's behaviour. The change of punishment was simply a means to expedite the process.

The general committee, due to meet at the end of September, now met on 14 October. They were presented with a *fait accompli*. The committee was being asked to rubber stamp the decision of the finance and general purposes committee that had taken place some 17 days earlier. They were asked to do this without reference to the players' statements. The next day, the press could report that 'the club's general committee has supported Mr Wooller'. *The Times*, no less, carried an article a week later, on 22 October, titled, 'Glamorgan Cricket in Turmoil.' It carried the news that Mr W. Evans, member for Pontypridd and Rhondda district, had resigned from the club's general committee in protest against the disciplinary reprimand which was issued to Bernard Hedges. Whilst he was approached by the reporter, Bernard made no comment, but after outlining the details of the affair, the article continued:

> 'It certainly appeared a strange quirk of justice that brought the player a reprimand when he had requested an apology. The first development has been the decision of senior players to hold a private meeting in west Wales to consider how they could wisely act in support of Hedges whose innocence they openly protest. This very action has made it a clear cut argument between the playing staff and administration, and already the general public are bandying stories of a players strike and the formation of a players union modelled on the professional footballers union.'

Mr Evans, a headmaster from Pontypridd stated that, 'It was not until we got to the meeting that we saw the findings of the sub-committee that had considered the Bernard Hedges case. Neither had the general committee seen the written statements submitted by the two players.' He could not identify himself with the decisions of a committee that had become 'largely ignored'.

Wilf Wooller, in response, was adamant that the matter had received 'democratic attention'. There had, admittedly, been six hours of discussions devoted to the Llanelli incident at the selection committee and finance and general purposes committee. Glamorgan was not, *The Times*' commentary aside, in 'turmoil'. Back in 1958 there had been 11 resignations from the committee after Wilf had triumphantly won the ballot over his future of the club. One resignation would not worry him too much.

Jim Pressdee, meanwhile, had left for South Africa and would make no further comment. Bernard was left to challenge the version of events presented to the press on his own. In the papers, he was quoted as having been given a 'raw deal'. He told the *Western Mail* on 25 October:

'I have posted a letter to the Glamorgan club's general committee seeking a personal hearing about my severe reprimand that was given to me by letter eight days ago.'

There had also been some discussion at the general committee on 14 October of setting up a small disciplinary committee. Such things were an indication of the club's unease at the way the whole issue had been dealt with. Wilf's attitude to Bernard's letter to the general committee on 11 November was uncompromising.

The letter was read out to the committee. Judge Rowe Harding believed there 'could be no useful purpose in dragging up the whole of this unfortunate incident again.' He had, unwittingly, used precisely the same phrase he had used six weeks earlier. Then, it had been used quizzically to bury the issue and save the club from poor publicity; now it was used emphatically for the same end and to bury any semblance of natural justice for Bernard. He continued: 'On his own admission in his letter to the club, Hedges had admitted that he had disobeyed the order of the Secretary and was, in effect, subject to the laws of trespass.' This is the first indication in the minutes that Bernard might have done something to have justified the Secretary's action in that little office at Stradey. Without Bernard's letter, it is difficult to say how accurate a reading of it this is. However, what we can say is that the chairman's language was not that of a benign administrator to a dedicated and long-serving member of the playing staff who, two years earlier, he had praised for his 'absolute loyalty'. It was the language of them and us; of master and servant. For those committee men who did not know Bernard but who revered the judge and the secretary, there was a clear message about how they should respond.

Wilf's intervention at the meeting typified the man. It was polite and reasonable with the steely resolve of someone who was determined to get his own way.

'The secretary said that if it would help the deliberations of the committee he would have no objection at all to Bernard Hedges making a statement to the committee but he felt that if they thought this was a reasonable line of action then the two committee men who witnessed the whole incident should also be present. If the committee subsequently decided that the action already taken by the club was a wise and just one, then he thought the whole matter of punishment should be revisited and something more fitting than the modest letter of censure should be employed.'

Those committee members that took the secretary line could stand firm; those that had some sympathy with Bernard's situation were now fearful of what might lie in store if they voted to hear him speak. The outcome was almost inevitable. The committee decided not hear Bernard's appeal but rather to write him a further letter stating that he must not continue to break his contract as he had done by making statements to the press. There was nothing more that Bernard could do. This was not a 'raw deal' but rather no deal at all. The consummate professional had been caught up in an argument not of his making and had been made a scapegoat for a disagreement between Wilf Wooller and the wider playing staff.

Ossie Wheatley's reflections on the Glamorgan committee at that time help us to understand how matters developed in the way that they did:

'The committee were fine in the sense that they were all cricket supporters but they were not capable of making any difference. The game was moving on and the clubs had to become more organised and professional. The club stayed in the 1940s until about the 1970s.'

It is difficult to decide what Bernard's feelings must have been as he did not confide in anyone. Even Jean, his wife, was not aware of the outcome of these discussions and the impact they had had on him. His brother Peter drew his own conclusions about what happened:

'Bernard would never have stepped out of line. It used to amaze me that he was so pally with Jim Pressdee because Jim was a bit of a hell-raiser. Bernard took the rudeness from Wilf but Pres stood up to him. I always thought there was more to it than what you read in the paper.'

The incident did not remain in the papers beyond the meeting on 11 November, although it remains in the memory of many associated with Glamorgan to this day. The small group of players and officials who were aware of the events at Stradey and their aftermath simply put it down to 'Wilf being Wilf'.

It may be that Wilf's interventions with playing staff were always made with the best interests of the club in mind. His actions at Llanelli and in the weeks after were taken whilst he endured the sting of disappointment on the field, a sting that he felt more keenly than most. However, it must also be said that Wilf sometimes took affront to personal challenges to his authority and responded to them in ways that are difficult to justify. His perception that he needed to reassert his control over playing staff meant he was willing to discipline a dedicated and compliant member of the team who had, to all intents and purposes, done nothing wrong. All of this never affected Bernard's view of Wilf as a great man, but that it did affect him, of that there can be no doubt.

14
Retirement

'We were doing what we loved doing. When that comes to an end, it is very difficult to finish.'

Cricket is a game that is all too often played in the mind. Temperament, character and commitment; all important features of a player's style are, first and foremost, psychological features. It is difficult to say what impact the events at Llanelli and the subsequent disciplinary proceedings had on Bernard. That he felt let down by the club is undoubted. Would that feeling last through the winter and into the following season? There may have been other factors at work that affected Bernard's performance including his natural decline as a cricketer but the facts were unmistakable. 1966 was probably his worst season in first-class cricket. He only scored 659 runs at an average of 18.30 with just two 50s and a top score of 65.

The nadir of that season came in August when Glamorgan played Yorkshire at Scarborough. Bernard was hit whilst batting; as Roger Davis recalls: 'I remember Bernard got hit in the box. He had a nasty hit. He batted on after the injury and batted down the order in the second innings. There was a lot of swelling. When someone gets hit in the box you all laugh, don't you, but we knew it was bad.' Bernard did not play for the last two weeks of the season and needed an operation to remove a damaged testicle. He made a claim under the county's insurance scheme which eventually paid him £198. Typically, he gave the money to his mother-in-law so she could have a 'once in a lifetime' trip to see her son in New Zealand.

This picture of an injured and poorly performing player will have been in the minds of the three men who met as the selection committee on 22 September 1966. Club captain Ossie Wheatley, committee member Ken Prickett and Wilf Wooller. They discussed a year-long contract for Bernard, with Ossie believing that 'he was still a good player and could be useful to the club.' Wooller's view, however, was that Bernard 'had a very limited cricket career now left and that if he was kept on the staff it would prevent younger players gaining

Kent v Glamorgan 1965. Caught Hedges, bowled Euros Lewis. Was Bernard becoming a block to the development of young players? (© Glamorgan CCC)

experience for the future.' It was decided to give Bernard a year's contract but that he was to be considered as a 'reserve experienced player.'

Whether these contract discussions were put to Bernard in this way is unknown. Such situations were often the trigger for a player to quit the club or to quit professional cricket altogether. Bill Alley was to stop playing in 1968 after what he thought was a derisory offer to play just one-day cricket in 1969. He was also told that Somerset were looking to the future and were 'going to introduce some youngsters.' Instead, over the next few years, they recruited Tom Cartwright, Jim Parks and Brian Close, none of whom Alley believed could be described as 'youngsters'. Graham Atkinson, too, left Somerset to play two final seasons at Lancashire. Bernard's fierce loyalty and, perhaps, a little fear of the alternative, shaped his decision to stay.

That phrase, 'reserve experienced player' was viewed by some, rather disparagingly, with a greater emphasis on the word 'reserve' than the word 'experience'. That was not a view shared by new skipper Tony Lewis. Writing in his autobiography *Playing Days*, he recalled the advice he had wanted to give David Gower on England's tour of India in 1984-85. He wanted to tell him about 'Bernard Hedges and the lesson he taught me during my own dreadful first season of captaincy in 1967.'

The Glamorgan players had lost a county game in two days and so were using the match wicket for an extended net on the third day. Tony was struggling for form and had got out half a dozen times in 20 minutes. Bernard, a 'humorous and wise man' came to him and said:

> 'Look skipper, you're wasting your time out here. You may think you are trying, but you are not trying an inch. Now listen. It's harder when a touch player like you loses it, because you can get half way to the pitch of a ball and still work out some sort of shot and get away with it, but I'm telling you, you've got to get your feet going and to do that you've got to be thinking positively. Hit the ball somewhere. Okay, now try to get 12 runs to win the match off the next over.'

Something in those sharp insistent words of advice struck a chord with the future England captain. He achieved the target and further ones that Bernard set; his recollection finished with the statement: 'Two games later I got my first century of the season, 128 not out against Pakistan at Swansea.'

Coaching the captain aside, Bernard did not play for the 1st XI until the beginning of June and then, rather than a Championship match, it was in the friendly against the students of Oxford University at The Parks. The variegated tree-lined background and parkland setting make it one of the most beautiful grounds on which to play first-class cricket. It is also the only ground where admission is still free, and it was here where the 39-year-old Glamorgan veteran walked out to open the innings with Alan Jones.

If Bernard had not realised his career was coming to an end, then he would have done so after reading the match report on that opening day's play. It read more like a cricketing obituary than an analysis of the day's events. Firstly, it had a side swipe at those that might 'carp' about the quality of opposition presented by the Dark Blues. Bernard duly scored a career best 182 but the reporter chose to describe this as the highest score of a 'chequered' career. If that had not thrown a pall of pity over a brilliant performance he continued: 'the true cricket lover would not begrudge Hedges such a break. In his 17 years as a first-class player the Pontypridd man has had more than his fair share of illness and injury.'

The report went on to describe Bernard becoming 'accustomed to the first-class feel and atmosphere' as if he had somehow forgotten how to play and was returning for a swan song. It mentioned how he 'let the strokes flow', how he 'drove' and 'hooked' and how his 'cutting of the orthodox left-arm spinners became little short of monotonous.' All of this came before the final two paragraphs that could have been written for a memorial service. The first addressed itself to that universal subject, the fulfilment of a dream: 'every Welshman present willed him onwards to the first double century of his life.'

The second, invoking the pathos of a piece of natural history writing rather than a sports report, would have drawn a tear from the most reluctant of eyes. It spoke of a man, old and weak, whose body appeared to be fading like the light across the ground:

> 'During the final half hour at the crease, however, he became noticeably tired and finally, with the sun westering behind the great arc of trees, he aimed a weary blow at the bowler and was bowled.'

It was his 21st century in first-class cricket and the first 100 by a Glamorgan batsman that summer. It was also the highest score, at that time, in first-class cricket during 1967. All of that was lost in the funereal prose.

Ron Grimshaw, the sports reporter for the *Oxford Mail*, watched the innings and recorded a poignant moment between Bernard and his longstanding roommate.

> 'After a little over three hours at the crease Hedges reached his century, which included 15 boundaries and was taken a glass of refreshment by his teammate Don Shepherd. After toasting the applauding crowd, he drained the glass – then continued to take apart Oxford's attack.'

Proving that not only Welsh sports journalists imposed a certain agenda on the proceedings, the student magazine, the *Cherwell*, carried the details of the innings in one medium sized sentence before rapidly changing tack and declaring, with all the gravitas at its disposal that 'The burning question is ... are we good enough to beat Cambridge again?' Even the headline of the match report 'Win? – It's up to the schoolsmen' relegated the events at The Parks to a convenient platform for airing other concerns.

As if to confirm the airing of others' concerns, Bernard batted at number 11 in the second innings, giving other players much needed batting practice. He stumbled on through another seven matches before what was to be his final championship game against Worcestershire at New Road. There was to be no grandstand finish as with Hugh Morris in 1997, whose final innings came as the Welsh side clinched the county title at Taunton. Worcestershire were all out in their second innings leaving Glamorgan the unlikely target of 51 in just 16 minutes. Bernard opened with Peter Walker and was caught on the boundary for five in the first over. His 422nd match and 744th innings was over. He would not play first-class cricket again.

As John Arlott wrote in 1949: 'The life of a professional cricketer in the first-class game is possibly 20 years, sometimes more in the case of the great, often less in the case of the average player. Often the period is less dependent upon the prowess of the player than upon the availability of an adequate successor, a circumstance beyond forecast.'

Bernard had completed his 17th season for Glamorgan. There were younger players on the Glamorgan books but the more significant factor was the anticipated opportunity to recruit overseas players. Already a number of counties had one or two on their books and more were to arrive in the coming months. Keith Boyce at Essex, Mike Proctor at Gloucestershire, John Shepherd and Asif Iqbal playing for Kent, Farokh Engineer and Clive Lloyd at Lancashire, Garfield Sobers with Nottinghamshire, Rohan Kanhai and Lance Gibbs playing for Warwickshire, plus Barry Richards and Gordon Greenidge with Hampshire.

In 1967 the Pakistanis had toured the United Kingdom. Bernard did not play against them in the game at St. Helen's but he did attend the after-match party laid on for the players. With his wife and mother-in-law, he was introduced to the young Pakistan batsman, Majid Jahangir Khan. Born in India, he had been educated at Atchison College in Lahore, the Punjab University and Emmanuel College, Cambridge. His father, Dr Jahangir Khan, was the former Indian Test captain and Cambridge Blue, and a friend of Wilf Wooller's from his university days. He spoke the Queen's English and played cricket in a manner that would have delighted Royalty of any country.

Majid duly made an unbeaten 147 at Swansea in an innings which was pivotal to bringing him to Glamorgan. With the ball disappearing to all parts of the St. Helen's ground, his fluent and wristy strokeplay convinced Wilf to approach him about playing for the county in 1968. Bernard's mother-in-law, demonstrating the provincial outlook of many in Wales who had only seen people from the Indian sub-continent on TV, inclined her head towards Majid and asked, whilst nodding encouragement, 'You like it in this country?' His reply would have been polite. How else would a 20-year-old acting as an ambassador of his country respond?

The other overseas player that Glamorgan were making overtures to was Bryan Davis of the West Indies. Crucially for Bernard, the Trinidadian was an opening bat known to play with a zest and freedom which was always regarded highly in the Championship. Bernard's career had effectively ended the previous season. The decision of the selection committee, who met on 12 September 1967, was simply administering the last rites. There was an excited and prolonged discussion about the merits of Majid Khan and Bryan Davis. Bernard's fate was recorded in one sentence: 'It was unanimously agreed that the contracts of Bernard Hedges and W. Slade should be terminated at the end of the current year.'

A week earlier, Don Shepherd had attended the inaugural meeting of the PCA, the cricketers union. The minimum wage, a standard contract and insurance cover for all players were all things that the PCA would negotiate in

Majid Khan arrived at Glamorgan as Bernard was finishing his career. The new era of overseas cricketers was one that he would miss. (© Glamorgan CCC)

the coming years. They were all things that might have benefitted an average county cricketer like Bernard. Here was one aspect of the modern world that he might have welcomed but, alas, it came too late for him.

On the same day as the selection committee brought down the curtain on Bernard's career, the *Western Mail* trumpeted Glamorgan's potential new recruit. 'Brilliant Majid Keen to Join County'. It felt like the future was being welcomed in through the front door on a red carpet whilst the past was being quietly ushered out through the back door. In the same edition of the paper, Wilf Wooller noted that the Club's debt had increased from £10,000 to £14,000. He had told the committee two days previously that 'the 1968 season may well prove to be a season in which the staff should be very much more drastically reduced.'

There were, therefore, three main reasons why Bernard's career had come to an end; a decline in form, the possibility of recruiting better players from overseas and the financial position of the club. Whichever was the more important, all players know that the end is difficult to accept. Roger Davis sums this up:

'We were doing what we loved doing. When that comes to an end, it is very difficult to finish. There is no easy way to tell someone they are not wanted anymore. There will always be a little bit of bitterness about it.'

Ossie Wheatley believes that, 'Retirement is the most traumatic experience.' It was not only Bernard's career that died with the move to recruit overseas players. Wilf, speaking at the general committee meeting on 26 September

The Glamorgan side of 1967. Back Row: Alan Rees, Len Hill, Roger Davis, Peter Walker, Alan Jones, David Evans, Tony Cordle. Front Row: Bernard, Tony Lewis, Don Shepherd, Ossie Wheatley. (© Glamorgan CCC)

1967 would say, 'he would have liked to have seen Glamorgan develop an all Welsh-side, capable of challenging for the Championship, but for the time being this would have to be shelved.' Many now believe that the idea will never be taken down off that shelf. For all the excitement and exuberance that overseas players have brought to Glamorgan over the past 50 years, and there has been much of it, every Welshman must feel a tinge of regret that we have proved unable to produce a home grown side capable of challenging for cricketing honours.

At the finance committee meeting on 23 November 1967, Wilf responded to a question about Bernard's entitlement to redundancy. The Labour government had recently introduced the Redundancy Payments Act and everyone reporting to the Ministry of Labour, as Bernard had done, were advised of their new rights under the act. Wilf's answer was definitive:

'The secretary pointed out that he had gone into this very carefully with the treasurer and Mr Webb, who had knowledge of these matters and it was clear that Bernard Hedges was not being made redundant in the meaning of the Act. He was being retired because of a loss of cricket ability. A replacement was necessary to fill his place.'

Bernard receiving a presentation cheque from committeemen at Glamorgan. He would miss his days as a county cricketer. (© Glamorgan CCC)

The Glamorgan playing squad for 1968 numbered 17 rather than the 21 players they had in 1967. The only two new recruits were Majid and Bryan Davis. The team was changing and, of course, would go on under the captaincy of Tony Lewis to win the county title in 1969 with just 13 players who appeared in the Championship matches.

If the world of cricket was changing, then the world itself was being turned upside down. The Beatles had turned from clean cut boys into hippies in four years while film and TV were increasingly becoming populated with images of sex and violence. This was a world that was increasingly alien to Bernard's traditional tastes. In more ways than one, he was now an outsider, looking back at the life he had inhabited and the world he had lived in and wishing it all could have stayed as it was.

15

Life After Glamorgan

'He took on his career after Glamorgan as seriously as he took on his cricket.'

The winter of 1967 was looking like it could be a bad time in the Hedges household. With Bernard out of contract and having devoted all his adult life to professional sport, it was difficult to know where to go next. His clerical skills learned in National Service were now well out of date. Jean recalls:

'We looked at each other and said "what are we going to do with the rest of our lives?" He was a relatively young man and we had nothing to fall back on. We were very concerned about what he could do at the end of his career. He started applying for positions. One was with a brewery in Neath as a rep to go around getting orders. He went there and the man who was meant to interview him was drunk. He walked out. He was very much against those that over indulged with drink.'

Although cricket could have been seen as the source of all his problems, it turned out to be the source of his salvation. Again, Jean remembers:

'It was a case of who he knew not what he knew. Wynn Jones was a follower of Glamorgan cricket and had met Bernard and other players on a number of occasions. I think he lived in north Wales. Out of the blue the telephone rang. He was on the phone for ages. 'You'll never believe' he said. I've got an interview with Barclays Bank. They're bringing out a card called Barclaycard and they're looking for a rep in west Wales. He was over the moon. He was first interviewed in the Kingsway branch of Barclays Bank. Then he went to London. They offered him the position. He started to work in Swansea; shops, opticians, anywhere he could walk in and show the card. He took it on as seriously as he took on his cricket.'

The Glamorgan committee man who had been caught up in the Llanelli incident, sports shop owner Bill Edwards, had intervened along with another

Bernard with a Glamorgan supporter. His good reputation with supporters and committee-men alike helped him on retirement. (© Glamorgan CCC)

committee man Mr Gwyn Craven, to help secure the job offer. The committee minutes of Thursday 23 November 1967, noted 'with satisfaction the continued assistance given by the club to helping players find suitable employment on retirement.' It had been slightly over two months since Bernard's contract had been terminated. This was quick work indeed. As Tony Lewis relates:

'I knew Bernard had a good education, a good mind so I knew he would succeed. You wouldn't have to worry about Bernard. But there were those who were not so successful.'

Bernard retained his friendship with Bill Edwards right up until he moved away from south Wales. Some of my earliest childhood memories were of visiting Bill's shop near St. Helen's. The door opened with an old fashioned bell like you would have on a grocer's shop or a newsagents. When you ventured inside it was like entering an Aladdin's cave of cricketing riches. Pads, bats and gloves were crowded across the floor and up the walls. The colours and names sounded almost as exciting as the players that we could see using them on our TV screens. Stuart Surridge, Gunn and Moore, Gray-Nicholls and Duncan Fearnley. Behind the counter, which was littered with the debris of the latest sale, were small box drawers filled with cricket balls, bails and numerous club badges.

The Barclaycard was introduced into the UK in 1965. It was a new concept in paying for goods. An early colleague of Bernard's, Brenda, recalls that not everyone was impressed with the new card:

'Credit was a new idea that had been brought over from Bank of America. The reaction in nearly every branch was 'this new-fangled idea will never catch on'.

The life of a rep was tough. The credibility of the card relied upon it being accepted in a wide range of retailers. The reps had to go out on the road, visiting numerous shops, clubs and restaurants and convincing sceptical retailers that there was something in it for them. Bernard's past as a professional cricketer was his unspoken weapon in this task, as his former colleague Brenda Peck explained:

'When he was first on the road as a rep, he made sure he wore his Glamorgan tie because it got him into places. It was a passport into the business. Barclays also employed a couple of other professional cricketers somewhere down south [Brian Langford worked for Barclaycard]. What we were taught to do is telephone for appointments. I never did. I went from shop to shop, up and down high streets but I was unusual. You didn't get women on the road in the 1960s so I could get into businesses. I never took no for an answer. The men used to tease me and say "they only signed to get rid of me", but I said "at least they signed".'

Brenda showed me a appeared in the *Barclaycard Merchant News* of Spring 1969. This was over a year after he had started work for the firm. His pen picture went as follows:

'Former county cricketer, played for Glamorgan for many years. Married with two children. A splendid raconteur with a vast fund of tales from his cricketing and rugby days. Keen philatelist and interior decorator.' Counsel for the defence would have taken issue with several elements of that profile. Bernard had his stories and as we grew up we got to hear a few of them but he would never have described himself as a raconteur. Words were a highly regarded currency with Bernard, not to be shared easily or without purpose. He must have raised a smile at the description of himself as a keen interior decorator, particularly remembering the incident during the winter of 1961 when he put his hands through a plate glass window after painting it the previous day, nearly destroying his cricket career in the process. As for philately, if he was keen on it he kept it hidden from his wife and children. We never saw him with any first-day covers or hovering over the kitchen table with a magnifying glass, searching for a Penny Black or other rare offering. For Barclaycard, he was a marketable property and, like many sportsmen in south Wales, his sporting profile gave him the opportunity to cash in on his sporting past. Having a reasonably well known face amongst the south Wales public was a key attribute for his new career.

Brenda showed me a photograph of the Barclaycard team at a training event in Wimbledon taken in 1968. There are 60 or 70 men and only two women. Brenda was the only female sales rep in the country. The other

Bernard Hedges. Former county cricketer — played for Glamorgan for many years. Married, with two children. A splendid raconteur with a vast fund of tales from his cricketing and rugby days. Keen philatelist and interior decorator.

The Barclaycard newsletter of Spring 1949. The description of Bernard was somewhat wide of the mark. (Courtesy of Stephen Hedges)

woman in the photograph was a secretary whom they had asked to be in the photo not to let Brenda stick out like an extremely sore thumb. She was used to being patronised and took it all in her stride. Many today would find some of her treatment less then appropriate. Her male colleagues were not averse to using her femininity against her, especially as she was more than a match for them in the business: 'The men in the office started a campaign titled 'Get Brenda Ever So Slightly Pregnant' to get her out of the way. When I was getting remarried they sent me a letter saying the GBESSP group has now ceased to operate.'

All of this was done in a jovial way and much of it was inspired by Wynn Jones, the man who had been instrumental in getting Bernard the job. He is described in that same *Merchant* newsletter in 1969 as 'An ebullient Welshman who sets a very fast pace, indispensable at parties. Bi-lingual, Mr Jones firmly believes in calling a spade a *rhaw*.'

Cricket was no longer his living but like many ex-county cricketers, Bernard found that his services were still much in demand. League clubs in south Wales were always looking for older experienced players that could give their club a lift. Bernard surprised everyone at Ynysygerwn Cricket Club when he accepted their offer to come and play for them for the 1968 season. They were a small club wallowing in the lower reaches of the second division of the South Wales Cricket Association. Bernard was to play for the club for two seasons, 1968 and 1969. He played 34 games for them in total, scoring 1,001 runs at 38.5. His highest score was 98 with eight 50s. He also took 16 wickets at 18.4 each. Perhaps far more important than these figures was the impact he made on the club and one of their most talented players, Lawrence Williams.

Lawrence had been born in Tonna in 1946 and attended Neath Grammar School, following in the footsteps of Tony Lewis. He made his first-class debut in the Championship winning year of 1969, taking 56 wickets with his fast-medium seamers. Known as the 'Tonna Terror' he became a regular part of the Glamorgan attack during the early 1970s and was capped in 1971 after taking a club record of 33 wickets in a Sunday League season. Long before all of this, Lawrence remembered his first outings with Glamorgan and his hesitancy about committing to the life of a county cricketer:

'I started work when I was 16. I worked in the rates section of the council. At the end of the year as the new boy I carried the bags of money from the council building down to the bank. I was carrying a quarter of a million pounds down to that bank. I played for Glamorgan's 2nd XI in 1964. My first wicket was Ken Barrington who was turning out for the Seconds on his return after injury. In 1965, we won the 2nd XI Championship. We had a little button on our jackets. Phil Clift approached my father about me playing for Glamorgan but I had a job for life in the council.'

Lawrence Williams. It was Bernard who helped make up his mind to be a professional cricketer. (© Glamorgan CCC)

At the same selection committee meeting that terminated Bernard's contract with the county, the following minute was recorded:

'Phil Clift stated that Lawrence Williams, who worked in Neath, might be considered as a replacement fast bowler. Whether or not he would be regularly available would remain to be seen, but he had certainly bowled well in the 2nd XI. The committee decided to keep an eye on this fast bowler.'

Lawrence remembered encountering Bernard at the indoor school at Neath where Ynys had a regular net. 'Run to like a rabbit' he remembers him calling out to the players as they moved between bowling and batting in the nets. He also recalled the impact that Bernard had on Ynysygerwn CC: 'Ynys were in the second or third division. By 1973 they went to the first division and have stayed there ever since. He taught us how to stay at the wicket and accumulate runs. He put the light into the lads. He made us into a much better side. We got to Lord's twice.' (the appearances at Lord's were in the Samuel Whitbread National Village Cup Competition). The club's first visit to Lord's took place in the summer of 1979. Labelled the Welsh 'super village' they lost to the Yorkshire club East Bierley. It was the same weekend that Glamorgan experienced one of their most humiliating defeats, being bowled out for 42 by Derbyshire in a John Player Sunday League match at St. Helen's.

The club captain at Ynys moved aside for Bernard. As club professional, he was paid every time he played. He used his match fee to buy the players on both sides a drink in the bar after the match. He made a massive impact on the club, an impact that was honoured when they made him an honorary life member. For Lawrence, he was the ultimate arbiter for his decision to accept terms with Glamorgan. Bernard would have had every reason to be downbeat about Lawrence's prospects as a county professional. It was less than 12 months since he had been let go. That makes his clear and unequivocal advice to Lawrence to 'give it a go' all the more impressive. 'He was my final decider about joining Glamorgan', the bowler told me.

It was probably one of the best decisions Lawrence ever made. He picked up a Championship winners medal and his own treasure trove of stories. He remembered arriving for a game against Somerset where Tom Cartwright was the coach. Tom asked him to watch a young prospect he had to see if he could improve his action. The youngster 'was bowling everything down the leg side with his front chest on. I encouraged him to get more side on.' The youngster's name was Ian Botham.

Bernard's traditional outlook on all things was taken lightly by the other members of the team. He appeared naïve and rather surprised at some of the more hedonistic aspects of club cricket. There was one member of the team who was a particularly capable drinker. 'No common sense but he could drink', remembers Lawrence. Bernard would monitor his drinking and on one occasion asked, incredulously, 'You know you've drunk 42 pints today, don't you?' On a club tour to Ireland, Bernard was charged with organising an attempt on the world record for the quickest time to drink a pint of Guinness. Showing all the preparation and thoroughness of the McWhirter twins, Bernard lined up the pints and recorded each attempt using a stop watch. Lawrence and the other members of that Ynysygerwn team roared with laughter recalling the scene.

Jean's recollection says a great deal about Bernard's commitment to playing and being part of this village club. 'He loved playing for Ynysygerwn.'

There were also other opportunities to play cricket against old foes from the county game. Charity and benefit games were a familiar part of life as a county cricketer with every Sunday during the season being taken up with appearing for scratch teams or playing with a Glamorgan IX. One such opportunity came at the end of the 1968 season when Harry Secombe hosted a game at Sutton CC in Surrey. Harry Secombe's XI comprised Ken Barrington, Alec Bedser, Eric Bedser, Roy Castle, David Evans, Jeff Jones, Richard Mills, the West End theatre producer, Harry himself, Don Shepherd and Bernard. The 12th man was the Welsh golfer Brian Huggett. As a thank-you for playing, Harry arranged for some complimentary tickets for the Barclaycard staff and Bernard to see his new musical *The Four Musketeers*. Brenda was impressed. 'It was the only time I have ever been in a box at a theatre.' There were other games and other opportunities for his Barclaycard colleagues to be impressed with his contacts. 'Bernard took us down to Worcestershire and we ended up at Basil D'Olivera's house.'

Phil Kempton, who was at one time captain and secretary of the Barclaycard cricket team, remembered several matches where Bernard turned out for his employers, including one at the sports ground in Ealing where he got 'quite a number of runs'. He remembered both Brian Langford and Robin Hobbs guesting in these games. There was an annual game between Barclaycard and their main credit card rivals Access. There was a great deal that rested on the game and when the opposition were late turning up one year Phil was panicking. 'I thought my career had gone up in smoke.' After this match, he recalled that competitiveness got the better of the Access management when they turned up with many of the Essex county professionals.

Back in Wales in 1969, there was more than sport to distract

harry secombe

46 st. james's place,
london, s.w.1
18th December 1968.

Dear Bernard

Thank you so much for your letter. I have pleasure in enclosing herewith a ticket for box CC for the evening of Wednesday January 8th. This box will seat four as you requested.

I hope you and your colleagues enjoy the show. I shall look forward to seeing you after the show if you would care to come to the stage door.

Yours ays!

Harry

Bernard Hedges Esq.

The letter from Harry Secombe with some complimentary tickets to see his show in the West End. (Courtesy of Stephen Hedges) the general public from their daily lives. The Queen's eldest son, Charles, was to be invested as Prince of Wales at the beginning of July at Caernarfon Castle. The *Rhyl and Prestatyn Gazette*, felt the investiture would assist the Welsh in discovering a 'new sense of Nationhood'. One of the events organised to celebrate the occasion was a cricket match between a Wales XI and the International Cavaliers, who staged regular exhibition games in the 1960s featuring Test and county stars in their line-ups. This would be the first time a Welsh national team would have played against any opposition and would provide a great platform for the newly formed Welsh Cricket Association.

Bernard was invited to captain the side and took to the field at the home of Colwyn Bay CC in Rhos-on-Sea. In the International Cavaliers side that day were Graeme Pollock, Lawrence Rowe, Saeed Ahmed, Godfrey Evans, Fred Trueman and Hallam Moseley. They were captained by Ted Dexter. When I spoke to Alan Jones, he recalled playing for an Australian XI against a touring South African side in 1963. The recollection was more poignant as it was in the days after we had all received the sad news of Richie Benaud's death. Alan was struck by Benaud's pithy comment, 'that boy can play', when summarising the young Pollock's ability. Alan continued, 'Graeme played in the Rest of the World match I played in at Lord's,' said Alan. 'He played a lot for the International Cavaliers because South Africa were not playing Test cricket. We never saw the best of him just like we never saw the best of Mike Procter or Barry Richards.'

Pollock hit a barnstorming 161 in only 88 minutes that afternoon in Colwyn Bay with four sixes and 24 fours. Although outshone with this kind of scoring, Bernard still made a hundred, getting 110 and sharing a third wicket stand of 126 with Huw Jenkins of Swansea. All the Welsh players were presented with a special cap and the crowd of 2,500 was the second largest the Cavaliers had drawn that summer. The cap ended up in the toy cupboard at home alongside the cap he had worn when he made his Gillette Cup century. As boys, we used them as props in our made-up games of cricketing fantasy. It never occurred to us to wonder where the baggy green with the embroidered Welsh dragon and the brightly coloured hooped cap had come from. Dad never told us.

In 1972, it was Alan Jones' benefit year. Bernard was asked to play in a benefit match for him and took along his two sons, aged 12 and eight years old. We were attracted not by the prospect of a free pre-match lunch or of watching our father or Alan play. The main attraction at the Hoover's sports ground in Merthyr Tydfil was Welsh rugby star, Barry John. Alan recalls:

'Barry had just come back from the Lions Tour and he played quite a few games for me. He played at Clydach and he played at Hoover's.

He's from Cefneithin, I used to know him before he was famous. Eifion, my brother, used to play against him, Eifion for Pontarddulais and Barry for Cefneithin before he went to join Llanelli. He was a good cricketer.'

We sat down to a ham salad lunch somewhere in the bowels of the building. I never looked at my plate once. I stared across the table at this man who was, in the eyes of many Welshmen, the nearest thing we had to the footballing superstars that seemed to dominate our TV screens. The game that day is long forgotten in my mind, even Barry's contribution to it. I do, however, remember the improvised goalmouth we set up on the outfield and the penalty taking session me and the phalanx of little kids had with the great man at the end of the game. It was with some regret that I realised, much later, that this was the year that Barry had retired from rugby, stating that living with his fame was like 'living in a goldfish bowl.' With my straw coloured hair I must have looked, for all the world, like a tiny little goldfish, gaping wide eyed and open-mouthed at him form across that lunch table at the Hoover factory ground.

In 1972 the Hedges family moved to Somerset, where Bernard had gained promotion after five years on the road with Barclaycard. We bought a detached house in the village of North Petherton. It was some indication of how far Bernard had come in his lifetime. His early years had been spent in the close knit terraced and council housing of Pontypridd. His first house in Swansea was bought with the help of Glamorgan, as Jean recalls:

'We were paying rent for two years from 1957 to 1959. I believe Bill Edwards from the sports shop was on the committee and brought it up that Bernard Hedges wanted to borrow the money to buy a house. I think he was the first to borrow money to buy a property. I met a girl who I was friendly with in my dancing days. She said there was a lovely house going next to her. I couldn't wait for Bernard to come home that night. "How much is is?" he asked. I said "£3,000." So we made arrangements, and with the club's permission, to pay the whole sum. I don't know how it was repaid. Bill would come on a regular basis to the house to see Bernard.'

The loan from the county was £2,700 at 1% for 15 years. A year after Bernard's loan, in 1960, the finance and general purposes committee placed conditions on any further loans to players including a ceiling of £2,000, loans to be given to capped players only and repayment of any outstanding amount from a players' benefit or testimonial. When Don Shepherd was presented

Wimmerfield Crescent, Killay, Swansea. Bernard's first house, bought with the help of Glamorgan CCC. (© Mrs M.J. Hedges)

with his benefit cheque in January 1961, the outstanding amount of his loan of £987 7s 6d was recovered from the balance due.

The semi-detached house that Bernard and Jean bought was in the Swansea suburb of Killay. His neighbours in Pontypridd would have been miners, in the main. His neighbour in Wimmerfield Crescent was the trade union official Roy Evans. As deputy leader of the ISTC, Roy led steelworkers during their national strike in the 1980s. He became General Secretary of the union from 1985 to 1993 and was awarded an OBE for his services to trade unionism. It was while living in Killay that Bernard also bought his first car, a Morris Marina which he managed to crash into the wall on the day he bought it. He was taking Jean up to meet David from school.

The house in North Petherton had four bedrooms, surrounded by garden on all sides with a secluded patch hidden inside a ten foot high garden wall. The walls of the house provided excellent opportunities to play, usually tennis, mimicking the top players of the day, usually Bjorn Borg. Inside the walls, I would practise my cricket, throwing the ball up to myself and then executing a limited range of front foot strokes. As I was a right-handed batsman, I had to hold the ball and throw it up with my left or top hand. This became a convenient excuse as my batting developed; I played with far too much bottom hand and got out playing across the line. I was eternally frustrated that Dad did not seem to want to intervene in my cricketing development. He never really gave me any coaching. I saw Gary Palmer being given all the encouragement by his father Ken as well as receiving coaching from John Jameson at the local independent school in Taunton and I wanted the same. It never came. I appeared in the Somerset Boys Football Association Cup final two years in a row (1975 and 1976). Dad did not come to either final. My only recollection of him watching me play is of him screaming 'Get back! Get back!' as I ventured forward on the right side of midfield. Ossie Wheatley's comment on hearing this was, 'That is absolutely the professional in him. Don't let them in. You can score later but don't let them in.' It felt as if he could only offer criticism of the way I played. Perhaps that is why he kept his distance from both my brother and me in all our endeavours. It was as if he could not trust himself to say the right thing so he kept himself out of it.

A sportsman who was reluctant to engage with his sons sporting development was not the only contradiction that Bernard demonstrated. On appearance, he was quite a serious man who would not tolerate flippancy and yet, in private, he was the most enthusiastic lover of TV situation comedy. *Til Death Us Do Part*, *Steptoe and Son*, *The Likely Lads*, *Butterflies*, *The Liver Birds*, *The Good Life*, *Porridge*, *Dad's Army*, *Open All Hours*, *Are You Being Served*, *Rising Damp*, *The Fall and Rise of Reginald Perrin*, *It Ain't Half Hot Mum* and *The Last of the Summer Wine* all paraded their humour through our living room along with comedy duos *The Two Ronnies* plus *Morecambe and Wise*. There was something in all of this that was gently reassuring. Many of the comedy programmes we watched were either set in a time or had characters who reminded him of the age that was increasingly disappearing from sight. It was an age when traditional values of family and community were important; when even those who had challenging lifestyles or personalities still had a strong moral code. Ossie Wheatley had been acutely aware of that code whilst he had played with Bernard:

> 'A lot of professional cricketers led a very formal life. They were brought up in a hierarchical society and they were very formal people. They dressed immaculately, played perfectly, their manners were impeccable and that was part of the image of the sport. They were local celebrities, everyone knew them in the village and the town, and they behaved as such.'

Even the informality of TV comedy did not shift this strong sense that Bernard had of doing the right thing and behaving in the right way. He was no longer in the public eye but continued to live as if he did. The combination of comedy and tradition were found most strongly for Bernard in the Welsh entertainer Max Boyce. We had his albums *Live at Treorchy* and *We All Had Doctors Papers* and were introduced to his warm, rugby-inspired comedy and his folk ballads about life in the valleys. As a Welsh exile, perhaps Bernard was more prone to idealizing his Welsh heritage. For me, being Welsh was almost synonymous with playing rugby and I wore my heritage like a badge of pride throughout my secondary school years in Somerset, a fact made much easier by the fact that the Welsh team was experiencing an unprecedented era of success. Max's songs *Duw it's Hard* and *Rhondda Grey* were a reminder of the Wales of the valleys, of Pontypridd and Rhydyfelin. Max also sang in Welsh and Bernard, though not a Welsh speaker, would give a gentle rendition of *Ar Lan y Môr* more often than he would sing *Hymns and Arias* or *Sospan Fach*.

That familiar mix of rugby and comedy led Bernard to make one of his few errors as a parent. In 1978, BBC Wales produced a film entitled *Grand Slam*. It was the story of four men, members of a Welsh rugby union club, who fly to Paris as part of a weekend outing to see Wales play France in the Five Nations Championship match with a Grand Slam at stake. Billed as a comedy, Bernard thought he was on safe ground allowing his 14-year-old son (me) to watch it. By the end of the film, the rather prudish father had endured the embarrassment of seeing me exposed to homosexuality, striptease, prostitution and sexual conquest. It was a very funny TV play and in later years, Bernard would echo one of the more memorable lines delivered by camp boutique owner Maldwyn Pugh. "Go the whole hog, Mog!" he would say whenever a situation seemed to justify it. On the night, there was little he felt able to repeat as I went to bed with a whole new understanding of the term Grand Slam and the widest grin any 14-year-old had ever had!

There were other examples of his attempts to protect us from the evils of the modern world. He seemed to have a particular concern about hair. Like Delilah, but for very different reasons, he believed the less of it there was the better. His own was swept back with the aid of Vitalis, giving it a dark sheen and exposing his forehead and temples. If it was not for the kindness and soft lines of his face he would have made a passable stand-in for any Dracula film. His style had not changed, even through his youth. He always took us to those old fashioned barbers that seem to exist in fewer and fewer numbers these days. First, we went to Bryn's in Killay. He had one of those bobbing birds that would bend back and forth in front of you like a metronome, acting as a partial distraction as Bryn massacred your hair with scissors, comb and clippers. In North Petherton, we were sent to Sid's. His shop was about as welcoming as a mortuary, the faded cardboard boxes selling contraceptives hidden away in the corner suggested that the question 'something for the weekend sir?' had not crossed his lips for many years. With the look of an aging Stalin and breath that smelt of stale beer it may well have been a question that he had not asked himself for longer than that. There was no sense of creating something to suit the customer with Sid; one style fitted all. Even Bernard ended up calling him 'Sid Vicious'.

Bernard remembered, with fondness, the drill sergeant during National Service walking behind recruits on parade. 'Am I hurting you laddy? Well I should be, because I'm standing on your BLOODY hair! Get it cut!' The only thing I ever remember Dad saying about George Best was 'get your haircut!' One of his favourite jokes around that time was of the man who walked into a barbers and asked to look like George Best. When the barber had finished cutting his hair, he stood back to admire the short back and sides he had delivered. 'That's not what George Best looks like!' cried the man. 'It's what he would look like if he came in here,' replied the barber.

Rugby commentary was another area where he applied strict rules. Bernard hated the voice and the patter of Scottish commentator and 'voice of rugby' Bill McClaren. All the Five Nations rugby games were on terrestrial TV at that time with Bill commentating on most. Dad would turn the volume right down so that not only did we lose the commentary, we lost all of the atmosphere of the stadium as well. The championship winning Welsh team of the 1970s were all silent movie stars in our house, jinking, swerving and charging to success as we added our own sound. I had always thought that this aversion was solely a result of Bill McClaren. After all, even as a youngster I found his 'they'll be singing down in Stradey' or 'he's a wee man but he's got one helluva kick on him' a little annoying. My mum assured me, however, that in retirement, turning down the sound became habitual. There was something in the art of commentary that left Bernard cold. I found this out to my cost when, after attending a match between Scarlets and the Ospreys, I returned to Swansea with a gift. It was a book about Welsh rugby written by Eddie Butler. He had been promoting the book in the club shop and I got a signed copy personalised to Dad. 'Bloody Eddie Butler!' he muttered as I passed him the book. I do not think there was anything personal in this. It was commentary that Dad could not respond to. Adornment to any game was not necessary for him. He would turn down the volume on Bill Mclaren's rugby commentary and many others that came after. The game was enough, for him. After his death, I came across several books that had been sent to him. One was Tony Lewis' *History of the MCC* signed by Tony himself. Another was a copy of *The Flame Still Burns*, the biography of Tom Cartwright with a note from his widow Joan. 'He'd have wanted you to have this' it said. I do not know for sure if either book was ever read.

Tom Cartwright was a regular visitor to Bernard's home in Somerset. The two got on well and talked about many of the issues in the game. Tom tried to persuade Bernard to get more involved in the administrative side of the game without success. (© Glamorgan CCC)

Tom Cartwright was sometimes a visitor to our house in Somerset. He had started coaching the Somerset team in the autumn of 1972. We moved to the West Country the following summer. I remember the tall man who seemed to carry the wisdom of the world just in his gait having informal chats with Dad in the kitchen or the living room. Occasionally, Dad would take us to the County Ground at Taunton. I remember being in the Glamorgan dressing room with Graham Burgess, the Somerset player, catching up with old friends. It may have been then that Dad was given a Slazenger bat by Lawrence Williams. My brother and I were to make much use of it, although at the time it was too big for me. Dad had told us, with a smile on his face, that Lawrence would not have any need of it anyway. It was a joke lost on me at the time but I am sure would make sense to Lawrence, whose highest score in first-class cricket was 37.

If I had wanted confirmation of Dad the competitor, it came at a strange venue; the Annual North Petherton Horticultural Show and Sports Gala. It was held at the village primary school and after looking at the prize marrows and carrots Dad and I wandered outside to the sports field. After I had won the three legged race with a friend, the schedule moved ever forwards to the last few races, one of which was the over-40s 60 metre sprint. I persuaded Dad to take part and watched from a distance as he was shepherded to the start line with about five other dads. As if on purpose, he missed the starting gun, gazing around and giving all his competitors a two to three yard start. Then I watched in awe as his body seemed to rediscover what it had been used to doing in the first half of his life. With his head perfectly still, arms pumping like little pistons, he moved through the field before breaking the tape a clear yard in front of the second placed dad. When I saw the photograph of him sprinting in his National Service days I understood where that little sprint had come from. He was an athlete and a competitor and he still enjoyed experiencing competition and winning. We both marched proudly into the kitchen at home, presenting our certificates to my mother.

The young Hugh Morris crossed Bernard's path in 1982. They both appeared in the Glamorgan Past and Present XI against an Old England XI at St. Helen's. The teams were:

Glamorgan: Majid Khan, Geoff Ellis, Tony Lewis, Hugh Morris, Bernard Hedges, Greg Thomas, Eifion Jones, Tom Cartwright, Don Shepherd, Jim Pressdee, Jeff Jones.

England: John Jameson, Arthur Milton, John Edrich, Basil d'Oliveira, Tom Graveney, Roy Swetman, Richard Hutton, Fred Trueman, Robin Hobbs, John Mortimore, Harold Rhodes.

Hugh was named the 'Star Attraction' as the game raised £1,000 for the Welsh Schools Cricket Association. The reporter indulged in the briefest of descriptions of the cameo performances on the day. John Jameson was 'hitting forcibly', Arthur Milton was 'neat and tidy', Tom Graveney was 'stylish' and Basil d'Oliveira hit a 'splendid unbeaten 35, hoisting the leg breaks of Tony Lewis for two sixes in an over.' Geoff Ellis 'looked good enough to be recalled to first XI duty' and Bernard 'briefly revived memories of his heyday with a lovely characteristic chipped hook.' Showing the magnanimity of the old, the senior players selected the 18-year-old Hugh as man-of-the-match. He had 'swooped to make stinging stops' and had 'attracted attention with his unshakeable confidence, poise and technique'.

By the early 1980s, Bernard had received his final promotion with Barclaycard. We were now living near Camberley in Surrey with Dad now the area manager for the South East Area office of Barclaycard based in Woking. Covering London, the post had its perks. Mum and Dad were guests at an invitation-only event to see the newly refurbished British Airways Concorde. However, the early 1980s was also the time when all sales-focussed businesses were experiencing the impact of Thatcherism and the 'loads a' money' culture. It did not always mean a meritocracy but rather those that could 'talk the talk' got on, as Brenda recalls:

'Barclaycard closed all the sales offices and they had monthly team meetings. The teams changed, the age of them went down. It was a very competitive atmosphere. One boss used to tell new staff if they had any issues to 'ask Brenda'. He'd never been on the road even though he was promoted to area sales manager.'

It was not an atmosphere that sat well with the noble and straightforward Bernard. He could feel the young Turks biting at his heels and it would not be long before he jumped at the chance of taking retirement. For cricket, he showed he was more than willing to take the plunge and, at the age of 55, joined Eversley CC along with me in 1982. The club had a beautiful little ground next to the main road between Reading and Camberley. Cars would often pull off the road so their occupants could watch a few overs and a Sunday crowd would regularly top 50 or more. For Bernard, it was a chance to feel a bat in his hand once again. All those who saw him bat that season reflected on the time he had to play the ball and the positivity of his stroke making. Much of this was off the front foot emphasising the time he had at this level of cricket, to play the ball. Peter, his brother, had seen that quality that set him apart from club players back in the days after his retirement from county cricket.

> 'When he was finished and played with Ynysygerwn against 'Ponty', he was just a class player. You could see that he'd been a cricketer. So quick and so enthusiastic about the game.'

He surprised everyone by the athleticism he displayed for a man in his 50s. Fielding on the boundary in one game, he made ground to his right before reaching down to almost touch the grass to take a catch. You would have thought it was the act of a 20-year-old apart from the agonising grunt he made as his hands grasped the ball. The other Eversley players were not sure whether to applaud or run for a stretcher! In another game, two naïve batsmen decided to take on what they thought was an old man's arm. Rather than the laboured parabolic arc usually associated with village cricket out fielding they got a low fast arrow of a return that left one of them stranded yards from safety. For a few brief overs, at a ground whose name escapes me, it was Hedges and Hedges who were the Eversley batsmen. The overwhelming memory I have of the partnership was me saying to myself over and over again, 'For Christ's sake don't run him out.' That message blocked out anything else, including my ability to play any run-scoring strokes. I stayed for a while and watched him manoeuvre the ball around. It all looked so easy. For many of us, batting is 80% perspiration and 20% prayer. For a player like Dad, even in his twilight, there was less prayer and more purpose.

Andrew Renshaw, current President of the Eversley Club was captain of the 2nd XI in 1982. He wrote, with warmth and affection, in the club's history book, published to celebrate its bi-centenary in 1987:

> 'Former professional Bernard Hedges added to his 17,000 runs for Glamorgan a further few 50s when he turned out for the Sunday 2nd XI in recent years. Totally unselfish in his approach, he would ask his captain on reaching his half-century whether he should get out to allow

others a chance to bat, only to be told: 'No, Bernard, it's better that you score the runs.' And for those lucky to play alongside him, it was.'

Bernard was made President of the club and for several years after returning to Wales made that journey down the M4 to attend the club's annual general meeting.

The September after we moved to Camberley, Dad took me to Lord's for what was to be the last Gillette Cup final. I am not sure I was aware of the historical significance of the day. I was certainly not that aware that the competition had given Dad one of his best days in a Glamorgan jumper. 'Lord's was bathed in sunshine', was Gordon Ross' opening description of the final and it certainly was. We took the brief walk from St. John's Wood tube station and settled ourselves into our seats in what is now the Compton Stand. Surrey were batting and Dad reliably informed me that he had coached Graham Roope.

At lunch, with Surrey struggling to make headway against a Middlesex attack that comprised Wayne Daniel, Mike Selvey, John Emburey and Vincent Van der Bijl, we went for a walk around the ground. At the back of the old pavilion amidst the crowds of fans, we bumped into Tony Lewis. He was then broadcasting for the BBC and after an enthusiastic welcome he invited Dad and me to follow him up into the press box. This was the old box that clung to the roof of the Warner stand looking a like an elongated glass eye. Climbing the steep narrow staircase felt like ascending into heaven and when we arrived, it was indeed the cricketing Gods that greeted us. Fred Trueman and Geoffrey Boycott were there and we watched some of the afternoon's play through the huge windows, the colours of the day seeming somehow intensified through the plate glass. The strongest memory I have is of the steely blue colour

Bernard and Jean in front of his plaque in the Rhondda Cynon Taff Sporting Hall of Fame. (© Mrs M.J. Hedges)

of Boycott's eyes. Middlesex won the game comfortably with Mike Brearley winning the man-of-the-match award for an unbeaten 96. I had witnessed the end of an era. Dad had not only been a witness but an early participant in what Gordon Ross summed up as, 'an historical landmark in the folklore of cricket.'

Bernard retired in 1987 on his 60th birthday and within months, he had moved back to Swansea with Jean and Jean's mother who had lived with the family for some years. The quiet routines which he had established way back in Wimmerfield Crescent, Killay, now became the everyday reasons to keep going. He had washed the car every Sunday from as far back as I could remember. It had become as ritualistic to him as going to church was when he was a child. A proper lathered up sponge first, then a rinse with several buckets of clean water, mats taken out of the car, a proper clean inside and then drying with a chamoix leather. It was longer than any sermon to complete and he would sing quietly as he did it. Bernard also followed the maxim of not discussing either politics and religion to the letter by not voting in any general or local election or attending church. There was never a great discussion about these things and he never made an issue out of either. The day to day politeness and civility of being human seemed enough for him. Being a good person did not mean fighting for a better society or praying for one.

A withdrawal from these public areas of life may also have been at the heart of Bernard's reluctance to re-engage with cricket. Tony Lewis recalls: 'I did talk to Bernard when I was chairman about improving our scouting arrangements. He decided against it after giving it some consideration.' Tony

Bernard celebrating Christmas with the author and grandchildren Tom, Ellis and Lewis. He always enjoyed the company of his family. (© Hedges family)

Bernard and grandson Lewis both wearing his county cap. Note, Bernard is still standing with hands clasped behind his back, as if he is about to take to the field after the photo call. (© Hedges family)

also offered an explanation of why Bernard may have felt reluctant to re-engage with old teammates in the ex-players association. It summed up the contradictions of many professional sportsmen. The bitter-sweet of their memories:

'It's a love-hate relationship. It's not that you want to go back and do better. You do not want to see those players who you played with. It's like being in an orchestra where you've sat next to the same violinist for the last 40 years and you hope you'll never hear him play again.'

Bernard welcomed the opportunity to talk about the game but he did not seek out opportunities to do so. There were regular meetings with Tom Cartwright who had a coaching role for Welsh cricket and now lived in Neath. Tom encouraged Bernard to take a more active role but all offers were politely declined.

In the autumn of 2004, aged 76, Bernard was one of a number of Welsh sportsmen and women who were honoured by Rhondda Cynon Taff Council when they were inducted into the authority's Sporting Hall of Fame. The Hall was located at Hawthorn Leisure Centre in Rhydyfelin, close to the house where Bernard spent his childhood. The recipients reflected the changing nature of sport in the modern era with a wide range of sporting disciplines and able and disabled athletes represented. Local Mayor Albie Davies inaugurated the Hall of Fame by saying: 'The people honoured today set standards of sporting excellence that will act as an inspiration for generations to follow.' Of the 28 people honoured, 15 sportsmen and women were given illustrated stories. They were: rugby players Bleddyn Williams, Tom David, Paul John, Neil Jenkins, Russell Robbins, Cliff Jones and Glyn Davies, boxers Glenn Moody and Freddie Welsh, swimmers Jenny James and David Roberts, badminton player Kelly Morgan, powerlifter Emma Brown, karate expert Tracey Taylor, and Bernard.

Jenny James was a long distance swimmer who was the first Welsh person to swim the English Channel. In the year Bernard was making his debut for Glamorgan and reaching the back pages of the *Western Mail*, Jenny was hitting the front page of the *Pontypridd Observer* by becoming the first woman to swim the Bristol Channel both ways. She gathered at the opening ceremony with some of the other inductees. We got to speak with Tom David who told us, for what must have been the umpteenth time, how he had fooled a gullible supporter into thinking that the fabulous try the Barbarians had scored against the All Blacks in 1973 had been practised on the training field. It was a day of celebration, a day to reflect in the warm thanks of a local community, a day for meeting old friends and reminiscing. Though it would be another ten years before his death, this was the last formal occasion at which Bernard would have the chance to mingle with old friends and recall the good old days

16

The Amateur Professional

'It was an absolute privilege to have met the cricketer, but an even bigger privilege and an honour to have met Bernard the man.'

'If you could play and had the opportunity to play, why wouldn't you play? What else would you rather do? Where else would you rather be?' This is sports journalist Gary Imlach imitating, in prose, the voice of his father Stewart, Scottish footballer of the 1950s and '60s. The world could well have been spoken by a thousand different footballers, rugby players or cricketers of that era. They were words that summed up a simple view of what sport was all about without embellishment or import. It was a point of view, in cricket, that united almost everyone from the greatest of exalted amateurs to the toughest of hard-nosed professionals. They were words that explain why Bernard was able to rank an innings made against psychiatric patients alongside any he had made against teams bristling with cricketing talent. It also explains why he could slowly drift away from the game he loved whilst never losing touch with the 'simple routine joy of playing'. Bernard would never have considered his place in the history of his county nor wondered about how all that mattered in the history of the game he played for a living. Being paid to play was a privilege and playing was all that mattered.

It seems contradictory that although he always professed to care little about the fortunes of Glamorgan or the England team he always knew their position in the Championship or what the state of play in the latest Test was. In the last few months of his life, in what I had come to appreciate was his perfunctory style, he told me that he thought Australian fast bowler Mitchell Johnson was a 'chucker'. It was not a theory I heard given any credence on the TV or radio but it proved that Bernard still cared about the game, even though he may not have cared about his own place in the history of it. There was no contradiction here; just a mild compulsion that all the players I have met seem to have. It is a compulsion that draws them back to seeking to understand the game that they played and loved playing so much. It is a compulsion that began, for most of them, as soon as they picked up a bat or bowled a ball.

Bernard's raw talent, his 'gift', as Maurice Stallworthy put it, was harnessed and honed during his school years. The County School in Pontypridd and the wider Grammar School set up in south Wales acted as the university for his sporting talent, giving him direction and challenging him to be the best that he could be. Rugby was introduced into the grammar schools after the First World War as it was deemed better than football at equipping boys with the physical and moral qualities that would benefit them in later life. Self-improvement and self-reliance along with aspiration were qualities that Bernard knew well from his father who had learnt them, in turn, from the working men's institute. These qualities were offered to the many thousands of boys who moved through the grammar school system, even those for whom sport was not a major interest. Alun Richards, in his autobiography, was acutely aware of the sporting dimension of the County School when he talked about the 'tiers of performance, 2nd XVs, form teams, club and cadet teams, an infrastructure of groups whose buzzing enthusiasms formed cadres from which the progress to stardom and its concomitant glories began.'

These 'cadres of sporting talent' delivered a rich source of recruits for Glamorgan. A number of players in their ranks during the 1950s and '60s came from this source including Bernard, Don Shepherd, David Evans and Tony Lewis. Ossie Wheatley believes that, 'When I was at Cambridge more than half the people came from grammar schools, and they had all come through the system with excellent teachers. Wales was well equipped with these teachers.' Despite the efforts of many to replicate this infrastructure, its demise has adversely affected the development of home-grown cricketing talent.

A Glamorgan batsman before the 1970s had to contend with impediments of both time and place. Combined, these impediments restricted their run making and need to be considered when looking at their career record. Uncovered wickets affected all counties until the end of the 1970s. They made for exciting cricket, with the fortunes of batsmen and bowlers being transformed after an opening of the heavens. Good wickets metamorphosed into raging turners or lethal 'skidders'. Batsmen's technique, temperament and bravery were sorely tested under these conditions. This was the impediment of time. The average number of runs scored by Glamorgan in a first innings at home over the years 1950, 1960 and 1970 was 206. The same average for the years 1990, 2000 and 2010 was 301. With covered wickets have come more trustworthy surfaces where batsmen can play down the line of the ball without fear and hit through it with more conviction. Add to that longer Championship matches and the improvements in bat manufacture, amongst other things, and you can see batsmen now have considerably greater assistance in making runs.

Bernard batting at Lord's. Some pitches outside of Glamorgan offered tracks more conducive to stroke making. (© Glamorgan CCC)

Another one that got away. All batsmen have to learn to live with the disappointment of losing their wicket. (© Glamorgan CCC)

Glamorgan also played on a large number of club wickets where it had less control over maintenance and development. These slow–low wickets sometimes delivered brilliant conditions for the county's bowlers but were not conducive to stroke making or fluent batting as Tony Lewis remembers:

'Wilf used to get the groundsman George Clement (at St. Helens) to roll fine grass cuttings into the surface and dust. The first ball of a Swansea match often went 'puff!' That's what persuaded John Waugh, who married a Swansea girl, to say "more Glamorgan batsmen suffer from silicosis than miners". Wilf used to get George to prepare the pitch with roller and rake, in that order. You can imagine what batting was like.'

Bernard developed his batting on these kinds of pitches. A comparison between Glamorgan and Surrey in the 1950s and 1960s makes interesting reading. Batting at The Oval, which was almost exclusively where Surrey played their home games, was worth, on average, 60 more runs in the first innings than batting at The Gnoll, Ebbw Vale, Stradey or the Arms Park. When you consider that sides could be bowled out for totals on or around this figure, this is a significant difference. Whilst still in existence in 2010, that gap had narrowed to 30 runs and the trend is for it to narrow further with most Glamorgan home games being played at Sophia Gardens in Cardiff.

These impediments of time and place are understood by many but were perhaps felt most keenly by Bernard's contemporaries. England Test batsman and a friend of Bernard's on the county circuit Peter Richardson saw it this way:

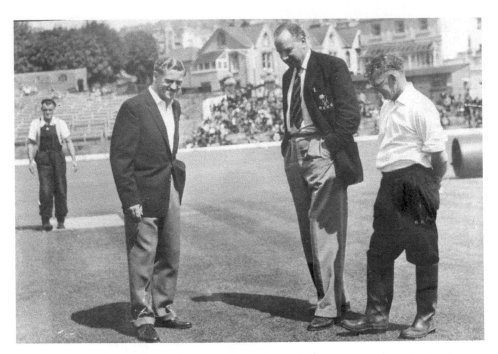

Wilf Wooller inspecting the pitch at Swansea, with George Clement to his left. 'The first ball of a match there often went 'puff'.' (© Glamorgan CCC)

'The wickets there (in Wales) were so low and slow. I used to watch players. He was the best player at playing on those wickets. Very few people bothered to work out how to play on them. But Bernard did. He was a real worker at it. He could manoeuvre it anywhere. If Bernard had played for another county, he would have got more recognition because it was bloody hard work getting runs in Wales.'

Tony Lewis also battled with these conditions:

'For batters it was a struggle because you were always changing venue. No one ever got a hundred in Ebbw Vale but you could fight for a heroic 35 and you could win the match. Bernard and I could certainly have got more runs if we had batted somewhere else but we became committed to winning matches on a smaller scale.'

Roger Davis puts it more succinctly, 'To batters now, if you're averaging 40, you can knock ten off. With Bernard, you could add ten onto his average.' Tony's aside during our interview was that 'Colin Cowdrey never got a hundred in

Glamorgan' and he was right. Neither did Denis Compton, Peter May or Ken Barrington. Some of the cream of English batting struggled on Welsh wickets.

All external impediments aside, there were clear limits to Bernard's game. A number of Glamorgan players who scored fewer first-class runs than him scored more hundreds. Allan Watkins, Steve James and Maurice Turnbull all fall into this category. Putting to one side the tragedy of Maurice Turnbull, who died in the Second World War, these players may have had other qualities that made them Test batsmen, but perhaps one that they had but Bernard lacked was the consistent ability to turn good scores into hundreds; a better conversion rate, as it is called in the analytical, results-driven prose of the modern game. Of the 13 men who scored more runs than Bernard in 1961, all of them except one scored in excess of 2,000 first-class runs more than him. All of them scored more hundreds. Whilst many would not agree with Bernard's own estimation that 'he just was not good enough', it is possible to say that against the best of his time, he was a little short on quantity. His batting came in fits and starts and he never achieved the sort of consistency or profligacy that would have brought him greater attention.

Falling below the standards of his peers cannot be said of his attitude towards playing and the spirit in which he played the game. Wilf Wooller was famously quoted as saying that the 1948 Championship winning Glamorgan side 'cannot compete with Middlesex in batting or Derbyshire in bowling. But in fielding we give first to no side.' In Bernard's case, he could not compete with Peter May in batting or Derek Shackleton in bowling but in sportsmanship he gave first to no one. Ossie Wheatley, as Bernard's captain, observed the more unusual ways in which this commitment to playing the game the right way would express itself: 'He was one of the few people who would come up to me when he was out of form and say will you drop me. We didn't, usually. Bit of luck here and there and you'll be away again. He took his social responsibilities as a team member very seriously. If he felt he wasn't pulling his weight he'd want to back off. His modesty was overpowering sometimes.'

Ossie saw Bernard and Don Shepherd as both sharing the same philosophy and

Bernard pictured at Neath in 1956. His ability to complete the crossword may well have been inversely related to his ability with the bat! (© Glamorgan CCC)

this not only shaped the way they played the game but also how they viewed the game as well, 'Bernard and 'Shep' had a lot of the same principles really in terms of the way the game should be played. They both found it distasteful if people were messing around with any aspect of the game.' Peter Walker, interviewed for Bernard's obituary in *Wisden*, remembered Bernard in this way: 'He was very proud to have played as a professional in the 1950s and '60s, in the manner of an amateur in the 1930s.'

The title of Bob Barber's biography, the Lancashire, Warwickshire and England Test player, was *The Professional Amateur*. Colin Schindler, Bob's biographer, used the title to capture the contradictions of a cricketer who started out playing quite conservatively as an amateur but ended his playing days being an explosive opening batsman playing as a professional. Such contradictions were not unusual when dealing with the worlds of the amateur and the professional during a time when these descriptions of players were dissolving. Bernard could quite as easily have been called the amateur professional. His Corinthian values flew in the face of the widely held view that all professionals were hard-nosed career cricketers that sought to win by all means. Bernard was always an ordinary county cricketer, someone who earned his living from the game. However, he recognised his responsibilities in upholding the spirit of the game he loved so much and this was always the pre-eminent thought in his head. Play the game properly. It did not make him especially different from a lot of cricketers but it did earn him a lot of credit amongst them.

Speaking to colleagues, neighbours, relatives and friends it is difficult to know where Bernard the cricketer ended and Bernard the person began. The values that he cherished in his playing career were the same ones he carried into his working life with Barclaycard and in his private life. There was no distinction for him between what he did on the field of play to uphold the spirit of the game and what he did off it in his day to day relationships. Life was all about doing the right thing and there was nothing that would shake him from this conviction. His personal philosophy would have matched that of the most privileged and wealthy amateurs who ever played the game. Lord Harris, a man who could not have been further away from Bernard in social position and life experience, set out his credo in 1932 in an appeal to all those involved in the playing of cricket:

'You would do well to love it. It is more free from anything sordid, anything dishonourable, than any game in the world. To play it keenly, honourably, generously, self-sacrificing is a moral lesson in itself ... protect it from anything that would sully it, so that it may grow in favour with all men.'

Bernard felt that cricket had been sullied. The modern one-day game with its coloured kit (pyjama cricket, he called it), flagrant commercialism and razzmatazz was not for him. He favoured the longer form of the game and the purity of the battle between bat and ball that it delivered. He would have agreed, though not using the same words, with his old friend Tom Cartwright, who described the development of one-day cricket as 'detracting from excellence' by undermining the 'quality of the interaction between bat and ball.' Bowling has become a 'chore' shared around by players looking to complete their quota rather than a responsibility undertaken with a determination to take wickets. That, in turn, affected the batsman's approach and the whole contest was diminished. It does not mean that the sport cannot produce excitement or enthralling passages of play but it does mean that cricket 'shrinks in its artistic form.'

Interviewing Ron Headley and Jimmy Gray, I was struck by how their recollections became a physical re-enactment that was almost artistic in its execution. Ron smiled in the late summer sunshine as he described his battles with Bishen Bedi, his wrist cocked in imitation of the Northants spinner's delivery, 'Bedi. If he bowled today they wouldn't know what to do with him. He'd come down and say "well played". You'd hit him for four and he would come down the wicket [Ron gently applauds]. He'd bowl again and you'd think it was the same but he'd make it a little bit shorter or a little bit fuller, dipping etc. I'll never forget those skilful battles. Sometimes you lose them but you learn something. There was subtlety about Bedi. He'd finish bowling and you'd both smile at each other.'

Jimmy, more circumspect than Ron, his flat hand pointing back towards his body as he demonstrated a solid backwards defence, 'I was a back foot player, basically. Sometimes you had to get in there [Jimmy moves his hand in front of his body and grimaces], drop your hands or work the ball with your wrists. It was quite an art.'

There was something sublime, almost spiritual, in watching these old men re-living the encounters of their professional past with a rigour and a joy that would shame many an adolescent. It was as if they were transported back to those moments, reliving them in the present like a well-choreographed dance. This was what Mike Brearley has described in Rob Smyth's book *The Spirit of Cricket* as 'a unity of shared striving' or, in more philosophical terms 'the duality of opposition.' It is what most of us would call, more humbly, part of the spirit of the game. Lord Harris and Bernard would have both seen the honour and the greatness in them.

If Bernard worried about cricket then it was nothing compared to his worries about the world in general. He believed that there was much that was 'sordid' and 'dishonourable' about modern life. He kept it at arm's-length and tried, where possible, not to let it impinge on him. In some ways, his life had reflected the economic and social transformation that Wales had undergone in the last 50 years of the millennium. The working class boy from a council house had ended up a retired bank manager living in a private mews. The change in his social position, however, did not alter his social outlook which remained conservative in all things. Simple, innocent and unadulterated, was how he liked his food, his TV consumption, his clothes and, indeed, his cricket. He almost always wore a tie when outside the house, kept a pair of driving gloves in the car and always held the door open to allow a woman to go through first. Nothing would have suited him more than for the world to reflect the lyrics of all those beautiful melodies he remembered from his young days listening to the radio and that he sang nightly as he washed the dishes at the kitchen sink. The world, according to the 'street singer', Arthur Tracey, or the tenors Richard Tauber and Jussi Bjorling was sentimental and straightforward; its rules always easy to follow; its essence always wholesome and uncorrupted. My suggestion to Ossie Wheatley that Bernard would have been happy if the world had stopped in 1955 was met with a one word answer, 'Sooner!'

The anxieties of the external world that Bernard harboured had their corresponding internal ones, with him often worrying about his physical health. The most consistent of these worries was a belief that he had an arrhythmic heart beat caused by an allergic reaction to a dye given to him in the mid-1970s in order to monitor a recurrence of his kidney stones. This affliction affected him throughout the last 40 years of his life.

David Foot, in his biography of Harold Gimblett, quoted a consultant psychiatrist who 'found cricketers to be happiest when on the field' and prone to depression in a sport where there was 'too much time left for them simply to sit and mope.' That time, for the retired cricketer, increases exponentially. Though never a depressive, it appeared as if nothing ever quite matched the happiness of playing for Bernard. A lifelong stoic, he met the pleasures and pains of life with a similar level of indifference. For his children, this meant our errors and mistakes were not greeted calamitously which was a relief but similarly, our successes were not heralded or met with great praise. As a keen young footballer and cricketer, I felt this absence of praise most keenly. Bernard, although friendly and approachable in company, preferred his own. He was not anti-social but asocial. He sought a quiet life and though not solitary would appear reserved. He wanted little fuss, especially around himself. Birthdays were celebrated without great occasion and it appeared sometimes as if he stood outside his own life, enduring it as a spectator rather than experiencing it as an engaged participant. On the few occasions we discussed his death, he quite seriously suggested that his final journey could be made totally on his own. Although it was a request he never formally made, the idea of his coffin winding its way to the crematorium without us or anybody else there to see him off was never seriously considered by either Jean, my brother David or me.

Bernard was diagnosed with cancer in 2012. Before he was confronted with the first of a series of indignities that marked the last period of his life he was required to undergo an exploratory operation at Morriston hospital. Dutifully, he and I arrived at 7:30am and sat in the already crowded waiting room for day surgery adjacent to one of the wards. After several minutes, a nurse arrived and called out the names of those on the list for that day. After she left, the old gentleman sitting opposite us with his daughter leaned over and said 'I couldn't help over-hearing but are you the Bernard Hedges who used to play for Glamorgan?'

Bernard's exact words in response were typically self-effacing. 'Yes, and if they're asking, I'm not available for selection!' he said. Time passed and before too long Bernard was ushered off to a store cupboard that was doing its best to double as a pre-op room. After several interruptions, with staff plunging into cupboards for paper towels and unusually shaped plastic tubing, the anaesthetist arrived. Having had operations requiring anaesthesia myself I knew that the first of many questions to Dad would be, 'Have you had anything to eat this morning?' This consultant's first question was not that; neither did he check Dad's personal details or ask him how he was feeling. He

Bernard on the cliffs above Caswell Bay in the Gower. Walking around these cliffs gave him much pleasure in old age. (© Stephen Hedges)

sat down, looked straight at Dad over his horn-rimmed spectacles and asked, 'Are you the Bernard Hedges who used to play for Glamorgan?'

This is how it is for many ex-professional sportsmen and was how it had been for Bernard ever since returning to Wales. When you least expected it, someone would pop up who remembered him from their childhood and wanted to talk about misspent days at St. Helen's or a slow turner at Stradey. It was most certainly a characteristic of Welsh sports fans. In my interview with Ossie Wheatley he referred to the 'clear, strong identity' that Glamorgan had. When they were in London they were entertained by Welsh MPs at the House of Commons and when they won against Australia in 1964 they went to the Eisteddfod in front of cheering crowds. 'I didn't speak a word of Welsh but it was great stuff. It is important in Wales to have a Welsh side.' The Welsh revere their sportsmen and hold them pre-eminent in their memories.

This desire to explore the past is also, most certainly, a characteristic of lovers of cricket. It was J.B. Priestley, writing in *The English Journey* in 1933, who wrote, 'I cannot believe that there is another game in the world that releases so many floods of nostalgic reminiscences.' There was the gentleman who stopped to talk over the garden wall in Newton who produced, from his jacket, a cigarette card that he had kept for 40 years and was only now getting it signed. Then there was the amateur artist who presented Bernard with two sketches of Don Bradman, both of which he had drawn himself and had signed by the great man on visits to Australia. The two drawings were separated by several years and the second one had a handwritten note on it drawing the viewer's attention to the fact that the Don had suffered a stroke in the intervening period, the evidence of which was the deterioration in his handwriting. Talking about cricket was, for many of those who sought out Bernard, not just about remembering the game or those that played it but remembering a time when things were different. That time may not be better and indeed was often worse, but looking back it felt like a time when life was simpler and sport was too.

Ossie Wheatley outlined how this time was also marked out by the closeness between the Welsh and their sportsmen: 'They really were different days. There were no school children in Wales who didn't know the names of the Glamorgan side. It was a much more important part of the community. Whether it was soccer, cricket or rugby, these players belonged to the community because they were from the community. They weren't imported from anywhere else. One of the big problems now is that you forgive your own if they fail but if you see the imported star coming in you don't want to see him fail too often, do you?'

Brian Roberts, who married Bernard's youngest sister Lynne, was in the Army. He knew Bernard in the years immediately after his retirement and expressed Bernard's local hero status in a way only valleys people could. 'Every bugger knew him. Our regiment was basically from around the valleys. Everybody knew of him.'

In 1991, the *South Wales Evening Post* carried an interview with Bernard in which he was encouraged to reminisce about his cricketing career. His greatest cricketing memory was that August Bank Holiday victory over South Africa at St. Helens in 1951. Bernard was in no doubt that the credit for that victory did not lie with bowlers Jim McConnon and Len Muncer but with his captain, Wilf Wooller:

'I can still see him standing in the dressing room during the tea interval telling us there was still a chance because the top had gone from the pitch and they could be bowled out. I still don't know whether he believed it at the time. I know I didn't and most of the boys shared my view. But once we got out to the middle things began to happen so quickly the Springboks were in trouble almost before they realised it.'

Wilf had not only rallied his men but had led by example. Bernard recalled: 'Clive Van Ryneveld, one of the hardest hitters of the ball, drove straight at him. Somehow Wilf managed to stop the shot which almost knocked him over, then clung to the rebound inches from the ground.'

South Africa defeated, the St. Helen's crowd famously celebrated by singing *Hen Wlad Fy Nhadau*. The players were also carried away with the moment and this made a huge impression on the young Bernard. 'It was quite an experience, and so were the celebrations that followed. I vaguely recall doing a turn perched on top of a piano.'

Alongside the article was a photograph taken of Bernard at the time of his interview, cutting the grass in his Newton garden. Jean always said that the grass had looked after him for 18 years, so now it was his turn to look after the grass. Bernard was a diligent rather than a talented gardener but he took great pride in the neatness and tidiness of his patch. It came as a great emotional sacrifice when he was no longer able to mow the lawn and hoe the border. Indeed, throughout his last few years, he was reminded time and again of the way in which old age was taking its toll on a once athletic body. 'Don't grow old' was his mantra whenever I came to stay with my children. These visits would end with a customary shake of the hand before some banknotes, always too many, were slipped to me, out of Mum's sight, to 'just cover the petrol'.

Those that have spoken to me about Bernard have often been drawn to comment on his personal characteristics alongside his cricketing ability. Peter Walker, summing him up, said 'Bernard was a good player and a brave man.

The photograph that appeared alongside Bernard's reminiscences in the local press. (© Hedges family)

To be a good opener you needed brains and heart. He had both.' Roger Davis, who knew Bernard at the end of his career, thought that, 'Bernard was short, strong; a fighter. A funny man but not a comedian. A good man. A traditionalist. He was very proud to play for Glamorgan.' Lawrence Williams bumped into Bernard after his career with Glamorgan had come to an end. 'The last time I saw Bernard I was working for the council. He was in there in the Con Club in Neath. He was the same as he always had been. There could have been an earthquake and it wouldn't have affected him.'

Geoff Williams, from Ynysygerwn CC wrote to me after Dad's death saying, 'It was an absolute privilege to have met the cricketer, but an even bigger privilege and an honour to have met Bernard the man.' Ron Headley called him 'a decent man'. To Tom Cartwright's widow, Joan, 'he was a very nice man' and to British Lion Russell Robbins he was 'one of my favourite men.' This final tribute struck me as something rather special. For one man to describe another in such a way, even though their friendship had ended some 60 years previously, showed the impact Bernard had on people. There were many older men I met in the weeks after Dad died. They all began their conversations with me with four words. They were words that were more often than not the pre-cursor to an anecdote. They were words that carried more than a just a recognition of the name. They were an invocation of Welsh camaraderie; the summoning of a spirit that people see embodied in those they look up to. They were always spoken with frankness and often some levity. They were the words that every grieving son longs to hear. 'I remember your father.'

A word familiar in cricketing circles was used to describe Bernard in life, during his career, and in death, from admirers and those with an affiliation to Glamorgan cricket. The phrase 'Glamorgan stalwart' is inscribed on my copy of Stephen Chalke's *Summer's Crown* by the author himself. That word, stalwart, is one that bears a little closer examination. Its dictionary definition is that of an adjective that describes someone who is loyal, reliable and hard working. A letter written to the county after their Championship success in

1997 quoted a newspaper which described the team as having 'no airs, no graces, no pretensions, no aloofness.' They were 'the people's champs'. This closeness to the community; the down to and salt of the earth quality that he had were also part of Bernard's status as a stalwart. He never forgot where he came from and the values he had learnt in his community became part of the way he played his sport. Ossie Wheatley, trying to sum him up at the end of our interview, felt compelled to repeat himself using a term that implied not only talent and skill but also those values of loyalty, honesty and generosity that marked him out. 'He was a popular guy. He was a proper cricketer. A *proper* cricketer.'

Such qualities must have been in the mind of R.S. Thomas when, in an early poem, he tried to capture the essence of the men who worked the land in the remote areas of north Wales where he ministered. The poem, entitled *A Peasant*, describes Iago Prytherch, 'an ordinary man of the bald Welsh hills,' The figure was one he would return to time and again in his poetry; an archetype of these simple, toiling men of the land who at once both attracted and repelled Thomas. The final lines of the poem appear to broaden and speak more widely, not just of those who find themselves 'churning the crude earth' but to all those, however they live, who appear to us as 'loyal, reliable and hard working':

'Yet this is your prototype, who, season by season
Against siege of rain and wind's attrition,
Preserves his stock, an impregnable fortress
Not to be stormed even in death's confusion.
Remember him, then, for he, too, is a winner of wars,
Enduring like a tree under the curious stars.'

This was Bernard. 'A winner of wars'; a sporting soldier who was happy to be part of the ranks and would stay true to the cause whatever the outcome of the battle. A historical glance at the sporting landscape of Wales reveals, in an instant, thousands of men like Bernard; men from Colwyn Bay to Cardiff; from Newcastle Emlyn to Newport; from Pontypool to Pontypridd. They turned out week in, week out for their club, county or, occasionally, their country. They played rugby or football or cricket, or boxed or ran or jumped or threw. They were characterised by their rugged permanence, like scars on the mountain. They were the 'enduring trees' of Welsh sport; always there but not always noticed. Solid, dependable and true. Unwavering, they stood together, growing side by side and securing the ground. Reaching upwards, they acted as a scaffold for those amongst them, and those that would come after, who would grow beyond the rest, bursting through the canopy and piercing the starlit sky.

Epilogue
The Boundary of Wales Walk

Bernard died on 8 February 2014. For the next 24 hours, his death was minor news, being carried on the BBC and Sky news channels. The modern world had a final trick to play on him. Sky carried the news of his death alongside a photograph of Alan Jones. Bernard would have tutted and shaken his head at the shabbiness of it. At his funeral, Glamorgan were represented by seven of the Championship winning side of 1969, some of whom had played very little cricket with him. Their presence was greatly appreciated by my mother, my brother and myself.

After the funeral, I still felt the need to do something that would mark his passing. Something that would reflect his interests in life and the gritty and determined way in which he faced up to adversity, both on and off the

The author with son Ellis, Jean Hedges and Don Shepherd in Swansea on Day One of the Boundary of Wales walk, 5 July 2014. (© Stephen Hedges)

cricket field. I had discovered walking for pleasure some years previously and had taken an interest in long distance walking with a friend. I knew of the existence of the Wales Coastal Path, which had opened in 2012. This was a walk of 870 miles around the coast of Wales, beginning in Chepstow and ending in Chester. It had already been completed by around a dozen or more people, a number of whom had combined it with another National Trail, Offa's Dyke Path, which follows the border between Wales and England. This was a further 177 miles making a grand total 1,047 miles.

Such a walk sounded like the kind of memorial I wanted. I had never done more than one day's walking consecutively and had never completed any of the National Trails that exist throughout England and Wales. This walk would represent the most serious physical and mental challenge of my life. It would take me to places that had, previously, just been points on a map so through it I would be able to discover Wales for myself. 'The Boundary of Wales' walk was born. Its title, in my mind, neatly brought together the world of cricket and long distance walking. With the help and encouragement of Andrew Hignell at Glamorgan Cricket and Peter Hybart, of Cricket Wales, I prepared for the walk, using the National Charity 'Chance to Shine' as the conduit to raise money for the future of junior cricket in Wales. Friday 4 July was the date for Glamorgan's T20 game with Somerset and was planned as a launch for the walk which would start at the Mumbles the following day. The game was a wash out but I did manage to be interviewed by Rick O'Shea on BBC Radio Wales which made me feel I had spoken to Wales itself!

The first few days took me round the Gower Peninsula and through Carmarthenshire, staying with my cousin Jocelyn and her husband Andrew. Their son, Aneurin, is now a professional cricketer with Hampshire having started his career with Glamorgan where, during his first season, he made 234 from 123 balls in the county's match against Derbyshire at Colwyn Bay, equalling Ravi Shastri's record for the fastest double hundred in first-class cricket. We are all very proud of him. I was just glad he and his father did not get too upset when I asked to be returned to the house five minutes into our journey to drop me off at the beginning of my days walk. I had forgotten my phone!

In Pembrokeshire, my brother had arranged for me to drop in on the cricketers of Neyland as they prepared for their Welsh Cup zonal semi-final against Dafen. I was ready to spend the afternoon with the only other club in the world (after New Zealand) that has permission to use the silver fearn as its logo. I watched the first eight overs of the match as Dafen raced to 40 for no wicket, then nipped into the bar for a bite to eat where I heard, less than 30 minutes later, that Dafen had collapsed to 68 all out. I collected over £50 on the day, but my visit to Neyland had demonstrated the depth of enjoyment

The author with Neyland CC after 180 miles of the walk. (© Stephen Hedges)

of cricket in the towns and villages of Wales. It was a great day seeing how a cricket club functions as part of the wider community.

In Solva, I had my major brush with fame. I arrived on the day that they were filming a modern production of *Under Milk Wood*. As well as providing a band, the production company had arranged for a number of 'personalities' to act as extras with the cast which already included Charlotte Church. I managed to get my photo taken with Charlotte, Gareth Edwards, J.P.R. Williams and Dewi Pws of *Grand Slam* fame. I also managed to speak with Gareth, Neil Kinnock and Graham Price. Both Gareth and Neil remembered seeing my dad play at the Arms Park. Gareth's face after he scored his solo try against Scotland and the sight of him flying over the All Blacks try line, Grant Batty clinging to his legs, are two of the clearest memories I have of my sporting childhood. It is difficult to express how great it was to hear one of my childhood sporting heroes describe my dad as a great player. Neil Kinnock was effusive about Dad's fielding, saying he was the quickest player he remembered seeing in the outfield. Neil's and Gareth's words rang around my head for days afterwards.

After Pembrokeshire it was Ceredigion, Meirionnydd and the Llyn Peninsula. The weather was warm and humid; there was to be less than a day's rain on the

Charlotte Church in Solva. I never did get round to talking with her about cricket. (© Stephen Hedges)

Gareth Edwards. He remembered Bernard from his days watching cricket at the Arms Park. (© Stephen Hedges)

whole of the walk. On the Llyn, I switched to a new pair of boots and within days developed three nasty blisters.

I had grown up thinking Anglesey was a rather glum place with a single main road that ran through it to Holyhead and the cross channel ferry. How wrong I was. This was an island full of beautiful beaches, quaint fishing villages and frequent hints at a history that went back long before the Holyhead-to-Dublin crossing. On the day salvation came to my feet in the form of some new Merrell boots, I visited Menai Bridge CC. If you have never been, I would venture that there are very few cricket clubs in the world with a better view from the pitch. It tilts down towards the water of the strait, and beyond to where *Yr Wyddfa* (Snowdon) towers behind to form a gigantic grandstand. The clear blue sky and the rich green of the outfield combined to make a ribbon of colour that stretched itself around the ground. Only cricket truly delivers this colour therapy.

I met Nicola Williams, a Cricket Wales coach who takes the Chance to Shine programme into schools on Anglesey. I also met Kain Holdsworth, the Australian club professional who assists Nicola with the programme. The fruit of their labours was visible on the afternoon of our visit as boys who had played in a recent Chance to Shine tournament turned up at the ground to use the club nets. This was no formal practice session but boys just desperate to bat and to bowl. Nicola's enthusiasm for the game of cricket and her energy made me realise that every penny I raised with the walk would be well spent. This was Mathew Maynard's first club and amongst his shirts and bat that were on display in the clubhouse there was a lovely framed photo of him with his dad and his late son, Tom; three generations of talent in one family that had played for the club.

Menai Bridge cricket ground. A beautiful place to play the game. (© Stephen Hedges)

It took me six days to walk the 132 miles around Anglesey. I was now 34 days into the walk and ahead of the schedule. Across north Wales I was fortunate to stay with Cricket Wales Board member Richard Penney for three nights. His good cooking and positive attitude were worth more than a hundred of the leg raises I had taken to doing at the end of each days walking. 'Finish it!' he yelled after me as I left his car for the last time in Llandegla. I had covered over a 100 miles in four days and was now well over half way.

I completed the 182 miles of Offa's Dyke in nine days and now there were only five days to go. As I covered the ground quickly from Chepstow to Newport and on to Cardiff, I stayed with Bernard's sister, my Aunty Jean. It was lovely to spend some time with her, talking about Dad and the rest of the family. All Dad's surviving brothers and sisters lived close enough together for me to try and get them to come to Pontypridd CC's social event on Friday 22 August. We were joined there by Pontypridd MP and then Shadow Secretary of State for Wales, Owen Smith. He was so welcoming, it was great. He identified me straight away as I was the only man in the room in shorts with a tan and an unkempt beard. One of my more eccentric decisions had been not to shave until I had finished the walk. We had a fabulous evening at the Central Hotel in 'Ponty' and raised over £300.

A current player of Pontypridd CC came up to chat as the evening wore on. His grandfather was a young boy during the 1950s when Dad was the talk of the town and a young cricket professional. The boys, like those in every town and village, grabbed every opportunity in every open space, to play their own game of cricket. Dad would be leaving the house, Glamorgan blazer and cricket bag packed, bound for the Arms Park or a train journey to one of the great Test grounds like The Oval or Lord's. He would always, without fail, stop, put down his bag, take off his blazer and spend a few minutes playing with the boys. One of those boys never forgot that and made sure he told his grandson of the kindness and humility he saw in Bernard. It was another lovely story to lock away in the memory bank.

The final night of the walk was spent at the house of Peter Hybart of Cricket Wales. He had been an enthusiastic supporter of the walk from day one and had helped lift my spirits when I had become a little pessimistic and gloomy. It was so interesting to ask him about the current state of junior and recreational cricket in Wales and to hear his views on the game, Glamorgan and England. I valued his advice throughout the walk and it was pleasing to know that he would join me at the end of it in Mumbles.

And so to Swansea and the Mumbles. The previous day, I had bumped into Lee Byrne walking his dogs with his wife on the cliffs by Ogmore-by-Sea. I tweeted his picture saying 'Great to meet Lee Byrne and his wife.' I only found out later that his wife is the anchor journalist for ITV Wales' evening news programmes. With my desperate need for publicity, I realised I should have tweeted, 'Great to meet Andrea Byrne and her husband!'

The walk finished at Mumbles CC. I had walked over a 1,000 miles and climbed four times the height of Everest in what was, I believe, to be the fastest time at that point. A woman had run the distance in 41 days. I had taken 50 and felt I could have done it faster, but records were not really on my mind. My mum was waiting at the cricket club. I returned to her the lucky cats and horseshoe from her wedding day which she had given me

With Lee Byrne on the Wales Coastal Path near Ogmore-by-Sea. I never realised his wife was on the telly more than he was. I should have had my photo taken with her! (© Stephen Hedges)

With Peter Hybart of Cricket Wales and Chairman of Mumbles CC Mark Portsmouth. The framed photo is of Dad. I presented it to the club in thanks for their support at the beginning and end of the walk. (© Stephen Hedges)

Receiving a cheque from Alan Jones, Dad's opening partner, at the Glamorgan Balconiers end of season dinner, September 2014. It was a very proud evening and receiving the cheque for the walk from Alan topped it all! (© Stephen Hedges)

at the beginning of the walk. They were battered, but I had carried them all the way. Also waiting at the finish were my son, who had walked several sections of the walk with me and Paul and Bev, neighbours of my father in Newton who had given much energy to making the walk a success. Also there, with Mum, were my brother David and his partner Julie. It was a small but dedicated group whose help and assistance were invaluable.

Standing at the gate of the club was one man I was overjoyed to see. Don Shepherd. I know Dad's death had affected him greatly and I know how pleased he was that I had undertaken the walk. The best thing I did for Dad in those final days was to make sure Don came round to visit. His visits, I believe, strengthened Dad's resolve and helped him end his life with thoughts of his cricketing days.

The walk was over. I had experienced something that only a few others had; a walk around the whole of my country. I had raised nearly £4,000 for Chance to Shine which, through Cricket Wales would seek to introduce as many school pupils as possible to the game of cricket. As part of its core message the charity has committed itself to embrace the MCC's spirit of cricket in the work that it does with young people. As its website proudly states:

'We want children to play sport competitively, but in the right spirit and we strongly believe that cricket is ideal for teaching young people respect. Respect for teammates, respect for the opposition and respect for officials.'

Bernard would have been happy with that.

INDEX

BERNARD HEDGES – CAREER STATISTICS

1. Bernard Hedges – first-class career record

M	Inns	NO	Runs	HS	Ave	100	50	Ct
422	744	41	17,733	182	25.22	21	84	200

Balls	Mdns	Runs	Wkts	BB	Ave	5W	10W	S.Rate	Econ
572	24	260	3	1-16	86.66	0	0	190.66	2.72

2. Glamorgan CCC – top seven first-class run scorers

Name	Glamorgan Career	Matches	Innings	N/O	100s	50s	Total Runs
Alan Jones	1957 - 1983	645	1168	72	56	194	36,049
Emrys Davies	1924 - 1954	621	1032	80	32	141	26,564
Mathew Maynard	1985 - 2005	395	643	60	59	131	24,799
Gilbert Parkhouse	1948 - 1964	455	791	49	32	129	23,508
Tony Lewis	1955 - 1974	409	708	76	30	113	20,495
Arnold Dyson	1926 - 1948	413	697	37	24	92	17,923
Bernard Hedges	1950 - 1967	422	744	41	21	84	17,733

3. **Glamorgan CCC – players who have scored 2,000 runs in a first-class season (displayed in descending order according to runs total)**

Name	Season	Matches	Innings	N/O	100	50	Total Runs
Hugh Morris	1990	25	46	5	10	10	2,276
Gilbert Parkhouse	1959	28	49	3	6	12	2,243
Tony Lewis*	1966	32	61	8	5	8	2,190
Alan Butcher	1990	23	41	5	6	15	2,116
Javed Miandad	1981	22	37	7	8	7	2,083
Bernard Hedges	1961	34	65	2	3	10	2,026

*Tony Lewis also scored 2,188 runs in the 1961 season.

4. **Bernard Hedges and Gilbert Parkhouse – batting partnerships in first-class cricket**

Year	Matches	Innings	Runs	Average	100	50
1955	1	1	76	76	0	1
1956	6	11	117	10.63	0	0
1957	17	29	897	32.03	1	5
1958	30	38	923	21.29	2	1
1959	29	45	2025	46.12	3	12
1960	35	41	1202	29.07	2	6
1961	29	42	1727	41.11	5	5
1962	2	4	92	23	0	1
TOTAL	149	211	7079	35.28	13	30

5. **Bernard Hedges and Alan Jones – batting partnerships in first-class cricket**

Year	Matches	Innings	Runs	Averages	100	50
1959	1	2	90	45	0	1
1960	1	1	12	12	0	0
1961	4	7	278	39.71	1	1
1962	0	0	0	0	0	0
1963	18	32	1103	34.46	3	4

1964	14	22	752	34.18	1	3
1965	22	38	1172	32.55	3	0
1966	14	26	681	26.19	1	3
1967	9	15	518	34.53	1	0
TOTAL	83	143	4606	32.33	10	12

6. Glamorgan CCC – opening partnerships in first-class cricket (displayed in descending order according to runs total)

Partnership	M	Inns	Runs	HS	100	50	Ave
D.E. Davies and A.H. Dyson	389	439	12,716	274	32	61	29.92
A. Jones and J.A. Hopkins	189	230	8,525	253	14	50	37.24
H. Morris and S.P. James	120	177	7,392	250	17	38	43.48
B. Hedges and W.G.A. Parkhouse	149	211	7,079	207	13	30	35.28
H. Morris and A.R. Butcher	99	115	6,592	269	25	23	59.38
B. Hedges and A. Jones	83	143	4,606	201	10	12	32.33

7. 1959 First-Class Season – batting statistics for opening partnerships of the top six teams

Team (Position)	Main Opening Partnership	Innings	100s	50s	Not Outs	Runs	Ave
Yorkshire (1)	W.B. Stott, K. Taylor	32	1	6	0	1,086	33.93
Gloucestershire (2)	D.M. Young, C.A. Milton	40	4	7	0	1,560	39.00
Surrey (3)	J.H. Edrich, M.J. Stewart	28	1	6	2	1,033	39.73
Warwickshire (4)	W.J.P. Stewart, N.F. Horner	26	0	5	1	754	30.16
Lancashire (5)	A. Wharton, R.W. Barber	28	3	6	0	1,206	43.07
Glamorgan (6)	W.G.A. Parkhouse, B. Hedges	44	4	12	2	2,024	48.19

BIBLIOGRAPHY AND SELECTED READING

There have been a number of books that I have read during the writing of this book. Those that I found both informative and enjoyable have been organised into areas of commonality. I hope the interested reader will find time to explore at least some of them.

Pontypridd
Granfield, Alun: *In Black and White: Pontypridd RFC 1876 – 2003*, Pontypridd RFC, 2007.
Powell, Dan: *Pontypridd at War 1939-45*, Merton Priory Press, 1999.
Richards, Alun: *Days of Absence*, Michael Joseph Ltd, London, 1986.

Glamorgan Cricket
Hignell, Andrew: *The Skipper: A Biography of Wilf Wooller*, Limlow Books Ltd, Royston, 1995.
Hignell, Andrew: *A Who's Who of Glamorgan County Cricket Club 1888-1991*, Breedon Books Publishing Company Limited, 1992
Hignell, Andrew: *The History of Glamorgan County Cricket Club*, Christopher Helm Books, Kent, 1988.
Hignell, Andrew: *'Lucky' Jim Pleass: The Memoirs of Glamorgan's 1948 County Championship Winner*, St. David's Press, Cardiff 2014.
Jones, Alan with Stevens, Terry: *Hooked on Opening*, Gomer Press, Llandysul, 1984.
Lewis, Tony: *Playing Days*, Stanley Paul and Co Ltd, London, 1985.
Lloyd, Grahame: *Daffodil Days: Glamorgan's Glorious Summer*, Gomer Press, Llandysul, 1998.
Miller, Douglas: *Born to Bowl: The Life and Times of Don Shepherd*, Fairfield Books, Bath, 2004.
Morris, Hugh with Smith, Andy: *To Lord's with a Title: The Inside Story of Glamorgan's Championship*, Mainstream Publishing, Edinburgh, 1998.

Autobiographies / Biographies
Alley, Bill: *Standing the Test of Time*, Empire Publications, Manchester, 1999.
Bird, Dickie: *White Cap and Bails: The Adventures of a Much Travelled Umpire*, Hodder and Stoughton, London, 2000.

Barrington, Ken (as told to Phil Pilley): *Running into Hundreds*, Stanley Paul and Co. Ltd., London, 1963.

Chalke, Stephen: *The Flame Still Burns: Tom Cartwright*, Fairfield Books, Bath, 2007.

Foot, David: *Harold Gimblett: Tormented Genius of Cricket*, WH Allen and Co Ltd, London, 1982.

Schindler, Colin: *Bob Barber: The Professional Amateur*, Max Books, Nantwich, 2015.

Westcott, Chris: *Class of '59: From Bailey to Wooller, The Golden Age of County Cricket*, Mainstream Publishing, Edinburgh, 2000.

County Cricket

Allen, David Rayvern (ed): *The Essential John Arlott: Forty Years of Classic Cricket Writing*, Willow Books, London, 1989.

Birley, Derek: *A Social History of English Cricket*, Aurum Press, London, 1999.

Chalke, Stephen: *Summer's Crown: The Story of Cricket's County Championship*, Fairfield Books, Bath, 2015.

Chalke, Stephen: *Runs in the Memory: County Cricket in the 1950s*, Fairfield Books, Bath, 1997.

Ross, Gordon: *The Gillette Cup: 1963 to 1980*, Queen Anne Press, London, 1981.

Smyth, Rob: *The Spirit of Cricket*, Elliott and Thompson Ltd., London, 2010.

Wales and Welsh Sport

Johnes, Martin: *A History of Sport in Wales*, University of Wales Press, Cardiff, 2005.

Johnes, Martin: *Wales Since 1939*, Manchester University Press, Manchester, 2012.

Richards, Alun: *Carwyn*, Parthian Books, Cardigan, 2015.

Sheers, Owen: *Calon: A Journey to the Heart of Welsh Rugby*, Faber and Faber, London, 2013.

Williams, Gwyn A.: *When was Wales?*, Penguin Books, London, 1985.

Miscellaneous (these were either referenced in the text or were used as background reading)

Hamilton, Duncan: *A Last English Summer*, Quercus, London, 2010.

Imlach, Gary: *My Father and other Working Class Football Heroes*, Yellow Jersey Press, London, 2005.

Morrison, Blake: *And When Did You Last See Your Father?*, Granta Books, London, 1993.

Norgay, Jamling Tenzing (with Coburn, Broughton): *Touching My Father's Soul*, Harper Collins, London, 2001.

Thomas, R.S. *Selected Poetry*, Everyman, J.M. Dent, London, 1996.

ST DAVID'S PRESS

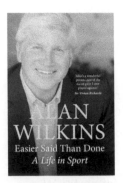

Easier Said Than Done
A Life in Sport

'Alan was an excellent county cricketer ... He may be Cardiff born and Cardiff bred but, in a broadcasting sense, Alan is 'a citizen of the world'.'   **Tony Lewis**

With great honesty and humility, Alan Wilkins tells the fascinating story of his seven years as a professional cricketer with Glamorgan and Gloucestershire - taking over 370 wickets and playing in the 1977 Gillette Cup final - and how his career was brought to a devastating end in 1983 by a debilitating shoulder injury.

Determined that his *Life in Sport* would not end after his enforced retirement, Alan Wilkins then embarked on a new and successful career in sports broadcasting, which has made him one of the most recognisable faces and voices in sports broadcasting in SE Asia, South Africa and in his native Wales.

978 1 902719 610   336pp   £20 hb

Not Only, But Also
My Life in Cricket

'People should remember that Malcolm was a wonderful opening bowler...in many of his peers' minds the best new ball bowler in county cricket.'   **Peter Walker**

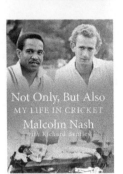

Malcolm Nash achieved sporting immortality as the bowler hit for a world-record six sixes by the legendary batsman Garry Sobers at Swansea in 1968 but, as Malcolm himself notes, although this single over made his name well-known, it should not define his long and distinguished cricketing career.

In *Not Only, But Also*, Malcolm explores and celebrates his wider achievements with ball and bat - Malcolm played over 600 matches for Glamorgan between 1966 and 1983, took over 1,300 wickets, had an England trial - painting an intriguing and nostalgic picture of county cricket, and the life of a county cricketer, in the 1960s and 1970s.

978 1 902719 719   256pp   £19.99 pb

Front Foot to Front Line
Welsh Cricket and the Great War

'recommended reading...nicely produced and well illustrated'   **CricketWeb.net**

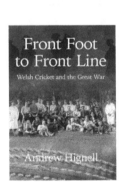

'this is a book that I have enjoyed more than any other on the subject of cricket and the Great War'   **Association of Cricket Scorers**

'perceptive...absorbing...poignant...there is pride, excitement and amusement here - then grief again with more tales of fine, innocent, young cricketers whose luck ran out.' (4*)
David Frith, The Cricketer

Front Foot to Front Line commemorates Welsh cricket's contribution to the Great War by chronicling the lives of 55 professional and amateur cricketers who left the friendly rivalry of the crease for the brutality and horror of the trenches, and lost their lives as servicemen on the bloody battlefields of Europe.

978 1 902719 429   209pp   £16.99 pb

'Lucky' Jim Pleass
The Memoirs of Glamorgan's 1948 County Championship Winner

'fascinating ... I can but only admire Jim's contributions during Glamorgan's Championship-winning summer of 1948 ... but Jim was not only an unsung hero on the cricket fields, he was also one of many thousands of people who heroically took part in the Normandy Landings of June 1944.'   **Robert Croft, from his Foreword**

Jim Pleass was the last surviving member of Glamorgan's County Championship winning team of 1948, the first time the Welsh team won the highest honour in county cricket.

978 1 902719 368   128pp   £14.99 pb

Lightning Source UK Ltd.
Milton Keynes UK
UKHW031825270619
345151UK00006B/249/P